RAISING LESS CORN
AND MORE HELL

"What you farmers need to do is
raise less corn and more HELL!"

—Mary Elizabeth Lease
from her campaign speeches
on behalf of the Kansas People's party
in the campaign of 1890

RAISING LESS CORN
AND MORE HELL

Midwestern Farmers Speak Out
JIM SCHWAB

University of Illinois Press
Urbana and Chicago

Library of Congress Cataloging-in-Publication Data

Schwab, James.
    Raising less corn and more hell : midwestern farmers
speak out /
    Jim Schwab.
        p. cm.
    Includes index.
ISBN 0-252-01398-0 (alk. paper)
1. Agriculture—Economic aspects—Middle West—Case
studies.   2. Family farms—Middle West—Case studies.
3. Agriculture and state—Middle West—Case studies.
4. Farmers—Middle West—Interviews.   I. Title.
HD1773.A3S38 1988
                                338.1'0977—dc19 88-1173
                                                      CIP

The chapters on Lou-Anne Kling and Anne Kanten appeared
in different form in a single article in Blair & Ketchum's
Country Journal in October 1985. Appendix A is an update of
material previously contained in a February 1985 report for
the Iowa General Assembly, *The Farm Credit Crisis in Iowa,*
published by the University of Iowa's Legislative Extended
Assistance Group. The chapters on Bruce Schmaedeke and
Delmar Carlson appeared in a different form in a single article
in *The Lutheran,* March 15, 1986.

To my wife, Jean,
who was patient enough to outlast
the writing of this book

and to my parents,
whose timely gift of a 1974 Maverick
made possible the travels that
made possible this whole project.

empty barns

empty barns dot the iowa countryside
  like polka dots
    on my grandmother's sunday dress
who is going to replace the broken glass
  oil the rusted hinges
    pull the weeds out of the cracked foundations
a no trespassing sign tells it all
empty barns are nameless tombstones
  in forgotten cemeteries
    their memories hang in dusty cobwebs
      like trapped flies

  no more milk bucket calves bawling
  no more squealing pigs nursing the sow
  no more free-from-the-axe bantam rooster welcoming dawn
  no more whisker-licking cats fat from spilt milk
  no more barking dog guarding his barnyard empire

  and when all that is left are empty barns
  who is going to teach the young how to farm
    hand down to another generation
      the legacy of being an iowa farmer

michael andorf
a rowley, iowa
farmer

Contents

Foreword

AFTER reading Jim Schwab's *Raising Less Corn and More Hell,* I was filled with two conflicting—but connected—emotions.

First was a feeling of anger and frustration. The testimonials in this book capture vividly the pain and anguish so many rural families feel as they are forced to give up not only their livelihoods—but their way of life. From my own travels across the Midwest, I know these stories ring true. Schwab does an excellent job in bringing them to life.

But the second emotion was a feeling of hope. Instead of a documentation of despair, Schwab has given us a testimonial to the triumph of the human spirit. Here we have men and women, young and old, on Main Street as well as the farm, who have turned their trials into positive action—either with a helping hand for their neighbors in need or by speaking out boldly in the political arena.

One person can make a difference. Take that one step further, and it means that a lot of people working together can move a nation. This, I think, is the central message of Schwab's book as well as the guiding principle behind the farm protest movement.

It's true that farmers are independent people. That is the source of their strength. It can also be a source of their weakness, unless they bind together to protect their independence.

I'm reminded of a story from the Laura Ingalls Wilder series, *The Little House on the Prairie,* which I've read to my daughters. In one chapter, Laura Ingalls Wilder was trying to talk her husband out of getting into farming because life was so tough. He said, "No, farming is the life for me. I'm independent, nobody tells me what to do. I can do everything on my own." And that was the end of the chapter.

The next chapter began with all the farmers coming around to help him thresh his grain. They all got together and threshed one farmer's grain and then they moved to the next farm and threshed the next farmer's grain. Sure, they were independent. But they were independent because they bound themselves together to help one another.

Obviously, since then the nature of farming has changed dramatically. Much of the manual labor has now been replaced with machinery. Yet the principle of "independence through cooperation" remains the same.

We saw it in action, beginning in 1984, when farmers across the country began to realize the only way they were going to get a decent farm policy was to write it themselves. And so they did, in dozens of grass-roots meetings across the country.

The result was the Farm Policy Reform Act of 1985 (now called the Save the Family Farm Act). This bill would establish a nation-wide referendum—one farmer, one vote—to give farmers a voice in their own destiny. A referendum is the key to reform because it takes farm policymaking out of the hands of high-paid Washington lobbyists and puts it back in the hands of the farmers themselves.

If the referendum passed, farmers would be allowed to join together cooperatively in a marketing-certificate program to bring their supply in line with demand. This way, farmers could earn a decent income from the marketplace, and not have to subsist on government subsidies.

Our bill did not pass in 1985, but we will try again. The pressure for a new approach will continue to increase as the farm crisis worsens, and the $26 billion failure of the current "free-market" approach becomes more and more apparent. In addition, the elections of 1986 resulted in a change of control of the Senate and brought several new senators to Washington who were committed to a "fair price" for farmers.

A new farm bill is just a start. We also need a new trade policy which will put American commodities and products on an even playing field with other nations. We need a new budget policy to reduce the massive budget deficits and bring military spending under control.

The important thing is that we don't lose sight of the big picture.

Changing policies only comes when you change people's ways of thinking. Our message to the American people is simply this question: How many farmers do we want to work the land?

Do we want two to three million farm families living on and working the land and preserving it for future generations? Or do we want our farms run like giant corporations, owned by absentee landlords and operated by day laborers?

Since the 1950s, the motto of our agricultural policy has been "get big or get out." We condemn, and rightly so, the forced removal of rural populations in communist countries. Yet, what is happening here in America? In communist countries, military force was used. Here, it has been economic—a laissez-faire approach in which the big and rich get bigger and richer.

Our farmers have survived droughts, floods, hailstorms, even recessions—but they cannot survive farm policies designed to drive them off their land. This is what we must unite to fight.

At stake is whether we will be a nation that continues to place value on human dignity and worth—or whether individual Americans are to be swept aside by the consolidation of economic wealth in fewer and fewer hands.

Thomas Jefferson once wrote: "I trust the good sense of our country will see that its greatest prosperity depends on a due balance between agriculture, manufacturing and commerce." Today, if Jefferson saw how our economy and society are out of balance—he would say we have taken leave of our senses.

Raising Less Corn and More Hell is more than the living, breathing stories of courageous rural Americans. It is a call to action to restore this balance. It is a tribute to the hope that we can and will succeed in preserving not only what is best in rural America, but what is fundamental to the freedoms and liberties we enjoy in a democracy.

—SENATOR TOM HARKIN

Acknowledgments

ORAL history, by its very nature, requires the cooperation of a small army of other human beings willing to talk, to share experiences, and to suggest other people to talk to and other sources of information to turn to. The only real difference in the case of a rural topic like the farm crisis is that most of those people and sources are down the road at least a few miles. Urban historians have a few advantages resulting from geographic density.

While the shaping of the subject matter in this book is purely a product of my own thinking, I can claim no monopoly on the information. I should, then, perform the ritual of acknowledging those who suggested ideas, reviewed material I had gathered, provided ideas, or simply helped with overnight hospitality or a cup of coffee. Clearly, I must thank all of those whose interviews appear in this book.

There is another group of interviewees who, for reasons of space, repetition of theme, or other considerations, did not appear in the book, although some of those have been quoted or cited in magazine and newspaper articles I have done since this project began in late 1983. They include: David Senter, Washington, D.C.; the Rev. Ron Kitterman, Aurelia, Iowa; Fr. Gene Sitzman, Cherokee, Iowa; Dan Schmidt, Marshalltown, Iowa; Jim and Helen Ormesher, Cody, Nebraska; Gary and Linda Connot, Sparks, Nebraska; Robert Simon, Winterset, Iowa; Don and Eileen Paulsen, Exira, Iowa; Edgar and Ida Morse, Winterset, Iowa; Cheryl Parsons, Memphis, Missouri; Shirley Borah, Wecota, South Dakota; Jim White and Keith Schippers,

Monroe, Iowa; Herb Jackson, Kellerton, Iowa; Bob and Tim Sullivan, Dunlap, Iowa; James and Marilyn Galloway, Redding, Iowa; Bill Kjeldahl, Brooten, Minnesota; Matthew Keller, Mike Laidlaw, and Joe and Renee Schramel, all of Belgrade, Minnesota. The information and insights all these people provided were invaluable.

Farm organizations were another constant source of ideas and information, and I can safely say that virtually all of those listed in Appendix B helped in some way. However, a few organizations stand out as being of regular assistance almost throughout the entire duration of the project: Prairiefire Rural Action in Des Moines; the North American Farm Alliance in Ames, Iowa; and Minnesota's Farm Advocates, organized by the incomparable Lou-Anne Kling.

Finally, there were various individuals who reviewed chapters, took the time to sit down with me and evaluate ideas and the directions I was taking, pointed me in the direction of books, periodicals, and reports I needed to read, and otherwise served as backstops for a book project that could easily have been impossible without their help. Among them are: Melvin Schneider, Washington, Iowa, volunteer farm credit counselor; Ellen Huntoon, Des Moines, case worker for Sen. Tom Harkin; Gary and Mary Beth Janssen; Dr. John Fuller, Iowa City, professor of urban and regional planning at the University of Iowa; Dan Levitas, staff worker for Prairiefire Rural Action; Carol Hodne, director of the North American Farm Alliance; Marilyn Fedelchak, Chicago, rural program director for the Midwest Office of the National Trust for Historic Preservation; the Rev. David Ostendorf, director of Prairiefire Rural Action; and Gary Lamb, Chelsea, Iowa, currently president of the Iowa Farmers Union.

There have been others too numerous to recall who have helped in various little ways, but the list must end somewhere. To all those who may remember making a suggestion but are not specifically acknowledged, you, too, may take a bow, and I apologize for the omission.

Introduction

I think we have not been irresponsible here as we've listened
to this testimony. I think it depends on which part of the elephant
the blind man got hold of, and we have had interesting testimony from three Secretaries. I'm the fourth one and I think there's
something ulterior and sinister about having a man named Butz
as the speaker on the tail end of this program. [Laughter.]

> —Former Secretary of Agriculture Earl L. Butz, at the opening
> of testimony before the Subcommittee on Agriculture and Trans-
> portation of the Joint Economic Committee of the United States,
> Monday, March 29, 1982.

JULY 1984. I am sitting in the driveway under a tree at the Edgar
and Ida Morse farm in Winterset, Iowa. Sipping our Cokes, we
are discussing Edgar's deteriorated relationship with a local banker.
It is not an unusual story. Low farm income and low farm product
prices, coupled with declining land values, have strained many formerly cordial farmer-banker relationships.

But Edgar points across the dirt road that runs alongside the
backyard of his house. On the other side are steep hills rising at least
at 40-degree angles from road level, heavily forested, with a handful
of cows munching grass in the meadow below.

"The banker wants me to plow those hills and plant crops," he
says.

I stare at those hills rather blankly.

"You've got to be kidding."

Edgar assures me that he is not, that, as part of a plan to get more income to pay his loans, the banker wants him to plant fifty acres of this land. It will produce more income than a few cows roaming the hills. And cattle haven't been so profitable, anyway. In fact, Morse had been pushed to sell his cows. "Why," he asks, "would a banker, knowing that this land is sitting here idle, push a man to sell his cows?"

"Has this banker ever seen this land?" I ask in astonishment. "Those hills wouldn't last more than a year or two if you plowed them up."

"He never came out and looked at them. He just looked at the map and asked me what I was doing with that land."

Throughout that summer and beyond, other farmers, perhaps in less starkly ridiculous situations, relate much the same story to me. "I know I shouldn't be planting that land," they would say, "but I don't have any choice if I want to hang on to it. I need the money to survive."

Common sense dictates that conservation cannot succeed when a farmer's choice is between giving up the farm and planting Edgar Morse's hilly acreage as a short-term stopgap for hanging on just one more year. The dust bowl of the 1930s may have been a product of ignorance. The tools are there today to prevent it. What is lacking is the integration of economic, sociological, and biological knowledge—in other words, crossing academic and bureaucratic boundaries and challenging agribusiness shibboleths—to make a sustainable and prosperous American agriculture a realistic prospect. We have allowed our modern technical skills to erect barriers in our minds, rather than to foster holistic thinking.

Edgar Morse's dilemma is symptomatic of a larger paradox whose consequences are all too common throughout the Midwest. This vast breadbasket has for some time been capable of producing far more than the nation can either consume or export profitably (or even unprofitably, so far as many farmers are concerned). In the absence of either production controls or expensive set-aside programs,[1] American farmers can almost invariably produce surpluses of the storable commodities generally associated with midwestern and much southern agriculture: wheat, corn, rice, oats, soybeans, and cotton. The surpluses depress market prices, and individual farmers feel pressed to produce more to earn the same income. The cycle inevitably leads to financial insecurity and unrelenting pressure to exploit the land at the expense of its own long-term productivity. No land can be eternally productive in spite of abuse. Ethiopia, after all, was once the breadbasket of the Roman Empire. Farmers in the Midwest, in escaping near-term consequences of soil nutrient depletion and erosion, have only the limited advantages of unusually rich topsoil, a relatively short history of exploiting it, and the relatively recent availability of abundant petrochemical fertilizers.

Until recently, despite a long-term legislative drift toward "free-market" principles, federal farm policy has sought to insulate family farms from some free-market pressures. The philosophy behind the basic structure of the programs established under President Franklin Roosevelt's New Deal was not hard to understand. Surplus commodities throughout the 1920s and 1930s had depressed prices to disastrous levels and led to widespread rural unrest. The cycle of spiraling surpluses and plummeting prices was little different from the likely result of abandoning all federal intervention in the farm economy today. As economist John Kenneth Galbraith observed:

[The free market] does not exist because left to market forces, agriculture has a relentless, wholly normal tendency to overproduce. This is for two elementary reasons. First, agriculture is an industry of truly extraordinary productivity gains; these over the last 50 years have widely exceeded those of industry. This has been the source of a persistent pressure of supply on price. But that is not all. Uniquely, or nearly so, in the modern economy the individual farmer has no influence or control over the supply and price of what he produces. The individual farmer is one among thousands and tens of thousands responding to a market price and situation on which not even the production decisions of the largest individual operator have any appreciable effect.[2]

But it is not federal farm programs responding to farmers' need for a stable market, nor is it the market itself, that created the family farm system. Throughout much of the world, the historical pattern of rural development has been one of concentrated land ownership, often long before the introduction of modern farm technology. Latin America's predominant social and political problems have revolved around its inherited system of huge ranches and estates held by an elite land-owning class. That situation should refute forever any assumption that the United States achieved its dispersed pattern of farmland ownership through some natural response to the vastness of its resources and open spaces. The same social stratification that has retarded land reform—and democratic government—for centuries in Latin America bred large slave-serviced plantations in the American South before the Civil War. Due to a failure of federal will to address the resulting inequities during the Reconstruction, that system has left its mark on much of the South ever since.

America's family farms are products of policy that resulted from a widely shared political ideal. Although public lands policy in the nineteenth century was often rife with speculative activity, not to mention some corruption, the prevailing public goal was the Jeffersonian ideal of widespread land ownership that would foster a democracy of independent small farmers. The single clearest manifestation of that goal was the Homestead Act, which enabled hundreds of thousands of settlers to stake a claim on acreages of prairie grasslands throughout states like Iowa, Kansas, Nebraska, Minnesota, and the Dakotas, forging what had to be the most democratic pattern of land ownership in the Western world. But as Galbraith notes, it is also a system of farmers uniquely vulnerable to the free-market forces that Reagan administration policymakers sought to make the hallmark of international agricultural trade.

Despite the complexities of federal farm law and farm programs, there are some basic structures that have been in place since the New Deal to respond to the classic issues that Galbraith and others—like University of Missouri agricultural economist Harold Breimyer—raise. Most of the storable commodities mentioned above have had a system of loan rates and target prices to sustain farm income. The loan rates work quite simply: Farmers can "lend" their grain to the federal Commodity Credit Corporation at a preset price per bushel for up to nine months at a prescribed interest rate. This allows the farmer to wait for improved market prices, which historically have responded to the floor those loan rates established. If the farmer fails to redeem the grain by paying the loan plus the accrued interest, the CCC takes possession of the grain, which becomes part of the government-owned surpluses, at least until the federal government chooses to release some of it into the market. Whether this measure specifically helps family farmers has been debated because, obviously, large producers can benefit in proportion to their size. That it has introduced some stability into farm prices is less debatable, although some have argued that it encourages greater production. On the other hand, so does the pressure of the combination of low prices and high debt.

Target prices were a measure introduced long after the New Deal to ameliorate production problems and to compromise with critics of the loan rates. They simply constitute farm income enhancement by compensating farmers for the difference between the established target price for a commodity and either the loan rate or the price a farmer receives. But the arrangement is tied to participation in any acreage set-aside program, thus enrolling the farmer in production controls. Farm programs have steadily moved in that direction in recent years, especially in the 1985 farm program. A major criticism, of course, is that target prices constitute a drain on the federal treasury. They also introduce the opening wedge for an issue that has often divided farmers and environmentalists and even farmers themselves: cross-compliance, or the requirement that participation in such farm subsidies be conditioned on compliance with relatively unrelated goals such as soil conservation or production controls. The former won acceptance in the 1985 farm bill; the latter are part of the Harkin–Gephardt proposal, which would replace subsidies with higher loan rates but require production limits if farmers chose them in referendums.

One of the oddities of the debate over the 1985 farm bill, which was negotiated amid an air of crisis, is that public pressure for an environmental component in the new law reached its greatest and most successful heights just as farmers were suffering their worst economic losses. American Farmland Trust policy director Robert Gray exulted over the inclusion of numerous provisions in that bill for dealing with soil conservation, including various programs for curtailing "sodbusters" and "swampbusters"[3] and for establishing a conservation reserve of highly erodible farmland retired from production. Yet later, when I met with National Save the Family Farm Coalition president Helen Waller, she complained that during the drafting of the bill, at a meeting of environmentalists that Gray chaired, she had tried in vain to encourage environmental groups to support provisions raising commodity prices through higher crop loan rates, arguing that farmers who could not pay their bills were unlikely to aid in the successful implementation of soil conservation measures. There was an obvious communication gap. As often happens, theoretically logical allies were divided by differing perceptions of their common interests. But Waller also indicated in the fall of 1987 that she and Gray were still undertaking efforts to talk out some of their differences, realizing that each would need to do further work to bring their constituencies in line.

The disjunction between farmers and environmentalists—who tend to profess a common commitment to the land—reveals much about the many disjunctions between the public's desires for agriculture and the actual results of our farm policies. While public support for the institution of the family farm runs consistently high in the polls,[4] the family farm itself has been hemorrhaging for some time—even before the onset of the 1980s farm crisis. Despite strong public support for preservation of our soil resources, there is little solid research on the kind of farm ownership patterns or economic conditions that will best foster effective soil stewardship. But conservation experts have offered educated guesses that a stable farm economy predominantly characterized by owner-operated farms is our best bet.[5]

If that is the case, statistics from the Midwest do not provide us with a comforting picture. The trend is toward a bipolar pattern of agricultural operations consisting of a small number of very large farms and a large number of very small, commercially nonviable "hobby farms" that tend either to be tax dodges or the part-time fancy of exurbanites. There will be little in between—and in between has traditionally meant the full-time family farmer whose income depended upon his crops and livestock, but who is increasingly unlikely to survive. Those who do will increasingly join what Washington, Iowa, farm credit counselor Melvin Schneider calls the "stompers," large operators with hired labor whose farms far exceed the four-hundred-acre average that prevails today.[6]

The traditional middle-sized family farmer is likely to become an anachronism in two ways: culturally and economically. What makes them culturally anachronistic is that most are holistic holdouts in a world of industrial and postindustrial specialization. Many describe themselves as jacks of all trades: accountant, mechanic, veterinarian, soil scientist, entrepreneur, tiller of the soil, milker of cows. They cannot afford merely to know economics and farm, for soon the soil may laugh at their vaunted efficiency. They cannot merely know the soil and farm, for the market may laugh at their best-laid plans when the price of corn or wheat falls at an unpropitious moment. And they cannot afford to listen unskeptically to experts, for all have their intellectual disclaimers when problems touch a subject that is not part of their credentials.

But experts like to carve out pieces of intellectual turf where certain credentials are required for one to affect the discussion of public policy. Even politicians are overmatched in most debates unless they have credentials beyond mere public office. Throughout this century, as the walls one must climb to establish these credentials have grown higher with our technological advances, and as our economy has become increasingly complex, family farmers have receded into the background as a voice in agricultural policy at virtually any level. It is not only their declining percentage in the American population that has lowered their voices. It is a profound sense of being overwhelmed and ignored in the discussion. The ascendancy of a conservative organization such as the Farm Bureau, running counter to the radical tendencies of many earlier farm movements, is due in no small part to its ability to segment and echo the message of those with the credentials.

Unfortunately for middle-sized family farmers, few of those with the economic credentials—except for a minority like Galbraith—are willing to confirm their value as a lasting institution in our economy. More typical is the somewhat chilling statement (from such a farmer's perspective) offered by University of Michigan economist Kenneth Boulding:

"The only way I know to get toothpaste out of a tube is to squeeze, and the only way to get people out of agriculture is likewise to squeeze agriculture. If the toothpaste is thin, you don't have to squeeze very hard; on the other hand, if the toothpaste is thick, you have to put real pressure on it. If you don't get people out of agriculture easily, you're going to have to do farmers severe injustice in order to solve the problem of allocation."[7]

Injustice or not, Boulding's desired reallocation is indisputably taking place. In fact, it has been taking place for years and has only been accelerated during what has come to be regarded as the 1980s' farm crisis. During the seemingly prosperous 1970s, for example, while Iowa land prices more than quadrupled from their 1970 average of about $400 per acre and corn prices more than doubled, the number of farms was slowly falling and the percentage of tenant farmers was slowly rising (for the first time since the Great Depression). Iowa lost 11,000 of its 130,000 farms between 1975 and 1980 alone.[8]

Many of those who did buy farmland were off-farm investors seeking a way to beat inflation, which farmland obviously did—until the decline began in 1981.

It is not that sort of decline that arouses concern, however, even in the farming community. The dropouts were retirees and those who simply could not pay or finance the price of a farm. Foreclosures and an impossible debt burden hemmed in by swift declines in asset values are another matter. By 1981, tight money and high interest rates were pricking the balloon of tens of thousands of overextended farmers who had amassed a $216 billion mountain of debt for a variety of reasons. Many older farmers brought children into the operation at a very inauspicious time; many had been convinced by lenders, economists, and extension personnel that they had to get bigger or get out; many were caught in the cost-price squeeze affecting petroleum-based inputs and ever-larger farm equipment; and some had simply gambled dangerously on the continued inflation in farmland prices.

Whatever the individual reasons, it was clear by the mid-1980s that the farm market had collapsed, but that its impact was highly uneven. Troubled farms dotted the landscape like the black squares on a checkerboard, interspersed with healthy operations that simply were not saddled with debt. A *Farm Journal* survey published in early 1985 clearly put the Midwest in the eye of a national farm debt storm.[9] Agricultural economists generally regard a farm with a debt-to-asset ratio above 70 percent as in very serious trouble. A farm with a ratio above 100 percent, of course, is technically bankrupt. But in an economy where farm land values began to fall by double-digit percentages in most midwestern states after 1981, even the 70 percent ratio is an unstable one that could render a farmer bankrupt within a year or two. A 40 percent ratio represented trouble somewhere on the horizon. But the survey showed 12 percent of U.S. farm operators and 21 percent of Midwest operators with debt-to-asset ratios above 70 percent. Another 18 percent of U.S. and 21 percent of Midwest operators had ratios between 40 and 70 percent. In short, more than two-fifths of Midwest farmers were threatened with near-term or long-term insolvency. With land values falling precipitously and being forced lower by the volume of forced sales on the market, the struggle for survival by those laden with high-interest debt was a struggle to escape quicksand. The work ethic alone just might not be enough to save the day.

14

Introduction

But there was another story behind the immediate headlines at the peak of the farm crisis. It contradicted conservative assumptions that the losers were less efficient and that the farm economy was simply undergoing a necessary restructuring. Those who were surviving had one of two advantages, neither of which necessarily implied greater efficiency: preexistent large cash and land reserves to weather the storm or age. Age was an advantage for some simply because they had entered farming in a more prosperous era, they had paid off whatever earlier farm debts they had contracted, they had not taken on new debt to aid their children, and they were now biding their time until retirement. Iowa State University extension economist Robert Jolly, in 1984, surveyed Iowa farmers to establish a demographic profile of the debt problem. Those with debt-to-asset ratios of 10 percent or less had an average age of sixty-one but rented or owned *less* acreage on average than the other three leverage classes in Jolly's survey.[10] In the 11 to 40 percent ratio, the average age declined to fifty-three; for 41 to 70 percent, to age forty-eight; and in the deeply troubled category above 70 percent, to forty-six. Oddly, the percentage in each class providing aid to family members showed very little variation, ranging from 13.4 percent among those highly leveraged to 16 percent among the lowest. But the percentage receiving aid climbed rapidly as debt leverage increased, going from 1.5 to 12 percent.

Of course, family farm advocates raised the obvious question: In a farm economy where only the wealthy and the elderly could survive, and where the elderly were destined soon to retire, who but the already well-to-do would remain to farm? Farmers themselves seemed to sense the obvious answer, as the results of one local survey in Iowa's Cerro Gordo County in early 1985 seemed to show: Only 35 percent expected to continue farming until retirement, whereas 60 percent saw their survival horizon as five years or less.[11]

The U.S. Congress's Office of Technology Assessment was preparing a report then that supported those farmers' collective assessments of their future. Showing negative net farm income for small and part-time farms, and a steadily declining market share for medium-sized family farms, it concluded:

It is clear that if these trends continue, small and part-time farms are likely to disappear, to the extent that the operators of

15

these farms depend on them for income. The number of small rec-
reational, or "hobby," farms may increase. Large and very large
farms will completely dominate agriculture. The number of moderate farms may continue to increase, but they will have a small
share of the market and a declining share of net farm income.

Moderate farms comprise most of the farms that depend on agriculture for the majority of their income. Traditionally, the moderate
farms have been viewed as the backbone of American agriculture.
These farms appear to be failing in their efforts to compete for
their historical share of farm income.[12]

What caused the bust? The answer is not simple. A variety of
related causes converged to deflate a very vulnerable market. But the
single biggest flaw in the bullish agricultural economy of the 1970s
was that it was based on questionable expectations, many of them
promoted by the most powerful and influential voices in rural America.
A combination of a devalued dollar and large Soviet grain purchases
had raised expectations of enlarged export markets to a fever pitch,
causing American and Canadian farmers both to expand planted
corn and wheat acreage by well over 40 percent within little more
than a decade.[13] (In the midst of the farm crisis, *Des Moines Register*
farm columnist Lauren Soth suggested the real cause of overproduction
with a column headlined "Not 'Too Many Farmers': Too Many Acres
Farmed.")[14] Of course, the additional production, in classic fashion,
served as a damper on prices just as speculators bid up farmland
values. Agriculture Secretary Earl Butz preached the gospel of
"fencerow to fencerow," urging American farmers to prepare to feed
the world. Forgotten in the crusade was the simple fact that, just as
Americans talked of energy independence as they realized their reli-
ance on foreign sources, less-developed nations—and even developed
nations like Japan that had endured privation in recent memory—
yearned for food independence. The Green Revolution, despite its
severe dislocating effects for tens of millions of formerly rural poor in
third-world nations, gave it to most of them. Africa, which remained
an exception to the general achievement of food independence, was
generally too poor to buy our grain, and occasionally too poor even
to process it when we donated it. In short, the export boom became a
bust just in time to be aggravated by the strong dollar created by the
onset of Reaganomics.

It is probable that neither Edgar Morse nor his banker fully understood the pressures of domestic and international farm economics

16

that impelled the suggestion that Morse plow up his hills. I cannot speak for the banker, but I do know that, however haltingly, Morse was groping for some political and economic understanding of the forces that were changing his life and jeopardizing his livelihood. His background and skills for grappling with such a complex subject may have been inadequate, but one of his tools in the search was becoming increasingly common among his neighbors. He was attending meetings of the Madison County farm survival committee, chaired by his neighbor, Robert Simon.

I talked with Simon in July 1984. Simon was a bit exceptional because few farmers were prepared to admit they were in trouble that summer. The denial is usually total: If you don't tell yourself, you won't tell others. But Simon was different. He readily admitted that he had had a declining and negative net worth since 1980. In his first decade of farming, starting in 1956, he and his wife, who have always been tenant farmers, managed to feed a family without any off-farm income. They had a problem in 1968 that resulted in a farm sale, but they stayed in farming, raising sheep, cattle, and hogs. But the current problem seemed intractable. The Farmers Home Administration had already hinted at a possible withdrawal of credit.

"They are not going to do well selling me out with a negative net worth," he said. "They had better bear with me and hope things improve this fall. After all these years, it can work again." But, he concedes, "The numbers are all bad right now." His wife was working at a nursing home in Winterset. It was only the off-farm income that kept them afloat. The farm was bleeding money.

Robert Simon organized a local farm survival committee, a relatively new creature in Iowa that gathered those wishing to share their pains and trials as farmers for mutual benefit and encouragement. I attended three of their meetings in Madison County that summer. It was a place to watch a new voice struggling to identify its message at the most basic grass-roots level. It was an imperfect voice, but it was a rare chance for a handful of farmers to go public with their determination that these particular "excess resources on the land" would not be squeezed out of the tube without a fight.

Farming is a strange business. It is an endeavor in which individual effort has relatively little effect on the larger forces that determine world prices or bulging surpluses. It has no effect whatsoever on such eternal uncertainties as the weather, a relatively minor concern to most industries. Yet rugged individualism somehow became the philosophic cornerstone of rural culture, despite all the evidence to refute its validity. This individualism leads to a refusal to admit the need for cooperative political action because such an admission would suggest individual weakness or failure. The helplessness and the denial continue until a crisis erupts. Domestic violence and suicide, despite all the inadequacies of documentation, clearly were on the rise in rural America.

The farm crisis of the 1980s has gradually broken down much of the resistance to admitting the limits of individual effort, an obvious precondition to successful cooperative action. Perhaps the very fact that family farms seem to be self-contained units—although that has largely changed in modern times—led to the idea that working with others is superfluous.

But a deeper problem faced the nascent farm survival committees. As I spoke with farmers and toured the Midwest, I constantly witnessed a profound inability to define solutions. At meeting after meeting, problem definition would go on for hour after hour without leading to any policy resolution. "I don't know what the answer is" accompanied by a shrug of the shoulder and a resignation that allowed the powers that be to sort out the problems.

It was not always thus. There *have* been eras of mutual cooperation among farmers. In the 1870s, the Grange swept through many farm states like wildfire, and there was virtually no notion of shame or foolishness among farmers themselves about joining such movements. At its peak, the order claimed six hundred thousand adult members, no less than a hundred thousand in Iowa alone. In the 1880s, another wave of organizing, the Farmers Alliances, again claimed hundreds of thousands of supporters. By the 1890s, farmers throughout the South and the Midwest actively worked toward and dreamed of their own political party as a means of transforming the values of an entire nation. They began to break down, however temporarily, long-standing and seemingly impenetrable racial barriers. A black and a woman were both on the Kansas Populist ticket in an 1890 campaign that came only five thousand votes shy of winning the state's executive offices. Despite its share of tactical mistakes, it was a vast popular experiment that has seen no equal in our century.

Farmers still mounted political revolts on a smaller scale up to and during the Great Depression, leading to the New Deal programs that expanded the Farm Credit System, created the Farmers Home Administration, and ultimately established the parity pricing system at the onset of American involvement in World War II—the first system of government price supports with an explicit goal of putting farmers on an equal economic footing with their urban brethren.

In the 1980s, farmers seem to have an historical amnesia of massive proportions. Many do not know that such prior movements ever existed or what they accomplished or how our current farm programs came to be. Such rootlessness is politically debilitating. Is it possible that real power over the farmers lies in erasing their collective memory? Have farmers unwittingly—or perhaps in a desire to conform to certain modern expectations or to reassert an erroneous but appealing sense of individuality—allowed certain questions and ideas to be put beyond the realm of public discussion in rural society?

If so, to be divorced from one's heritage is, in a way, to be disenfranchised. The mere knowledge that one's forebears exercised power and influenced politics is a form of empowerment. It requires only a decision, an exercise of the will, rather than a complete reeducation process. It is the difference between political literacy and illiteracy.

Many of today's farmers, faced with a crisis they do not completely comprehend, are engaged in reestablishing their identity on firmer soils than the quicksand promises of the 1970s. But they have also learned that, in their days of innocence, they wandered down the wrong road and visited the inn of Procrustes.

In Greek mythology, Procrustes was an ogre whose roadside inn offered false solace to wayward customers. In it was an iron bed. Once they were inside, Procrustes made his customers fit the iron bed. If they were too tall, he chopped off their legs to fit. If they were too short, he stretched them.

The modern grasp of Procrustes lies with policymakers who will not admit that our free-market system fails to answer all the questions these newly aware farmers will pose. As one person put it when I mentioned this story in a church, "Procrustes has gone franchise." The new Procrusteans dismiss the new farm voice as naive and are determined to make agriculture fit the iron bed of preconceived economic theory, despite all the evidence of disastrous results. Farmers who cannot make it in the brave new world must be stretched or cut to fit.

Such pressures lead to many responses on the part of those who wish to fight back, however late their discovery that they have walked into a trap. Not everyone interviewed in this book will agree with everyone else about the answer to the farmer's plight in the 1980s and 1990s. A movement voice in almost any age is a potentially raucous and discordant one, and what is remarkable is the degree of unanimity that is emerging among progressive farm spokespersons. That voice needs to be heard because a farm policy crafted without farmers' input is ultimately a travesty, however much other voices must also have a say. It is ultimately today's family farmers who can best and most persistently raise the question articulated by economist Harold Breimyer on Charles Kuralt's August 16, 1987, *Sunday Morning* on CBS, in a segment titled "Who Will Own the Land?": "The main point is really your social and political image of what you think is better: whether one prefers a more egalitarian, democratic rural society in which each person on the land has some interest in his land and gets all the standing that goes with it or whether, instead, we go to a four- or five-layer-cake arrangement with big owners in the cities, managers in the state capitals, the straw bosses in the county seats, and then two or three layers of workers on the land. That's where we are headed if we do not do anything to arrest the trend."

In short, no matter how often the cry of "efficiency" is raised against the pleas of these newly politicized farmers, they will always be able to reply with another question: efficiency for whom and for what purpose?

NOTES

1. Readers uninitiated in agricultural issues should find that their progress through this book will steadily familiarize them with these terms of art in farm policy and render the terminology less foreign. Production controls are government-imposed limits on the amount of any commodity that individual farmers may produce. They are not part of current farm policy, except for tobacco, but were part of some of the experimentation of President Franklin Roosevelt's New Deal during the mid-1930s. Set-asides are acreages idled by farmers participating volun-

20

Introduction

tarily in government efforts to limit production in order to reduce surpluses, and may take the form either of direct payments in cash or in kind for idled acres or of percentage set-asides required for participation in crop subsidy programs. The 1983 PIK (Payment-in-Kind) program, which traded farmers supplies of surplus crops for their agreement to idle parts of their land, was a major recent example of a set-aside program.

2. John Kenneth Galbraith, "Agriculture Policy: Ideology, Theology, and Reality over the Years," remarks before the National Governors' Conference, Traverse City, Michigan, July 27, 1987.

3. Although these two terms are not new, they somewhat exploded into the general American consciousness with the passage of the 1985 Food Security Act. A sodbuster is someone who plows previously unbroken dry ground that is often highly erodible, and is particularly a problem on the Great Plains, where drought combined with questionable farming practices in the 1930s to create the Dust Bowl. (Nearly a century ago, the story goes, a Pawnee chief watched the first settlers in northeast Colorado plow such ground and commented sadly, "Grass not good upside down." We've had plenty of time to learn.) Swampbusters, in contrast, are farmers who drain wetlands in order to plant crops in their often fertile but vulnerable soil. A major environmental objection was that such practices often eliminated valuable wildlife and plant habitats. The law ended federal subsidies and incentives for such practices.

4. See *The Harris Survey,* no. 19, March 7, 1985; no. 99, December 5, 1985; and no. 8, January 27, 1986.

5. This is not the place for citing a specific quote, but rather to refer the reader to a more general source of literature:

Stephen B. Lovejoy, and Ted L. Napier, eds., *Conserving Soil: Insights from Socioeconomic Research* (Ankeny, Iowa: Soil Conservation Society of America, 1986). This book, which is merely a starting point, is based on papers presented at a symposium in Zion, Illinois, June 3–5, 1985. The speakers did not all agree with the statement I have offered, but some offered ideas that resembled it, and most agreed that the relation between macroeconomic agricultural policy and the soil conservation practices of individual farmers is an area inadequately studied and needing further examination. For another examination of the relationship between the farm economy and the environment, the following is suggested: *Agriculture and the Environment in a Changing World Economy* (Washington, D.C.: The Conservation Foundation, 1986).

6. *Technology, Public Policy, and the Changing Structure of American Agriculture: A Special Report for the 1985 Farm Bill* (Washington, D.C.: U.S. Congress, Office of Technology Assessment, OTA-F-272, March 1985), p. 19.

7. Kenneth Boulding, *Collected Papers,* vol. 3 (Boulder: Colorado Associated University Press, 1973), p. 164.

8. Iowa Crop and Livestock Reporting Service, *1984 Iowa Agricultural Statistics* (Des Moines: Iowa Crop and Livestock Reporting Service, 1984), p. 4.

9. Gene Erb, "42% of Iowa's Farmers Face Debt Trouble," *Des Moines Register,* January 26, 1985, p. 1A.

10. James Schwab, *The Farm Credit Crisis in Iowa* (Iowa City: Legislative Extended Assistance Group, The University of Iowa, February 1985), p. 45.

11. Schwab, *The Farm Credit Crisis,* p. 98, originally supplied by Cerro Gordo ASSIST. A *Des Moines Register* poll a year earlier offered much the same assessment of farmers' attitudes, though not quite so pessimistic. But 86 percent of farmers responding said it was not a good time to become a farmer (David Elbert and David Westphal, "Iowa Farmers Facing Worst Times Ever," *Des Moines Register,* April 29, 1984).

12. Office of Technology Assessment, *Technology, Public Policy,* p. 21.

13. Andrew Schmitz, "Agricultural Trade and U.S. Policy Response," in *United States Farm Policy in a World Dimension* (Columbia: University of Missouri, 1983), pp. 70–71.

14. Lauren Soth, "Not 'Too Many Farmers': Too Many Acres Farmed," *Des Moines Register,* February 18, 1985, p. 14A.

PART ONE
Looking Back

A Matter of Social Justice

MERLE HANSEN
Newman Grove, Nebraska

A grain and cattle farmer in central Nebraska, Hansen comes from a town that was a hotbed of the Farm Holiday movement in the 1930s that spearheaded many of the protests that preceded many of the New Deal farm programs. He is now president of the Ames, Iowa-based North American Farm Alliance, a coalition of numerous state and national farm groups.

UNTIL 1933, in the Roosevelt administration, we had the so-called free market, and for farmers, it was a boom-and-bust affair. For instance, in 1920, corn was $2.20 a bushel; 1921, it went to 23 cents a bushel. In the course of about twenty months.

I have a quotation that I use quite often from Hicks's *Populist Revolt.* It was about 1890, and it quoted an agonized farmer. He said, "We went to work and plowed and planted, and put in the big crop that they asked us to, and the sun shone and the rains fell, and we raised an abundant crop, and what came of it? Ten-cent oats and eight-cent corn, and two-cent beef, and no price at all for butter and eggs. That's what come of it, and the politicians said that we suffered from overproduction."

But this has historically been the way the free market worked for farmers. In 1932, corn went to as low as 10 cents a bushel, and hogs to 2 cents a pound. And a farmer just the other day—some of these farmers come up with the best stuff—he says, "Hell, I can remember when we had a strong dollar. A dollar could buy ten bushels of corn!" He wasn't very much impressed with a strong dollar! But the so-called free market is really a license to steal. And it never, never did work for the farmer. In 1933, Roosevelt initiated the first government intrusion, really, into the farm marketing system. Which, by the way, was at the time that a whole bunch of other social legislation came in. For instance, farmers could not get electricity. It was only the government intervention and financing that brought electricity to farmers because the private power companies didn't think it was profitable enough. And so REA [Rural Electrification Administration] was set up. The Wagner Act, which really gave labor the right to organize, was one of the things that came in then. The minimum wage idea, Social Security, whole bunch of social legislation.

Recently, the Farm Bureau vice-president spoke to President Reagan, and he called farm legislation entitlement programs, which proves again that it's a social justice issue. And proves again where farmers really belong in the scheme of things.

Roosevelt actually raised the price of corn from about 10 cents a bushel to 45 cents a bushel practically overnight. He brought in this loan program where farmers could go and take a loan on that corn. Since that time, the loan level has determined farm prices. If you took the eighteen years from 1935 through '52, which would be really the Roosevelt program—Truman really carried on the Roosevelt program—those eighteen years averaged 90 percent of parity[1] to farmers. The cost to the government on storable commodities: The government made $13 million. It's incredible. Eleven of those twenty years, from '42 to '52, farmers received 100 percent of parity or over. The cost was very minimal. The total cost of all price supports, including perishables, was about $1 billion. And most of that was due to a loss of potatoes, which was a kind of a fiasco.

But, for all of those twenty years, it was the most cost-effective program you could think of. That was in a period when you didn't see farm prices go down and food prices go up at the same time. Consumers probably got the best buy in food that they ever got. The cost to the government was the best.

Then, in 1952, Eisenhower was elected. Ezra Taft Benson, who was a John Birch Society member, became secretary of agriculture. He said that farmers needed the spur of insecurity. They needed to feel the market. Earl Butz was assistant secretary of agriculture

[1]A level for farm-product prices determined by the government that would give farmers the same purchasing power they had during the base period of 1910-14, when farm prices gave them a rough equality, or "parity," with nonfarm workers.

during those years. He said there are too many farmers. We've got a big pie here, and we need to eliminate a certain amount of farmers, and then we'd have bigger pieces of pie to cut. Parity during the Eisenhower years went from 97 down to 84.

From then on, we've really had a bipartisan farm policy, as we've had a bipartisan foreign policy. Even Truman was beginning to have a bipartisan farm policy, as well as a bipartisan foreign policy. There was very much of a tie between farm policy and foreign policy because, among other things, we used food as a weapon. Cheap raw materials are very much tied to foreign policy.

The Kennedy years: parity was 79 percent. The Johnson years: parity was 75 percent. The Nixon-Ford years: parity was 78 percent. The Carter years: parity was 68 percent. And this brings up an interesting question with Ronald Reagan blaming Jimmy Carter for just about everything, although we've had a Republican president for twelve of the last sixteen years, and it was Earl Butz, when he was secretary of agriculture, who told farmers to plant fencerow to fencerow, "You are practically in the Promised Land." The Reagan years have set a new record low of parity. Parity for those years has averaged 58 percent [as of 1984, but falling since then], which is even worse than Herbert Hoover's four years, which was 68 percent. And only one year, even under Hoover, did it get down to 58, in 1932. The Reagan years, parity has gone to 57 in 1982, and 56 in 1983, and 1984 averaged 58 percent of parity. So by any standards, the Reagan years are much worse than Jimmy Carter or even Herbert Hoover.

How do you find your way out of that?

We are not going to solve the farm problem in isolation from other social justice issues. We didn't solve it before, and we are not going to solve it now. I think farmers and other people have to come to the realization that, until and if we can turn this government around, it is not going to be solved. I see nothing but very hard days ahead for farmers unless there is an uprising in this country the likes of which we haven't seen for years. And that means an uprising of all people who are victims of this. It's got to come soon for farmers, or it's gonna be too late for most of them.

My Life in the Farm Bureau

SELMER HODNE
Manilla, Iowa

His son, Steve, is now the backbone of the family farming operation. His daughter, Carol, is the staff director for the North American Farm Alliance, an international progressive farm coalition based in Ames, Iowa.

O F course, I grew up on a farm. Had a touch of the depression. I was born in 1919, so in my very early teen years, I felt what happened to my folks in the thirties. One thing I knew was that I was not going to be a farmer. When I graduated from high school, there was nothing much more worthless than a teen-age youngster. There were no jobs available.

I graduated in '36—right in the middle of nothing. I was out of school for, I guess, four years. I had a high school classmate who, in the fall of '39, said, "You might as well go to school as sit, there's no work anyway." He'd gone to Ames for a couple of years, and he was the primary influence in my going to Iowa State University. I enrolled in science. I really felt that I was going nowhere in science, so, after about two years, I enrolled in agriculture. I felt comfortable in that study because I had a real understanding of the value of that topic and how it related, because here in this field, I already had a living background. School suddenly became easy, and naturally I had economics and farm management or business agriculture as a significant part of my formal study.

I went in the service, came home and, once again, had no money. I went back to school and then got a job teaching farm veterans. I had

28

an uncle, during about 1950, who stopped in one day. He had a farm about five miles from here and was going to change renters and wanted to know if I wanted to rent it. I said, "Well, I don't have any money to farm." He said, "Well, you don't need much." He rented us the farm, and that's when we started farming.

What had you been doing?

I was teaching farm veterans. I taught for them for about four years. The veterans were anywhere from my age to at least fifteen years older. It was a rather interesting experience of the typical college student trying to teach farmers how to farm.

I was at Corning, Iowa, to begin with; then I moved to Manning. They taught those programs out of the high school. And these were farm training programs because of veterans' rights. We were providing advanced training in, you might say, adult education. But we dealt directly with them on the farms. So, in that background—I'm once again back in school.

But I had to know what I was talking about because those guys were actually doing it, and they had the critical mind: "Does the guy know what he's talking about?" You know. That is atypical as far as agriculture is concerned because there's always been a lot of money in agriculture, and there's always been a lot of people trying to figure out how they can share in the use of that money—that wealth that agriculture creates.

Well, out of that background, we started to farm. And even in that time, there were not very many graduates of ag colleges. Not very many ag teachers, so to speak, that would get into farming, because even then it took a certain determination to be a farmer. At that time, most farmers really would rather see you fail than make it because it would prove that you didn't have to be educated to farm.

After I had farmed about five years, Farm Bureau, doing what they do—they look for leadership—zeroed in and made me a part of that. I was active in Farm Bureau at the ground level membership work, at the county level; from the county level climbed to county president; and then went on up and was on the state board about 1962. I was on that board for twelve years—in other words, four three-year terms.

Whatever my mindset is, I realized that there's politics. As I was told rather early in the game, those who were favored by staff people were people who made advances, who got the favors. Well, I guess,

29

within that first three-year term, I became quite aware of that. But by then I also had a strong belief that agriculture needed representation by people who believed in agriculture for its own sake, not by people who were in it for their own values. And I got that sense that some people who went on the board served because they wanted the prestige. They enjoyed the honor. I felt that my primary obligation should be to represent farmers rather than promote the vested interest of an organization.

I sensed you must know who the players are to realize where the power is and what the problems are. I saw some power plays. I came up on the short side of the popular politics, but that never bothered me because at that point I had to decide, Who am I, what do I stand for, and what are my principles? From then on, I did what I thought I should do. I saw many programs come on that I realized were not for agriculture, but for the organization. I would ask myself, Is it good for agriculture? Do I represent Farm Bureau as an organization or do I represent farmers?

And that became my chosen role: representing people who were engaged in agriculture, making a livelihood out of farming. From that viewpoint I saw many things. All the years that I was in Farm Bureau, I knew how key agribusiness and insurance were for the organization. I had come to realize that staff controlled the organization. I grew to find out that the politics of it was to learn who the people might be who would go on to the state board who knew the right people.

Farm Bureau had a period of what I call top-notch leaders, leaders elected by farmers to represent farmers. As the organization matured through age, staff became more and more the dominant force. And then you would note that the seniority of staff over the planned constant turnover of elected leadership left elected leadership with no control.

They never knew the background, never knew what was happening, why it happened. It was all a result of the organization's structure. I believe Farm Bureau had some excellent leadership, super leadership in the development stages, and then hit a period where its personnel took on increasingly dominant roles. Then you saw the leadership being handpicked. At that point the leadership deteriorated a little bit because they were being selected for a good reason. I believe that the turning point came in the late fifties.

That's a bit of the background of my personal situation. Now some observations that I've had. At no point did I realize how much internal power and control the people in the life insurance organization had. It seemingly was secondary, but it did have a lot of power.

So the insurance business, which came into being about mid-forties, by the time I was involved, was a big chunk of Farm Bureau's income. Farm Bureau as a farm organization had a huge business in life insurance and casualty insurance. The insurance companies played a dual role. Not only did Farm Bureau members help it grow, but they also maintained a loyalty for other people through the life insurance and mutual company ties.

Farm Bureau has a similar tie-in program today for members. I saw the health insurance program, Blue Cross–Blue Shield, develop. You had to be a Farm Bureau member to have the group insurance rate for Iowa. So they have a financial tie. There are a lot of farm families that have to belong to the Farm Bureau for the kind of rates that Blue Cross offered.

The staff moved into that totally with a desire and hope that that would be a membership retention device. So the program was brought into Iowa. The very people they're representing are the people they're using to create additional revenue for the organization.

Well, as I say, in the twelve years I was on the board, I never really believed the elected members understood how the role and purpose of the insurance business related to Farm Bureau as a farm organization. So who controlled? The staff. And, of course, the staff in turn benefits from that. As for the board members, they don't even know the organizational structure, the power of the total Farm Bureau activities.

This gets to the nub of a real problem we are facing today in many areas: Farm Bureau, as an organization, at one time working to get farmers an equitable share of the contributions they made to society, now has seemingly lost that mission with control by the employees.

The advertised membership totals for Farm Bureau in many states exceed the actual numbers of farms. What is Farm Bureau's future membership base in view of its declining numbers of actual farmers?

They still want them on the farm, fragmented. Farm Bureau as an organization still seems to want farmers fragmented and small. That's why they're for family farms. They want an agriculture that is dependent on them because that helps them justify their own existence. I've seen that trend, continued to see the programs—program after program comes on to sustain the parent organization, not help the farmer. Anyone who ever was close enough knew it was a grass-roots program that came from the top down, and if, down at the grass-roots level, it didn't come out the way they wanted it at the top, they altered it in the policy development process. They knew what they wanted people to do. They also never wanted the people to have a voice speaking for the farmers and what they wanted to do. They had to have a reason for their existence. As I saw staff people gain a larger say in who became leadership, farmers would surface as leaders and then were bypassed.

If that's true, aren't they in a bind between the objective of keeping farmers small and fragmented and the kinds of political positions they are taking on farm policy, which are eliminating many such farmers?

You are right. There is a conflict. They do want membership, to retain that as their right to be a voice for agriculture, so they completely tipped over the traces as to what a membership role should be. Membership role could be anyone with a paid membership can have group health insurance, or whatever other service. Membership has nothing to do whatsoever with bona fide farming.

I happened to sit alongside Dean Kleckner [president of the National Farm Bureau] on the state board. We were on the board for about eleven years. I think a year and a half ago [mid-1983], they were flattering him to be their household spokesman, and he was saying there was no farm crisis. A year and a half ago! And for anyone to read that, and he was telling the people this! No farm crisis!

I remember reading that in the Des Moines Register.

Yes. The head of a major farm organization says there's no farm crisis. At the same time they come out and talk about having a record out here.

They're not my voice, they're not Steve's voice. I know any number of people, Farm Bureau members by the fact that they're tied to it economically one way or another without an alternative choice that was desirable. And it's my hope that there's never any question that the farmer was always expendable if it helped the growth of the company.

There's a lot more money in insurance, and that's why I mentioned it. They also have a service company, too. Of course, in Iowa, the background of that was such that they had difficulty competing and managing. Ag business, fertilizers, all of that. Tied in again, I mean, beautiful tie of holding and retaining new members.

This, then, gets back to why we have a lot of the problems that we have. You go to the state legislature, and Farm Bureau still has a voice. You go to Washington, and Farm Bureau is the farm voice. The problem is their policies have been so bad for so long, they are a major part of the problem with the policies they take credit for. And I don't really know where you pin that, other than the fact that the people who are the policymakers are so far from the problem. Mentally, they've been isolated a long time. Today, they are physically isolated. They concern themselves with the survival of the organization and the machinery. For an organization like the Farm Bureau to survive, you have to have problems. Because if you solve the problems, the people become restive and may not have a need for you. So to continue it, you have problems even to the point of having controversy. You create your own need with the membership. Have some problems that they can work at—and you were always able to do that, but you work at them.

Such as?

One program on legislation one time which wouldn't address the problem, so that you could come back later and get the problem corrected. Never work toward correcting problems, but just stirring them. And that's been one of my observations over many years.

A Disturbing Theory

GARY LAMB
Chelsea, Iowa

"It probably goes back to something my father told me many years ago, before he lost his life in a cornpicker accident, that Roosevelt and the Democratic party saved our farm in the thirties."

Gary Lamb calls himself a "reluctant leader," but clearly there is some profound sense of political responsibility that was awakened in him in the mid-1970s.

A few years ago, I simply stood back and took a look at this industry, and it just appeared to me that there was something wrong. I didn't see very many young people coming in, and I always felt that every industry had to have a certain amount of young people entering just to keep it strong. This was about the time the American Agriculture Movement[1] was beginning and talking about price as the basic problem out here. It was in January of '78 that I did something I didn't think I'd probably ever do, and that was throw some clothes in a suitcase and go out to Washington.

I got probably the shock of my life out there. This was really the first time I'd ever run into this theory or this philosophy. It was described to me at that time that the basic problem in agriculture is that we have what we call unneeded resources. That's the numbers of farmers. With the modern technology and so forth, there simply are too many farmers out there trying to share in their piece of the pie. The nation can't afford to have that same number of farmers out

[1]A populist farm organization launched in the 1970s.

there, so we've got to eliminate a tremendous number of these people. When I first ran into this, and I believe Mr. Stockman[2] was the first one, I thought it was an isolated theory. I thought it was one man who happened to be a congressman from Michigan, who happened to have a philosophy that there's too damn many farmers out there, and if we get rid of a bunch of them, well, we'll have solved the problem.

But it wasn't just one man. I ran into it with several other elected officials, senators and congressmen, and I also ran into it at USDA. Howard York, for example, was one of those who seemed to be thrusting this same ideology out there that we've got to eliminate some farmers. He was the economist at the USDA at that time.

I became terribly alarmed when I ran into this theory numerous times in that first year. Of course, I ran into it numerous times since then. But the basic theory is that we've got to remove farmers and that there's really gonna be an added benefit to society because, as we remove farmers, they have to be absorbed by the work force, and we're basically going to lower the wage to the laboring man in the city and factory. Basically, the way I interpret it is: We're trying to adopt an economic policy that provides cheap labor both on the farm and in the factory. And it just seemed to me that, if that was the economic policy to adopt, Mexico should be a hell of a prosperous country at this point because nowhere is labor cheaper than in Mexico. I didn't think that was the kind of economic policy that we should be pursuing.

As I ran into that philosophy more and more, I became deeply concerned that these weren't farm policies that had failed, but that it may be an actual planned strategy out here to eliminate farmers. And that really began to scare me. Because if it was simply a mistake on someone's part, a bad program or a bad policy, you know, I figured at some point in time we'd recognize that and we'd correct it. But if it was a planned strategy from people in high levels in government, I don't define it as a conspiracy, but as simply a weakness in the free enterprise system.

The weakness that I see in the free enterprise system is that we're basically a people's government. When we—the people out here—are not influencing government, somebody else is influencing govern-

[2]David Stockman was director of the Office of Management and Budget during Ronald Reagan's first term.

ment. Those with the wealth and the power and the influence begin to dictate to government. For their own advantage, not for the good of the country or the good of the industry, or the good of the people, but for their own personal advantage. It doesn't mean that they're evil and corrupt and sinister, it simply means it's the free enterprise system, see?

It suddenly dawned on me that probably the one thing that affects the lives of us every morning that we wake up, whether we realize it or not, is politics and government. And I've always had, I guess, a little bit naive opinion that government's taking care of itself, and we don't have to be involved in that. We, as farmers, basically don't like politics or government involvement. We're basically very private people. That was the beginning of something I recognized was terribly important, that if we're going to bring about changes, a great part of that change has to come through the political arena. And then in late '81, some people approached me, asking if I'd run for Congress, and I thought it was probably the stupidest thing I'd ever heard of.

As I thought more about it, I decided it would give me an opportunity to explain what I thought was the economic problem at least in the state of Iowa: depressed agriculture. And I guess there were basically two reasons that I finally conceded and decided to run for Congress. I had a terrible premonition that if we didn't do something, and do something fast, we were going to see 1984 or 1985, where a tremendous amount of farmers were going to get forced off the land. So I thought it would give me an opportunity to at least express my concern. The second factor was: I had to learn more about politics. I had to learn more about how it works or how it doesn't work. I had to know more about the pressures, the influences that can affect somebody running for public office. It's kind of like running a farm machine. You got to understand the doggone machine, you know, if you're gonna make it work right.

It was a very educational learning experience. I'm certain I didn't find out all the answers. But I did learn a lot about how it functions, why it doesn't function, and those kinds of things. Looking back at it now, I'd say we didn't have the party, we didn't have the finances, and we didn't have the name recognition, and we got whipped pretty good.

But we got 30 percent of the vote. People that understand politics tell me that somebody in my position, if I'd have got 5, 10 percent of the vote, that would've been pretty respectable. We actually tripled

36

that. So I must've had a message. Somebody must have identified with what I was saying. And that was positive. The second positive part of it was that we got people motivated to get involved in politics.

A Change of Heart

HOLLIS PETERSEN
Sutherland, Iowa

He now farms alone and raises his young son, of whom he gained custody in late 1986.

I was farming with my father, but we weren't able to expand our land base, so I had the opportunity, I had a college education, and I talked with some people in the Farm Credit System. I had, I guess, a good image of the Farm Credit System. I was encouraged by one of the loan officers from Sheldon who asked me, "Have you ever thought about working in the Farm Credit System?" And I guess I could see that maybe that would be a good direction to go at that time, so I started interviewing. I went to the FICB [Federal Intermediate Credit Bank] in Omaha and interviewed, and they sent me a letter back after the interview, a very complimentary letter. They wanted me to work in the system, not to consider any other positions with any other lenders.

I had good aspirations about working with the Farm Credit System. I finally ended up down at Winterset, which is part of the Creston association. I started in December of '76, worked til July of '77. Then there was an opening in Storm Lake. I wanted to return to this area. So I talked to the branch manager in Storm Lake, and I worked with the Storm Lake association from July of '77 until my termination, which was October [1983].

My memories of working down there at Winterset are all good. That was back during a different period. Back in '77, farmers weren't experiencing the losses that they have been the last three, four years.

38

Just during the time when I left Winterset, they were very aggressive about putting new loans on. I remember they were making a campaign to increase volume. I think this was probably coming from Omaha, and from the FICB. I guess there was more optimism back then amongst the lenders and the other PCA workers, so they were campaigning through the counties, through the townships. And they would sweep through the townships, talk to all the farmers, and drum up business. It was the entire staff that would do this, all the loan officers and branch managers, they would just sweep the entire township. They were taking that approach at putting on new volume.

I moved to Storm Lake, and I could see the same aggressiveness on the part of the loan officers here. We were very volume-conscious. We were wanting to put new loans on. In fact, I can reflect back and can think of one farmer that I was trying to pick up as a borrower and was considered a good loan. I wanted to pick his operating line up, and I learned here earlier this summer that he's in bankruptcy now. He never became a PCA [Production Credit Association] borrower. So it shows that people that you were aggressive about going after, some of these people, solid farmers, they're having the financial problems today. We were encouraging farmers. I guess we were more willing, more optimistic. Farmers were capitalizing more, improvements, and maybe a hog facility, maybe a farrowing, maybe a finishing facility, or maybe replacing some machinery, maybe trading some land. I can think of one farmer that traded 80 acres for 110 acres, and so it increased his debt, but we were very volume-conscious back then.

But the associations are rated at different levels, and if you go up to a higher level, I'm sure your president is eligible for a higher salary, and he has more people working for him, more loan officers, more branch managers, more secretaries. That's how they determine the levels of the association. We were on what I guess you'd call the quota system in a way. The more volume we could put on, we thought that was constructive for the association.

I can remember where there was pressure coming from the FICB to encourage the farmers to go on Agrifax, which was a computerized accounting system. So we were promoting that and, of course, we were on hail insurance and credit life insurance.

And with the volume, you were seeing a lot of buildings going up, new buildings. We worked on Geneseo Street before they built the new building in Storm Lake, and we were not with the administrative office, we were with the branch. I was more comfortable with that. I was happy working away from the administrative office at that time, because fellows that I talked to in other associations told me that you were better off not being so close to the administrative office. But then we built that new building in '79. And then we moved in together, so they have a new building north of Storm Lake.

It covered five counties. And with the increase in staff, we saw new buildings, more company cars, and personalized license plates. Back in '80, we were looking at adding a third loan officer to our branch, and I told Jim Smith, the branch manager, "I just don't think we're going to see this volume increasing all the time." I really questioned whether we should be gearing up for all this volume that they were expecting, but, of course, no one listened at all to me. We did hire a third man, he came up from the Sac City branch, and he came up to Storm Lake, so I transferred some of my loans to him. I didn't transfer loans which I thought would be challenging loans because Dave had had some problems down at Sac City, so I didn't want to give him any loans that I thought would take more time and more effort to work with. I gave him some of the loans with low activity, maybe retired farmers or farmers that borrow very little.

But then in '80, we saw the very high interest rates and they've remained much at those levels all through [1984]—18, 20 percent interest rates.

Then we have the embargo, January 4, of 1980. And, of course, commodity prices slipped, drifted lower all during the year, and then later on in that year, in the summer of '80, we had some weather markets.[1] Commodity prices started to improve, and prices were quite high in November or December of '80, but they didn't remain there very long. So not all the farmers were fortunate enough to take advantage of the higher commodity prices.

So what happens then, you see a little buildup on the operating debt, and you see that happened to so many farmers. Then I was just seeing that change in the attitudes and philosophies. This debt had accumulated not in just one year; it had taken maybe three, four, five, six years for that debt gradually building up. And I think lenders since 1980 have become more impatient and more pessimistic every year. Every year, they're a little bit more pessimistic. And they're wanting cash adjustments. We were getting a lot of memorandums,

[1]Prices rising on expectation of a poor harvest due to weather problems.

like earmarking loans, to go through and earmark loans for liquidation, for collection, loans which would have major cash adjustments, and when you get memorandums like that, you start to see the attitudes of people changing. This was going right up and down the line.

Some of this is done on the part of the people in the associations wanting to make the impression on the higher-ups, people in the FICB, that they're making every effort to monitor loans, protect the association from losses, and we had memorandums concerning two-man-in-field reports, where before you worked as a loan officer by yourself. Maybe you worked as a loan officer with this farmer for five years, and you had a good relationship with that farmer, and you worked well together, but they were wanting you now, because this farmer's maybe rated "problem loan," which is a number two rating, to have two loan officers, or a loan officer and a branch manager drive out. Two-man it, they call it. I think sometimes when the farmer would see you drive in with the branch manager, he'd probably be a little suspicious.

But now, I think they've overreacted on the other side. I can give you a lot of specific examples that demonstrate the attitudes of the people in the Farm Credit System. In '82, I remember a particular farmer passed away. He was a man in his eighties, and he had a son who was in farming, a farmer-son operation, informal partnership. And he was being encouraged by the fellow employees, the branch manager that I worked with, and even by the attorney that was handling the estate, to sell land at that time. The loan was not a very large loan, and they had a lot of equity in the land, and I used to handle the loan before the third man came in, but I could see that that wasn't the right approach. They weren't going to be able to take advantage of use valuation[2] if they sold that land, and prices were already trending lower back in '80, and I thought there was another way to approach it—maybe restructure some of that operating debt with Federal Land Bank. They finally did that, but I think there's an

[2]"Current use" value is a method of valuing real property for inheritance tax purposes that Congress added to the Tax Reform Act of 1976, partly with the intent of making it easier for heirs of farmland to keep the land intact for farm use. There are two methods of valuing current use. The simplest uses a previous five-year average of cash rent for comparable local property divided by the average annual effective interest rate for Federal Land Bank loans. Thus, a cash rent average per acre of $50 with 10 percent interest rates would yield a current use value of $500. The law put some qualifications on this valuation, however. The one most relevant to what

example of their encouraging farmers to sell land—even farmers that didn't need to seriously think about selling land. There were other ways to handle it.

Or calling farmers up on the telephone and telling them to sell grain. Two brothers I know that were borrowing from the Storm Lake PCA were called by their loan officer, told to sell grain over the telephone, and at the time the grain was under loan with Commodity Credit[3], so there wasn't a lot of equity in the grain because prices were quite low then. They sold the soybeans. Heck, quite a quantity, too, I think about twenty thousand bushel. So there wasn't a lot of repayment coming into the association because they had been sealed already. From then on, we saw prices move higher. So they missed out on probably $70,000.

So how would you react to a loan officer or a branch manager that called you up and said, "You sell those beans," when he should have been able to see by looking at the financial statement that there wasn't a lot of equity in the beans anyway at the time?

Do you call that being impatient, or becoming very active in the marketing? You're telling this borrower, you market at this price, which can have long-term impact on your operation. Now just think if these brothers had $70,000 more to bring in. It would have materialized if they would have held about two months longer.

I was criticized the day I was terminated, and I was told one of my problems was I was too sympathetic with the farmers. Well, I guess I was sympathetic and am sympathetic for the farmers. I felt I always took the association's best interests at heart, and always was protecting the association against losses, but I just felt that these farmers were creditable people that I'd worked with for five, six years, and

---

Hollis Petersen is discussing is that the government "recaptures" fair market value of the estate for tax purposes if the property is disposed of, other than by death, by the heir within fifteen years after the death of the decedent. That fair market value, like the current use value, is that value at the time of death. Thus, during a period of declining land values such as the early 1980s, forcing an heir to sell such inherited property resulted in a disposition that could have had grave inheritance tax consequences for the farmer. The failure of some loan officers to consider the impact of those consequences on a farmer's financial viability when making that demand is the abuse of trust that Petersen is addressing here.

[3]Federal price support programs allow farmers to "seal" their grain in exchange for a Commodity Credit Corporation loan, at a rate fixed by law, payable with interest when the grain is sold. It is called a "nonrecourse" loan because the CCC's only collection method on the loan is to take possession of the grain.

that we could possibly take some other approach and try to work out of this problem over a period of three to four years. And if there was just no other way than to liquidate, I felt that I could sit down with that borrower and go through it, take the time and effort to explain it to him. And I think probably by the time it was all over with, we'd be in agreement.

Today, I don't think they take the time to sit down with the members and explain this process that they're going through, and say this is why we're requiring this and requiring that. They just make this demand, and maybe they don't know themselves why they're making this demand. They don't really offer any explanation.

A weakness that I feel that I've seen in some of the officers working in the system is that they didn't seem to have the interest to keep well enough informed. They didn't understand the commodity markets well enough, or they never had any understanding of the tax implications that they might cause by requiring farmers to do certain things. They'd make demands on some of the farmers, not knowing what kinds of repercussions they would cause by doing those things. I thought that I was maybe a little better informed in some of those areas.

When I approached a loan, I always tried to take into consideration, What is this going to do to the farmer's tax liability? Maybe having him liquidate something wouldn't accomplish that much in the end. A year from now, he may have a terrific tax liability. I know I would be upset if I was that farmer, so I tried to look at it from that standpoint.

I'll go one step further on that. We have loan officers today that don't know what a bushel of seed corn costs. They don't know even how many months it takes to get a hog to market. And I'm sure you've heard this before, that there's a lot of them, they know nothing about agriculture.

Well, you've probably met Melvin Schneider[4]. . . . He made a comment in Afton that several years ago, when they were interviewing prospective employees to work in the system, that it wasn't a concern then to hire someone who had a good understanding of agriculture and agriculture finance. It didn't seem to be a priority or a concern. And I think when I started working there . . . it was seen to be more important.

[4]A retired PCA loan officer who worked out of his home in Washington, Iowa, as a volunteer farm credit adviser for financially distressed farmers.

PART TWO
Down and Out on the Farm

Where Life Begins

PAT and ELMER STEFFES
Audubon, Iowa

Elmer and Pat Steffes used to operate a farm in rural Audubon, Iowa. Neither on first impression appears a likely candidate for political activism, but both have been active in the Audubon County Farm Survival Committee and the Iowa Farm Unity Coalition. In August 1984, Elmer was interviewed by Des Moines's WHO Radio shortly after the conclusion of a public farmers' meeting with Iowa Governor Terry Branstad at the Paulsen farm in Exira, about ten miles from their home. He has frequently found solace in aiding other farmers at rallies, penny auctions, and meetings.

The couple has been writing, with the help of a journalism student from Iowa State University, a book about their own ordeal in trying to hang on to their farm and what it has meant to them. Its title is Where Life Begins.

ELMER: We got married February 15, 1958. We moved onto a farm two miles east of Templeton that my dad had bought. We started farming with my dad and lived there.

Our income at the time was from a hundred chickens, and I worked for wages from my dad. Also, I worked part-time at the locker and for the railroad. I got enough money saved up and first bought a hundred acres in Templeton. I did custom chopping of corn silage with Dad's chopper, and we ate out of a big garden we raised, and milked cows. I built a dairy barn out of used lumber. We sold grade-B milk [used for butter and cheese].

47

We lost all our baby calves the first winter because I didn't have the barn fixed warm enough.

We were both born and raised on farms as were our parents and our grandparents. We had worked enough to get credit from my dad on our first farm. We got a Federal Land Bank loan. The best tractor we had at that time was this 400-Case. The year we bought this farm, in 1965, we got our first 930-Case. That was the first and only new tractor we ever bought.

Dad bought this place in August 1965 because my brothers were all getting growing pains. We all needed a place to go. We traded farms with him, using the one in Templeton. We moved here the last day in February 1966, and the next day we got a blizzard.

We moved machinery, cows, and everything from Templeton. And everything went along pretty good. We both had off-farm jobs for a couple of years. Things went along pretty good until about 1977. We built buildings and bought land and borrowed money. Our lending people taught us to "get bigger and get some volume."

Then, in 1978, our first son [Daryl] got sick. He had leukemia. This was the start of our letdown. One year later, our second son got sick. He had leukemia, too. They were both in Iowa City [at University of Iowa Hospitals] at the same time. They passed away twenty-eight days apart in 1979, in September and October.

So, now we had all these outside bills and tried to negotiate them, hoping for a good year. But in 1981, our interest skyrocketed and we lost control of the situation.

The Steffeses proceed to explain that they own 460 acres, on which they grow both row crops and dairy cattle. They use a hundred acres to grow hay with which to feed the dairy cattle.

Elmer: By the spring of 1982, the bank started putting a lot of pressure on us. I broke my arm in an accident and couldn't do much work. So we went to Alaska for ten days for a vacation because there wasn't much I could do anyway.

Pat: If he didn't quit working and rest his arm, he would have to have surgery, which would cost as much as the trip anyway. My sister lives in Alaska and invited us up, and we stayed with her. We used her pickup truck to drive up to the valley. His arm was broken in the elbow. If he was home and working, he would have aggravated it. Two days after Elmer broke his arm, the banker was out seeking a bigger milk check assignment.[1] He persisted until Elmer signed it over.

Elmer: When we came back, we found the banker had been on our answering service every day while we were gone. He came out the next day for an inspection of the farm because he thought we had skipped town. The bank gave us notice verbally that we would be off the property in thirty days. Then they brought brokers and bank directors out. The inspector who does inventories for the bank came out. He started devaluing everything. They would knock this off, knock that off, and our net worth on their books would decline up to $50,000 every two months. They worked out the values at the bank without any input from us.

Elmer proceeds to relate in detail the various forms that creditor harassment began to take, such as late-night telephone calls and reports in mid-winter that he had allowed his sheep to starve in the cold. On one occasion, the sheriff arrived to check out such a report, only to conclude that it was untrue, Elmer says.

As he relates the emotional stress of operating under such circumstances, Pat comments, "He wasn't fit to live with." Elmer mentions that he had almost wanted to punch his banker when he came to the house.

Elmer: It has just been constant harassment for the last two years. Reorganization[2] does not exist in the bank's eyes. But we filed Chapter 11 in the summer of '82. They had started in December of '81 to push us to sell out.

Our PIK check is still in the drawer today [June 1984] because we added names to it to pay the feed dealers we owed money to, and the bank won't cash it that way. They want it all. We have to pay for fuel and everything today, but we have to gamble on a crop when we don't even know what price we will get for it.

This interview took place in early June 1984. The farm is still muddy from extensive rain throughout May that flooded out thousands of acres of western Iowa farmland before the crops were even out of the ground. Elmer points to that and continues.

[1] A milk check is a monthly payment received from the dairy by milk producers for their production. An assignment is an amount regularly deducted from that check to pay a loan.

[2] Under Chapter 11 of the federal bankruptcy law, seeking the court's protection from creditors under a plan to reorganize the business.

49

Elmer: I think there is going to be a real short crop this year already, because of the rain.

Pat: It will be PIK without the PIK payment.

Elmer: The ground is sour and under stress right now, and this will hurt the yield. It might cut us from a hundred to sixty bushels an acre.

Having related the broad outlines of his story, Elmer insists that we visit the dairy barn, where his remaining son, Bruce, is milking cows. "If you're going to write about this," he says, "you have to see it, you can't just read about it or be told about it. Have you ever seen a milking barn?" I nod that I have, but add that I would certainly be willing to see his, so he leads me inside and with the enthusiasm one might expect from a teen-aged Future Farmer, explains all the machinery and how much production they get per day, and any other details I care to learn. After watching for awhile, I am led back outside.

"I guess I should let you go now," he apologizes. "When you write this up, be sure to tell it like it is."

On the first Monday morning in February 1985, Elmer and Pat Steffes are joined in court by over a hundred friends and supporters, many holding symbolic white crosses (for farms that had died), as they watched the Landmands National Bank, of Audubon, win a replevin petition, thereby gaining legal right to the couple's livestock and farm machinery, which had been collateral for a $168,081 debt, the ultimate legacy of their career in farming.

Among the supporters, Nevada, Iowa, farmer Loren Book may have put it most simply: "Whenever there's been a farm sale or a family facing legal problems, Elmer has been there, helping in any way he could. It's the least we can do to be with him here today."

"I don't know how much more we can take," Pat was quoted in a newspaper article. "I don't think the bank will be happy until we have absolutely nothing left."

On the following Friday morning, at 7:30, the couple was awakened when thirteen law enforcement officers from six counties arrived to enforce the seizure order. As Pat got to the door in her bathrobe, they began the process of hauling off pigs, sheep, cows, and machinery. They had sealed off the roads leading to the Steffes farm, so any neighbors wishing to join the family had to come on foot.

Throughout this period, Elmer had been getting psychiatric counseling for depression. When I interviewed them, they asked about the

Ronald McDonald House being constructed in Iowa City. Elmer said they felt they would be good at helping to counsel and comfort people under stress because they had been through so much themselves.

In June 1985, it was Federal Land Bank's turn, and again the Steffeses' neighbors and supporters turned out, this time for a rally in the downtown Audubon park. Speakers included Roman Catholic Bishop Maurice Dingman of the Des Moines Diocese, who had become increasingly active and vocal concerning the issue of farm foreclosures. The Rev. Jesse Jackson sent a message to the rally. Their son, Bruce, and daughter, Kay, spoke at the rally, although Bruce could not contain himself. For his parents, it was all over.

Bruce is now trying to farm, hoping to buy back 80 acres of the 370 most recently sold acres from their foreclosure. Pat says this "would get him started." Pat and Elmer retained 10 acres as their "homestead" in the bankruptcy settlement, and in early 1988 acquired 20 more acres from one of the new owners. Pat was working at a nursing home, but has quit her job. She joins Elmer on the road now; he is driving a moving van. They still live in Audubon.

A Christmas Feast

LOUISE and EUGENE WUCHTER
Delhi, Iowa

Eugene Wuchter reminds one in many ways of the depression-era labor leader, John L. Lewis. Bushy eyebrows and a deep voice complement a huge, muscular frame. Louise appears every bit the hausfrau. The two sit across the kitchen table in a simple old home atop a small hill that overlooks a county road.

Louise begins at the beginning by describing a new milking barn they built in 1975 to expand their herd, only to encounter problems with the pipeline that led to an outbreak of mastitis that killed eight cows and forced the sale of forty-two others. A lawsuit ensued, but "we didn't get enough money out of it to make any difference." Nonetheless, "we had the satisfaction that they fixed the line." In the meantime, they had to replace the cows in order to get back into the milking business.

LOUISE: I suppose '81 is where we first ran into the credit crunch. We were looking for a place to borrow money, and we had been with the Delhi bank, and the bank had been divided between the two Schmidt brothers. And we stayed with Art and the other brother went to Hopkinton, and Art sold the bank and told us that he would help us. We didn't want to do business with the new people, and he told us if we would go with Thorp [a finance company] temporarily, it would be a matter of a couple of months, and he would negotiate new financing for us, and not to worry about Thorp because it would be a short time that we'd have to pay high interest, and he would eventually get us a long-term loan. He had somebody flying in from Minnesota. The people had all our papers and agreed to come down and look at the farm and were interested in taking on our loan, and Art was sure that we were going to get it. Art died the night before or early in the morning of the day that he and Gene were to meet at the Manchester airport. So we've been left with Thorp ever since.

We went to Farmers Home, and they would always say that we had four sons in the operation, that there were too many people trying to make a living off the farm. They turned us down. Then the boys decided that if they went up and asked for a loan, and if they would take the operation over from Gene and me, that that would work. They were told that they couldn't because that would be a partnership, and FmHA would loan only $200,000 to a partnership, which wouldn't begin to buy us out.

So then Gene went to the Dyersville National Bank and worked with Cliff Knippel. He tried to work with FmHA, and Gene just ran back and forth between the two of them. They used him for a messenger boy. They would put this money in if FmHA would put in so much, and that wasn't agreeable, and finally, we just gave up on it. And then we saw a loan finder, who turned out to be a crook, and we had paid him up-front money. He was going to get a loan for us, but we never got a loan. He wound up in the Manchester jail for a month and a half.

Another fellow was going to put more cattle in, because the first thing everybody would say when they looked at the farm package was that the income wasn't big enough to cover our sons and ourselves. Well, we knew that.

Let's see, who'd we go to next? Oh, this fellow out of Connecticut. He was supposed to come out and give us cows to lease, and it was supposed to be a very good deal, and we only were to pay about $35 a cow per month, and we even would get the calves, wouldn't we? [Looks to Gene for agreement.] We'd build up the cash flow, and then we'd be able to get the money. Well, we had the cattle all sorted out. He was coming down to approve it and sign the papers. He was a crook, too. And he never did show up. Thank God we never took those cattle home from Wisconsin.

We paid Thorp five points over prime. The highest we paid was about 24 percent interest. And we had to pay them $7,025 per month out of the cream check. So the cattle herd was dwindling because, as something would happen to them, we'd sell them off, but we had no money to replace. We had hope. Every day we just knew we'd come up with something. For five months there was no money for us. It just went to Bell Investment and Thorp. They got all of our milk check. There was nothing left for us.

What were you living on during that time?

Louise: Ingenuity. [Turns to Gene, laughing.] What were we living on? I said, "Ingenuity." I canned everything in sight. I must have canned four hundred to five hundred quarts of tomatoes. We had a big garden, and we did a lot, and my folks were good to us.

Gene: We borrowed money from her relations.

Louise: Yes, we borrowed money from my folks, my sister, and Gene's cousin, and that helped us.

Gene: Our boys never got paid for one year.

So they were working for you for free.

Gene: Definitely. Definitely. They didn't want the farm to go down.

How old were the boys at the time?

Louise: Rick would have been nineteen, and Jake would've been eighteen, Ed would have been twenty-one, and Butch would've been twenty-two. Ed had a wife, and Butch had a wife and two kids. They got food stamps. We didn't qualify for food stamps.

And we just shared everything. The door out there on the porch was broken. We had two winters with the knob broken all the way around where it went in, so there was a hole out there this big around [holds her thumbs and index fingers together], and we stuffed it with a sock and nailed the door shut at night. In the winter! It was gross, the way we lived. We didn't go anyplace because we didn't have any money for anything. And the cars just fell apart. Everything just went to pieces, because we couldn't make even little repairs. We raised chickens and butchered chickens like crazy. We lived on chickens for the last five years, that's about all we lived on. And this last year, not the last three or four months, which have been different, but the year before that, we didn't have any beef in the house. We just couldn't afford it. We went without beef for a whole year. I went to visit my sister and helped her, and I joked about it. I said, "We haven't had anything but chickens." She sent me home with a package of steaks. And then this place where Ed works had a cow get hurt calving, and they were just going to call a truck to get her, and Ed said, "Can I have her?" And the guy said, "If you want her, take her." So he took that cow and got it butchered, and he brought us back three hundred pounds of hamburger.

And we're eating really good now! It's funny because we can laugh about it, but at the time it was pretty dismal.

As for our chickens, we put what we had here in our home freezer. We used them all up. Those we had stored over in the Dyersville locker became part of the bankruptcy because we couldn't pay the locker bill. We couldn't get any chickens out. They wouldn't give them to us because the bill wasn't paid. So we had two or three hundred chickens over there. . . .

Last spring [1984], we had new chickens coming on. We couldn't get the earlier chickens, and then we butchered another five hundred chickens. We filled everything up here, and then be damned if we didn't run into the same thing again this winter because [starts to cry]. . . . The lawyer, who was writing out the checks, didn't pay them again for this year. So here we have all these chickens, two-year-old chickens and year-old chickens [chuckles] sitting in the freezer. So we didn't raise any chickens this year. The heck with it, I said, we do all that work and we can't even eat. . . .

Some day you're going to have a lot of chickens. [Louise laughs hysterically.]

Louise: Then we finally went over and had a round with the lawyer because we have to get them home because who would want to eat them after they get any older? Who'd think of such dumb things?

My mom would come out, and she'd give me $25, which I used to buy toilet paper and other things we really needed. When my folks would come up from Dubuque, they'd always bring us 49 cent bread from Dubuque. So, even though it was really close. . . . This spring, when we didn't have any meat, before we got the beef, we must have had seventy ducks around here. We ate duck eggs every way you can imagine.

The really bad part was with our daughter. She was going to school in Dyersville, and she screwed up her school year. She shouldn't have, but she did, and she was upset because of the circumstances. The other kids had money for this and that, and she didn't have any money. We would try to see that she got more of a share than the rest of the family, but it was really difficult for her, and she was in the

55

psychiatric ward for a short time. She admitted herself to Mercy Hospital [in Des Moines] this spring, and I think it was when she realized that she blew her school year.

Gene: Tell him what else happened to her school year.

Louise: Well, she was thinking about killing herself.

Gene: Yeah.

Louise: Yes, she was thinking about killing herself. We were going to these farm crisis meetings, and they keep talking about suicide as being such a danger, and that really scared us.

She came home here about 5 o'clock in the morning and woke us up. She'd been into the hospital, and they wouldn't take her without us admitting her because she was only seventeen. I think *that* is asinine. They let her come back home again. She could've killed herself before she ever got here. She had to have her parents' signature.

Gene: She can have an abortion without the parents knowing about it, but if she tried to kill herself and kill somebody else, they won't admit her without the parents signing her in.

So you had to go back down there and sign her in?

Louise: Yes, I had to go back down. One of our big losses is that we lost all of Gene's insurance. Everything he's got. We don't have anything anymore, we don't have any health insurance, and so when she went in there, they only kept her four days because they said that she could get county health. And we have applied for county health, and they never contacted us yet. So she really has not improved. It's just that our situation has eased up a little bit this summer, with the boys going out there to help, because they were able to bring money around. Also, our daughter in Sioux City tries to get things we need. She's gotten clothes and shoes for me, and things like that to take the pressure off, but you know, I don't know what people do who don't have any friends or any family.

Well, maybe you remember when that Ray Starks got killed at Christmas time. He ran the pharmacy in Manchester.

I don't recall that.

Louise: He died Christmas week. He got killed on a new snowmobile that he got for Christmas.

I worked with him when he was on the Republican central committee, and for a little while I took over the central committee, and I offered to lecture at church when he died. I'd known the family; not his folks but his wife and him, and after I lectured I came home here, and they called me after the dinner and wanted to know if we could use what was left over. I said we'd take it if they didn't have a home for it, and she said, "Oh, we've got so much and I just know you've always got a lot of people coming and going. Maybe you'd like some of it."

And so I thanked her, and I went to the church, and I just bawled when I opened that refrigerator door. There must have been twenty-five pounds of roast beef. Aw! You've never seen so much food, and these guys here . . . roast beef! Like I said, we'd been eating chickens and eggs. And it was great! Must've been a gallon or two of mashed potatoes, and there was more gravy than there was mashed potatoes, and there was a gallon of corn! [Laughs hysterically, then cries.] It was our Christmas dinner. I was just absolutely floored, and there were all kinds of desserts and things, and I brought it all home here. After we ate, I packaged it up, and I put the rest in the freezer so we could have it different days instead of eating it all at once.

You just can't believe what it meant. I never had been in that position. We've always been the people all our lives that gave to everybody else. And it's an awful deal not to have anything, and then it really hits you when you really need and you get it. It makes you realize . . . I mean, we have done a lot for a lot of people over the years. We've opened up our home and taken lots of people. We've taken in kids that didn't have homes, kids that were kicked out of homes.

Gene: Well, what countries have we had?

Louise: Well, we had kids from Poland, kids from the Philippines, and lots of kids from France, kids from Panama and Brazil.

But we've also had a lot of people that didn't have anything, you know. They came and stayed, like the girl that stayed when her family kicked her out when she was pregnant. Three girls came to us that way, but we take them in.

Well, we've just done a lot for people, but now it's our turn to take back some of what we've given. But that funeral dinner really wiped me out when I saw that. Oh, that blueberry! And you hate to admit to anybody. . . . It's a funny feeling.

And then, I hear people in town say, oh, "So-and-so doesn't have anything to eat." Then they say, "Well, I just can't believe that."

Well, I know they'd never believe that we were that bad off, and that family that called had no idea that we were that badly in need.

They just knew we always fed a lot of people and this would be a good place to send the food.

And then, when I tried to tell them how thankful I was and how it really hit home, they were embarrassed and they couldn't understand it. So I just kind of dropped the subject because they had no idea what our need was. . . .

That it really meant . . . a lot to me.

Laughter with the Tears

RUTHANN HUGHES
New Virginia, Iowa

On one of many rapid sweeps through western Iowa, I meet David and Ruthann Hughes at a Saturday night meeting of a local farm survival committee in Winterset. Before the night is out, they are among four couples I have agreed to visit and interview the next day. Distances and the length of stories make it one of the longest Sundays I have ever spent in the field.

Both of the Hugheses were born and raised on farms. They are longtime Farmers Home Administration borrowers who rent land and earn a modest living. Both, at various times, have had off-farm jobs. After encountering loan problems with the local FmHA office—they say their file shows they were targeted for liquidation—they discovered both their access to fuel assistance to keep their home heated the previous winter and the farm survival committees of the advocacy organization Rural America, now Prairiefire, an independent organization, through Ellen Huntoon, a staff worker for then-U.S. Representative Tom Harkin's Indianola office. They also say that, before they were given their loan files by FmHA, they were warned that their insistence on seeing it would permanently change their relationship with the lending agency.

M ORE and more people have fallen in with the survival committee. We need the survival committee not just to organize and unite farmers.

A survival committee—and we're speaking from experience on this—helps you keep your sanity. It helps you keep your family life. It helps you keep your sense of humor because you get to the point pretty soon, you can laugh at it. And if you've ever seen a file of somebody from FmHA or a PCA, you'd see what I mean. You have to be able to laugh at it. They put personal remarks in there that has nothing to do with anything pertaining to the business. For instance, I don't think that any lending institution has the right to say that a farm wife who is working away from home goes to the beauty shop too often.

That was in somebody's file?

Our file, personally.

We know another family that had all boys, and in their file, it stated that these boys spend too much time in athletics in school. They should take them out of the athletic program. That's what I'm saying—you have to keep your sense of humor. I came home from work the day after we got our file, and I sat down there and started reading it, and, at first, I was so mad that I could've hauled off and busted the county supervisor. In the first place, it's none of his damn business what my family does. And I reached the point where they stated in there that they made a farm visit, and Mr. and Mrs. wasn't at home. They told the son that they wanted to look at the cattle. And we did have a mean bull, and our son told him that we had a mean bull. So he said, "I stood on one side of the fence and looked at the cattle over on the hill. They all appeared to be there. I asked the boy how old he was. He said he was a sophomore in high school." And this is quotes, mind you. "He said he was a sophomore in high school. He was chewing tobacco. I did everything I could to preserve my safety."

When I reached that point, I started laughing.

Now, to me, that makes it sound like my son is some kind of a hood, rabble-rouser, or something. And so you reach that point that you need this humor. You get to the point that you make jokes about it. It's either that or you're to go crazy.

Early Retirement

REVA and FRANCIS CROOKS
Corydon, Iowa

*Past the corner, they had said, turn right from the second stop sign
coming south from Corydon, Iowa.*

*So I turn onto a gravel road heading south out of Corydon. It is five
miles before I find a stop sign, by which time I am seriously convinced that I have profoundly misunderstood my directions. My
apprehension is fueled by the wooded, unbuilt landscape surrounding me: no points of reference. As often happens once one has a big
investment in a seeming mistake, I drive on. Five miles later, a
second stop sign finally appears. Thank God! I am almost to the
Missouri line, which would have confirmed that I had misunderstood.
I turn, and finally, atop a small hill, sits a house. But the place
appears unfinished. Climbing the driveway, I wonder again: Am I
way off the path? Surely the Crookses do not live in this place.*

*I get out of the car on a little gravel apron behind the house, and a
dog stares at me as though I am lost. Maybe I am. I scout around the
back side of the split-level, and Reva Crooks finds me. They live in
the finished upper half whose entrance was not visible from the road.*

*Reva and Francis Crooks are both sixty-two years old. They are
both lean and tall, with the look of hard work etched in their faces.
They are generous people. Their first concern is not the interview
but the condition of my stomach. Am I hungry?*

*Of course I am. After visiting a farm survival meeting the night
before in Winterset, Iowa, I had stayed in a motel. I had not eaten
breakfast, but interviewed the Hugheses in New Virginia, Iowa, at
nine that morning. It is now two o'clock.*

61

In their kitchen, I am promptly served roast beef, mashed potatoes and gravy, green beans, noodles, bread and butter, all left over from a Sunday lunch they have just finished themselves.

I get out my tape recorder. This is a couple that, before this story begins, had only a $1,700 debt on their entire dairy farm. But later they got involved in a $63,000 milking parlor loan.

FRANCIS: We had a loan from FmHA to build a milking shed and silo. And FmHA was gettin' milk assignment off of that to pay for it, and Production Credit knew this. So then we was wantin' a few more cows, and we found nine head to buy. And Production Credit loaned us the money.

We was supposed to make $211 a month payment on those for three years, principal and interest, that would pay them off in three years. We were making two payments in one, and that's a lot of milk to carry. It was taking us so long out there at the barn that we decided that if we had a few more. . . . We wanted to get up to a hundred head. If we could get twenty-five more cows, that would make the payment on the barn and pay for the cows just like these others. We went up to see FmHA, and they said they'd see if we could get a loan approved—if Production Credit would buy the cows.

We went up to Production Credit, and they said that they would buy the cows, and we could pay for them just like we did these others. They filled out the papers, twenty-five cows at $1,000 a head for $25,000. So then FmHA wanted us to have something in writing to show that PCA would agree to buy the cows. In a few days, we got a letter from FmHA that the loan had been approved. So we made arrangements and built the parlor.

The Production Credit guy was out here to look around when we were building it. And he knew we were building a milking parlor, but he never said a word. So we finished the milking parlor, and when we got it done, we went up to get the money for the cows. But before we got in the milking parlor, FmHA started holding the milk assignment out. Then we didn't have enough money to make the payment to Production Credit. But we was about six months ahead of them on the payments 'cause we was doubling up the payments.

So we went up to get the cows and PCA said no. Said, FmHA is getting the money, let them buy the cows. We never did buy the cows, and, of course, what cows we had couldn't do it [give them the production necessary to pay off the loan on the parlor], so we went up to Des Moines to the attorney general's office to show him our papers, and he said he thought it was fraud, to get a lawyer and go after them. So we went and got an appointment with one.

He said, "You've got a case, but I can't take it. You're the fourth one that's been here this morning with Production Credit. We took the other three. We can't stand to take any more. It wouldn't do you justice," he said, "because it needs attention, and we just don't have time to do it." So we took it to another lawyer. He said, "You've got something well worth pursuing," but he couldn't take it because it would be conflict of interest because he does work for Production Credit from Newton. Then we went over to this Rural America, and they told us about a lawyer from Cedar Rapids, and we went and talked about it to him, and he said he'd take it over.

But I had got another fellow to go in with me to see this fellow that was with FmHA when we got the loan. He quit and came over to the bank as a loan officer. I said, "Do you remember when we built the milking parlor?" and he said, "Yep." I said, "Did you ever talk to Production Credit about buying those cows?" He said yes, he did. "PCA agreed to buy the cows. If they hadn't, you'd never have got the loan."

And I said, "Well, if PCA hadn't promised it, we wouldn't have wanted it."

If we thought that the cows we had would've done it [made enough money to pay the loan], we wouldn't have been asking for more. Evidently, they thought that it would pay out, or they'd never have made the loan, either one of them, or even promised it. But anyhow, we just didn't get the cows, and, of course, the same cows we had wasn't gonna carry the whole load. He caused us about a $63,000 debt. That's what the milking parlor cost.

We've got the debt and two years behind. They didn't foreclose on it. They just shut your money off, and you haven't got any way to go, so you've got to sell out.

But that's a nice way of putting it. That's the fact at FmHA. You just get starved out.

We had sixty cows that we were milking. We had twenty-eight heifers ready to have calves this spring [1984]. We had another eighteen that was gonna be bred this spring, and twenty to have bred this fall.

We was breeding them to the best bulls yet, and the last two years

63

all our heifers was better than their mothers. Out of eighteen head, all but two or three was better than their mothers. So we was getting up there, but we just didn't have time. They wouldn't loan us no money to even buy semen to breed those cows or doctor those cows. So about half those cows wasn't bred.

Then we got mastitis. When you get mastitis, you should doctor them right then. If you don't, it'll just keep spreading from one to the other. I suspect about a third of them had mastitis. They wouldn't loan us any money, and that cold weather hit. Just like that Woods[1] up there, it hit us at the same time. We had a creditor that come in and garnished our milk check. FmHA was releasing the money to buy our feed because Production Credit wasn't. It was Production Credit's cows, but they wouldn't feed them. And we ran out of feed for two weeks and lost a bunch of cows, heifers, and calves. So we knew we was gonna run out of feed, and they wouldn't buy us any feed before we did. I said I wasn't gonna tell nobody no lie about those cattle 'cause I wouldn't want somebody to sell me a bunch of cows that was no good. There was some in there that was good, all right; they just wasn't taken care of. We just loaded them all up and took them to the packing plant and sold them. If you sold them to anybody, you couldn't recommend them for milk cows. So we lost money there.

Reva: These are some pictures we took.

A small batch of photographs shows dairy cows that lay down and died in the cold, emaciated, in the grass, alongside trees.

Francis: Those cows had all the silage they could eat. But that's just not enough with a milk cow. They've got to have some energy to go with it. And we didn't have it. So that's the reason we sold the cows.

Reva: They would just lay down some evening. . . .

Didn't stretch out or nothing, just like a cow lays, just the next morning, they'd be out here in the barn . . . [a long sigh]. So you've got to have that protein and that energy feed.

Francis: We had no other choice, so. . . .

Reva: They went down on their milk.

Francis: Of course, they didn't foreclose on us or nothing.

---

[1]An Iowa farmer being prosecuted at the time for allowing his cattle to starve to death during a snowstorm while he was vacationing in Florida.

Reva: No.

Francis: But what other choice do you have? We weren't just going to sit here and let them starve to death. What alternatives do you have?

Reva: I think we had a pretty good bunch of cows. We don't get them just overnight. It takes a long time. And then our son and his wife, they have two children, the trailer just to the side of us, right on the other side of the driveway. They lost their trailer, we had no wages, they had no wages, we had no income whatsoever.

Francis: We all worked for free.

Reva: We still owe last winter's utilities. Now we're still a month behind. We don't have any heat on now. I don't know how long they're [the rural electric cooperative] gonna let us go along like this. The whole thing slipped out from under you after you get this age? It just doesn't seem possible.

Francis: On the milk diversion, anything over nine months old is considered a cow. So [any cow] had to go some place. She either had to go to another producer in the program[2] or she had to go to slaughter. And it was up to you to prove, if they ever questioned you, where that cow went. So we sold everything under nine months of age.

So there's thirty head out there, heifers, plus we knew the cows that they was out of, we knew what bulls they was out of, we knew that they had prospects, so this guy bought 'em and brought 'em back here, and we're taking care of them. So there's thirty head of heifers out there yet. That's one reason we was waiting to get this lawyer on the ball. We don't even get any money out of the milk diversion. FmHA was gettin' the milk assignment, see? For the payment on those buildings, so we can hang onto the farm until the thirteen months is up. After thirteen months, we don't know what's gonna happen. That's one reason we was wanting to get this trial on the road.

What are you surviving on now?

Francis: Well, I was going to say, can you survive on $282 a month? That's what my Social Security is.

Reva: He had to take early Social Security at sixty-two, and he didn't want to til he was sixty-five.

[2]The federal dairy program for curtailing milk surpluses, or "diversion." The action he undertook was to avert the dangers they had just described and the resulting "lack" of documentation of what happened to a starved cow.

Francis: And that's it.

Reva: And that's it. Of course, when you're used to not having anything anyway. . . .

We don't know what we're gonna do. See, we don't have any of that milk diversion payment at all til March. We always thought we had good credit. But it got to where there was nothing to pay the bills with.

Francis: It all went into cows.

Reva: And they always got the best of care. They had veterinary care—to spray 'em, or worm 'em, we bred 'em to the best bulls, and it just seems like a . . . nightmare, really. . . . We're going to wake up and it was just a dream. But it isn't.

The Crookses' case, represented by Cedar Rapids attorney Peter Riley, went to trial in Iowa district court. Just before Easter, in April 1985, the jury began its deliberations. It returned with a verdict the following Monday. The Crookses won a $70,000 judgment against the Ottumwa, Iowa PCA, which did not appeal the decision and has since then paid the judgment to the couple, who are still farming. Nonetheless, accumulated debts and setbacks still had the Crookses' farm on the brink of insolvency more than two years later.

The Last Generation

DAVID JENNINGS
Ellston, Iowa

*Dave Jennings is no newcomer to farming. As of July 1984, when
we talked, he had been farming for thirty-nine years and had spent
thirty-two years on the farm where he still lives and will probably
retire. Around 1977, he began adding some new buildings to allow his
son, D. A., "a place to run the hogs . . . so he would be able to take
over when I quit."*

YOU go clear back to 1980. This young man at PCA made a
$40,000 mistake on my budget. He made me sign a note for
$40,000 more than I needed to. See? And I caught him on it. He
accused me of selling hogs and not turning them in. But I caught him
on the fact that he didn't read his paper right and didn't take the hogs
off that I turned in after the first of the year. And there's where the
friction started. Well, he started putting dirt in the file.

Oh, we've had some goodies. This kid got so vile and so bad that a
delegation went to Creston office, and the next day he lost his job.
Then they brought this guy in that was rotated so many times.

Well, this young man, when he got out of college, got a job with
FmHA, and him and D. A. didn't hitch. And he finally got a job at
PCA. But when he came into PCA, he didn't like D. A., and we was
already having trouble in our files because this young man was mad
because I caught him in his mistakes. And he lost his job, so he had
plenty in the file, I know. So this young man that didn't hitch with D.
A. in FmHA wouldn't renew D. A.'s note the next spring and put him
out of business. And they proceeded to work me over.

He proceeded in '81 to shut him off. That basically took away 50 percent of the land that we were farming, took away my health, and he gave me $50,000 of the debt with no assets for his share of the buildings, no extra assets for his machinery, all I received was a debt—to make me look bad. He also would not let me pay D. A.'s share of a feed bill that we had in partnership with a company I'd done business with for over twenty years with a good credit record. He waited a year before he let me pay that so he'd ruin my reputation with the feed company.

And then they decided that I wasn't smart enough to farm. They decided that I should sell my hogs and cattle. I needed to get rid of my sows and start a new breeding stock. I thought I'd try to go along, anything to go along, to try to work this out. The next spring, they informed me that I had to get rid of the cows. As I started to sell my cow herd down, why, I realized what was going on, so I set my heels and quit. And, of course, this made them very unhappy and mad. In the meantime, I had cashed a life insurance policy on my wife and bought a few sows. PCA informed me they had those hogs coming, and I told them they had nothing in the hogs, that they didn't get the hogs. So I sold a bunch of pigs and took the money and bought some more sows. And it wasn't long until the PCA man was out because I had sold those pigs and bought some sows instead of paying him. And I told him that I did exactly what I told him I was gonna do—buy more sows. If I was trying to dodge him, I wouldn't have sold them in the area, and I wouldn't have bought sows off a man who was doing business in *his* place. If I wanted to, I could sell those pigs, and he'd never find them.

I could buy a sow, and he'd never know where they'd come from. As we went on through the rest of the year, I realized I had a big problem. This was around August or September. So I didn't sell any beans, I didn't sell any corn. I didn't sell any calves. I waited. And they decided that they were going to close me down. They said, "You will sell out." And I said, "I will not."

So, I took some feeder pigs to a sale, and it had PCA's name on the check also, so I just folded it, put it in my billfold and kept it. And every little bit, I'd get a telephone call or a question, "Why don't you give us that check?" And I said, when we get something worked out, I will. Otherwise, I'd roll it up in my pocket because I will not sign it over to them.

I made an application to FmHA, which was turned down immediate-

68

ly. I think that FmHA and PCA decides who is going to be where. And I'll tell you why I think this: The next meeting I had with PCA, they leaned back, I had told FmHA that if I had my ruthers, I would sell grain and livestock, and pay interest on an operating loan this year. The next time I was in PCA, I visited a PCA man, and he said, "How would you rather operate? How would you rather do it this year?" He called me on the pretext of making out a new application for FmHA, and after one or two false starts, I realized what he was up to. He wanted me to say what I wanted to do.

So, I said, "Tell you what I'll do, I'll pay my interest and you'll release my hogs, my calves, and my grain, and I'll operate as I see fit." He just reared right up and said, "No way."

And I said, "All right." And I got up to leave, and he said, "What are you going to do?" I said, "You figure the alternative." "Well," he says, "come back here. Maybe we can make it work." He says, "You give me that check that you got in your pocket, so we'll see what we can do." I said, "You get that check when I get a letter releasing my livestock. When I get a letter of commitment from you, then you start getting the money. Until then, you get nothing." He stalled me for almost a month before I finally got my letter. And that's how I operated last year, and this year I basically went in and threw my hat down and said, "I believe I'll stay with you another year."

And we're operating the same as we did last year. The only thing is I never got a letter of commitment from them. So that's where I stand today. I tried for disaster money. I got a letter back from FmHA stating that I had neither management skill nor the industry to handle an operation of this size. And it seems strange to me that I'm still farming the same 530 acres that I have for thirty-two years. All at once I've become too lazy to handle it. So I don't know where things go from here.

So you're saying you were in perfectly good shape before you started that whole routine?

Well, basically, I was because I could've paid them off in '80. And would've paid them off, and never sold my machinery or my farm. I could've paid them off very easily. I couldn't have paid D. A.'s off, but I could've paid mine off and had money to operate the two farms. But they said, oh, no, don't do that, you're all right. So, you see, this is what strikes you. That's just like two fellows I know that paid almost $800,000 in three years' time to PCA, and they lost $600,000

69

worth of equity in the meantime. And they lost a million, four hundred thousand dollars in just three years' time.

The amazing thing was that after the heat got on PCA, they found a lot more equity than they had when they were just trying to make them sell out. I speak of the crooked pencil, the FmHA man that takes a pencil and totals your figures after you take the sheet in. I finally figured out why you want to make your Farmers Home plan out in ink, instead of taking a pencil like they ask you to. Because they can change the figures after you fill it in. I saw him do this in a meeting.

A lot of farmers really have been hesitant to speak up because they're worried about someone calling in their notes, and. . . .

Well, it is done. It is threatened. One man said, "My FmHA man told me not to write Tom Harkin another letter or go to another meeting, or he would call in my note." Now, I've had people come to meetings. In the bank, three men that I know of came to the first meeting we had in Mt. Ayr. They never showed up again. I commenced to inquire why, and the bank says, if you go to another meeting, we'll call your loan.

The thing that really gets to me is the underhanded way that some of them get names on notes. I was talking to one couple, they were worth $750,000 in '81. That's clear money. And they sold the farm at a sheriff's auction just the other day. The way their name got on a second mortgage was very underhanded. They'd had a little child, and his lung collapsed, and they were in Des Moines night and morning. He'd been there for two or three weeks.

They come home, and they didn't no more than get home with him, until her dad's in the hospital, ready to go on. And on their way back to the hospital they were to stop in and sign renewal papers. They thought it was just ordinary renewal papers. But two years later, they found out they'd signed a note for a second mortgage on the farm, and PCA was taking it. They didn't know til two years later that they signed a second mortgage.

How has your activism changed your own relationship with PCA?

It hasn't changed it. They can read a man's personality. And know that if he's bullheaded enough, he's gonna go ahead and tell the world about [his situation]. They won't push him as bad as if they intimidate him. Now, this one young fellow that PCA tried to can, I ran him

70

off my place. He started in on me, "You knew what you signed when you signed those notes." I said, "Yes, I knew what I signed. And I knew I signed to pay the money back. But I didn't sign to lick your boots every day," I warned him, "I'm tired of brown shoe polish. I'm not coming in there begging for any more food to eat. We're making our own living, and I'm not going to ask you for another nickel, and I ain't going to give you the check that's in my pocket, now you get to town. And don't come back." I said, "I know one young woman chased you off with a shotgun," and I said, "You better be looking out because I won't be as kind as she was, I won't warn you." [Laughs.] He left.

That's one time my wife was scared to turn in the driveway when she came home. She never seen me so mad in my life. He was backing down the driveway with my finger in his nose. Well, I was trying to get him to hit me, is what I was trying to do. Oh, that'd been ideal.

He later lost his job with PCA and went back to work for FmHA. And I promptly went to [FmHA state director] Bob Pim and told him that if this young man was sent to Ringgold County, it'd be conflict of interest handling disaster loans for the people he kicked out of PCA. So he had no business in Mt. Ayr, and if he did put him in there, I would go clear to Washington, D.C., if I had to to stop him from working in Mt. Ayr. And Pim promptly put him in there. We talked to Jepsen's people, and we talked to Grassley's[1] people, and two days later he moved. Now I'm not saying that we moved him, but it's kind of a coincidence as far as I'm concerned.

Now, a lot of these people that you see that are slow in getting in their crops, maybe not taking care of their homes like they used to or not looking after the cattle like they used to, if you'd get them to visit with you long enough, you find out the banker's giving them trouble. One young fellow I talked to said, "I'm out there in body but not in spirit." He said, "After they put so much heat on me, my wife left." And he says, "For six weeks I couldn't tell you what I was doing." And just like one man told, that he was all upset, the way things are going, he'd go out there and he was planting beans. And he made the same mistake filling boxes three times in one afternoon. Just because his mind was someplace else. When they harass you so much, your mind doesn't function as sharp as it should.

[1] Iowa's two U.S. senators in 1984.

71

The thing I found, though, is the people with a deep religious conviction about faith carry through this better than people who are not strong, committed Christians. The ones that have a deep faith come through with a different attitude, they have just a little brighter outlook on life, and a little stronger approach. I find out that some, even though they have got strong faith, they get revenge in their heart, and the first thing you know, they've got a problem. But after they commence to get a little faith and do a little more studying, then they start to find the solution. And I've found this to be true in my case. The more studying I done, the more prayer I had, the solutions commence to surface. I can do this, or I can do that, or I can do something else.

He expounds at a modest length on farmers' responsibilities as citizens, a subject on which he has strong opinions. He reads. "Now I get a lot of material, and my wife gets upset with me. I lay it next to my chair, and I'll turn on the television, and I'll set there, and I'll pick up this material and read it while the television's going on."

Reading, in fact, is an activity that he thinks Americans in general do far too little. As a result, he says, we are too ill-informed to participate meaningfully in politics. "We hire a legislator and expect him to take care of us. We don't take part. That's the biggest thing that's the matter with this country. Just like sports, we want to be spectators."

I need to tell you a little bit about the reaction of our son and his wife. She's a schoolteacher, and when they got pushed out, he went to work for a marina down here at the lake and made nothing for three years. There's times when he'd come, and we'd just have to set and visit and counsel by the hour. And he's commenced to find himself now to the point where he's doing some carpentry work, finding jobs to do. This is one of the things that I see so drastic is these young people pushed out because if they don't know someone, they can't find a job. You have to know someone in a position to find a job. I see them as the casualties of this. And I feel that our economy is losing a generation of farmers. Or more than one, because these boys when they leave the farm don't bring up their kids on the farm. You don't learn it through a book. That's all there is to it. So these are the things that bother me, much as anything: the generation of farmers we're losing. And if we don't do something fast, we've lost it.

72

The Sod Story

DICK MYERS
Maxwell, Iowa

"That's another problem that this state has got," Dick Myers said almost as soon as we began to talk. "If it ain't corn, beans, and hogs, it's a death offense." Myers contends that while a 1976 purchase of three hundred acres in Melcher, Iowa, to accompany his two hundred acres in Maxwell, added to his debt load, his real problems with his lending institutions began when he chose to convert his farm from a corn and soybeans rotation to sod. "They didn't understand it and had no way of counseling me on it because they knew nothing about it." But, he adds, "If it wasn't for the sod, I guarantee I wouldn't be here now."

Guarantees were the core of the problem. Although many Iowa officials and political candidates have talked of crop diversification, many lenders have been reluctant to abandon the tried and true. Myers did. In 1984, he harvested his last bean crop. During his gradual conversion from corn to sod farming, corn prices had fallen almost 30 percent and would plunge by another 50 percent within two more years. The bottom fell out. Meanwhile, Myers worked with a contractor to sell his sod. There were short-term risks: "You see, sod is always a year behind. It takes two years to raise sod, so that put us behind, and I'm going to be the first to admit that we made mistakes, too."

Myers also says the bank's practice of making notes on a yearly basis conflicted with the longer-term credit needs of a sod operation, although "I don't blame them." But he contends that much of the financial pressure was a result of the bank's internal problems. Accord-

73

ing to Myers, the final break in their longstanding mutual relation-
ship came when he removed a medical negligence trust fund for his
deaf son, Michael, to a Des Moines bank. Whatever the cause, his
bank accelerated collection of his loans. His story is of the events that
followed before he eventually succeeded in finding another source of
credit.

W E were down where we had very little money, but my wife had received $3,000 as a gift. We had that in a local bank here, not the one I was doing business with, but another local bank. I realized that any grain or livestock or anything did belong to my bank, so we weren't moving that stuff around. But my bank sent out a letter to all the banks. I don't know who all received it, but I do know of several that did receive this letter, saying that if we had any funds in that bank, be advised that those funds might belong to them. When this other bank got hold of that letter, of course, the first they done was lock everything up, we had no access to that money.

You see, that was a gift to my wife. The bank had absolutely no call to do that. This money that we would have lived with through the winter was gone; we just had no means at all.

We've always been sort of hard up. I mean, we've always had enough, we've always had plenty. But then, you get to this point, you've been married for twenty-some years, and you've got a family and the sod here, and, all of a sudden, you don't know how you're going to buy groceries, you see? And man, that's traumatic. And how you're going to keep heat, so what are you going to do? I had a chain saw, and, of course, there was no work anywhere. I played music professionally for many years, and I was making a little money doing that. No big thing, but that, and the fact I took a chain saw here and went out, and we cut wood, and sold wood enough to buy a few groceries, what we needed. My son and I went out and shot rabbits, .22 rifle. We lived like people had lived in depression times. We hung rugs up at all doors and heated just what we had to heat. I've heard people talk about depression times, and I'm sure it was something comparable to that. Well, not that bad.

It got to that point. I felt good at that time, physically and mentally. I still felt good. We were fighting, we were mad. When the fighting's over and we got the loan, I started getting sick. I mean mainly sick mentally. I started having depression, and I just wouldn't have believed it. When you hear of someone having depression and stuff, I think I must admit that I feel, well, there must be a weakness there. You'd have to be kind of weak to let this happen to you. Well, I started experiencing this thing myself. And boy, you go to bed at night, and you'd be afraid to go to bed. I started experiencing fear all the time. I was afraid, afraid of everything. I still am today but it's not like it was. Afraid to get up in the morning, scared to death all the time, and it just got to the point where I knew I needed to talk to somebody. I was the kind of person who would read a lot of self-help books. I'm basically a religious person, and the faith there came through, but eventually I knew I had big problems and I needed to talk to somebody. Then there's things, well, I never even told my wife about as far as that goes, but. . . .

When your farm has been in business all these years, you have a certain amount of confidence in yourself. You have your judgment. When your lenders won't talk to you, you think, boy, you're a no-good bum, and it works on you. So, as I said, I had occasion to run across Rural America. From there on, it was just a matter of finding someone. Just a shoulder to lean on, that's basically what they were at the time. Then they put me on to Joan Blundall.[1] I went and talked to her at Fort Dodge and basically just kept carrying on that way. She advised me eventually to go to mental health, and I did. I went there for several weeks, then we got busy and I quit. But when I got busy, I started feeling better, and I'm a lot better than I was.

The emotions you feel, I don't know how you put it in words, really. The emotions are just fantastic. You look at your kids, and you wonder what they think of you. We just pulled together. I mean, it brought us closer together, but I know what happens to so many of these guys. It pulls them apart. I mean, the husbands and wives start feeling the conflicts and pressure. It pulled us closer and I just thank God for it, but there are so many people that experience it the other way. Then start grafting that thing on top of all the other problems. . . .

I had a lot of feelings about it, feelings I'll never get over, certain amount of anger and stuff. But I know there's definitely a lot of people in worse shape than I'm in.

You said you had been done an injustice. Did that bolster your determination?

---

[1]A counselor with the Iowa State University Extension Service at its Fort Dodge office, who later joined the Northwest Iowa Mental Health Center staff.

It made me want to show these people that we had a viable thing going here. It got me mad enough that I thought, by gosh, I just wasn't going to let somebody who didn't know anything about this situation tell me this and tell me that. We was going to fight it to the end because it's in my particular makeup—and I think most farmers' makeup—that you'd have to fight it anyway. You just couldn't let them walk over you.

I think the thing with the sod itself was just a culmination of things. But I could understand where I stood, and I knew that they didn't particularly like that.

Farming was always a real stable thing. If you were a farmer, you pretty well knew about where you were going to be in the next fifteen to twenty years. A lot of times, a factory man didn't have quite as much security. It seemed like a farmer did. It always seemed that the factory man had a little more money in his pocket than the farmer did.

But as a farmer, you owned the land that you were working.

Right. But that picture's changed, and there's no security in farming anymore, nothing you can count on. Political manipulation with markets and stuff. You know, it used to be everybody knew that if you put your grain in a bin in the fall, for example, and you kept that grain for a few months or a few weeks, you would just eventually pay for that bin and be money ahead by keeping that grain. The last few years, you have no control over what you're doing anymore. I'm disillusioned with corn and bean farming. I don't see any hopes down the road. Cattle, terrible, poor cattle people went broke by the dozens around here and all through the Midwest. Hard work but it was honorable; cattleman was the type farmer you looked up to. He was a good man. They're just going broke like flies.

What is happening to most of those people?

Hanging on by their teeth and toenails. Maybe they should've gotten out, but how you gonna know? It's that instinct, within a farmer especially, that says one more year, let's try our one more year. Invariably, it's like grain farming. When spring rolls around, weather starts changing, you're gonna dump those seeds in the ground because this has got to be the year. It's in your blood.

76

Breaking the Ice

DARLOS BURKHART
Memphis, Missouri

The summer of 1983 brought a searing drought to southeast Iowa and much of northeast Missouri. As commodity prices and land values had already been in a steady decline since 1981, this added disaster put the entire drought area on the cutting edge of the farm crisis. A bank failure in Bloomfield, Iowa, intensified an already gloomy atmosphere.

The Burkharts found their nine hundred acres yielding only nine bushels of soybeans per acre, a mere fraction of normal production, because the intense dry heat burned fields to a crisp. They worked with four other farm families to form the steering committee of American Farmers' Survival—Save Our System (AFSOS). More than three hundred farmers attended the first of many monthly meetings. A year later, members of the group who had done telephone counseling from their homes opened up the office of Farm Counseling Services in Memphis, Missouri. It is a telephone and drop-in center for farm families needing emotional support or advice on finances or social services.

WHEN we got to traveling and got in contact with farmers, we got called all hours of the day and night. Many had no money to buy groceries, or the utilities had been shut off, and we had one farmer who had seven kids and he had no money to buy groceries. We had a seventy-year-old farmer come in, and he had enough money—he had about $70 in his pocket—that he could probably go about two weeks. And that was it. He had nothing else.

77

So we decided we needed to find out if we could get help for these farmers. We tried looking at legal aid; there is nothing in Missouri for legal aid to farmers. So we went to the welfare office in Scotland County. We had called beforehand to find out about it, and they said, well, yes, farmers may qualify. We asked them what we had to have, and they told us to bring our last year's income taxes, and our utility bill, our fuel bill, and we need to have information on your vehicles and stuff.

So we gathered all that up and went in. And my taxes showed, from the year before, that I had lost $130,000. And what they do, if you've got depreciation on your taxes, they will subtract that from our loss. But even subtracting my depreciation, I still had about a $90,000 loss. So while we were in there, we also found out that we could get fuel assistance, so we just went ahead and applied. We were thinking that we wouldn't qualify. And they told me it would be forty to sixty days before I would know anything.

In ten days I had my food stamps in the mail, and I was in shock. In more ways than one, really. I was ashamed, and I said to my husband, "No way, I will not spend those." I was going to take them back. It's hard. I had them a month before I spent them.

Were you thinking of going to the next county with them and bringing the groceries back?

Yes. A lot of people do, and I'm guilty of it, too. I think the warehouse market is where I go and get all my groceries, it's cheaper. I didn't want anybody to know I was getting them. I wasn't going to tell anybody.

But we had a meeting that Saturday in Paris, Missouri. And most of the time we just sat out in the audience. The men done the talking.

And as my husband and I left the house, we stopped at the mailbox and got the mail. We had applied in November for our FmHA disaster loan, and this was April, and I got the mail, and there was a letter from FmHA, and it was our turndown. For a disaster loan. And needless to say, I was furious. I sat and bawled a little, and cried a little. And I don't really know who I was mad at, I guess everybody and everything.

And we got down there, and we picked up Bill and Donna, and I told Donna, I want five minutes on that stage. And there was quite a bit of the legislature there that day. We had some congressmen and, I think, an FmHA fella, some bankers.

78

And so, they let me go up there on that stage, and I stood up there on that stage. In one hand, I had my food stamps. In the other hand, I had my turndown from FmHA. And I told it like it was. And what they were qualified for, I think I got $280-some fuel assistance by applying, and I got food stamps from April through September.

And I could have got them again in September. I got a thing in the mail if I wanted to reapply. But I thought, you know, I got crops, I don't need 'em. I did too need 'em. Because the crop is spent, you know, it's not money in your pocket. There's so many people with their hand out, so many year-before bills and this one.

But I had so many people come up and tell me that that really took a lot of guts and courage and everything, to get up in front of an audience and admit that you were getting food stamps. But by doing that, and we had it on the radio then, now the farmers have to get an appointment. Family Services is so busy you can't just walk in, you've got to have an appointment. And I believe it's because we have let them know that they can get some help.

Suffer the Children

MARY BETH JANSSEN
Rudd, Iowa

Mary Beth Janssen has frequently joined her husband, Gary, on the farm rally speaking circuit. "I do the tear jerkers. He tells them what to do about it." But as an adoptee who was an adult before she learned the identity of her biological mother, she has long had a cause of her own: the rights of adopted children. The sensitivity she has learned clearly cannot be confined to that issue.

NOW, we tried to protect the kids as much as we could. They were nine and twelve at the time when we were going through this [bankruptcy proceedings]. But they knew what was happening. My heavens, when the sheriff comes to deliver papers every other day, and Mom and Dad are tearing each other apart, it's hard not to know what's going on. Now, they were young enough, they didn't hear about the bankruptcy from their friends at school. They weren't teased or made fun of, thank goodness, contrary to what I see happening to other kids now.

We've met a little boy who hides his farm toys and tractors under his bed at night because he's afraid the banker will haul his toys away just as his father's machinery was hauled away. Or the little girl—the daughter of a banker—who simply refuses to ride the school bus because she constantly is ridiculed and tormented and told what a lousy man her father is. And one day we sat on a bale of hay with a little girl who was saying good-bye to the dairy cow that she had bought and raised and considered her own. The bank was forcing the family to sell the herd of dairy cattle at a fire sale. Haul them off and

80

slaughter them. And this little girl couldn't understand why her cow was going with it. And I sat on a bale of hay and held her as she cried and said good-bye to her cow.

Or the young man who, when he was in high school, all he ever wanted to do was farm. He was a Star Chapter farmer in Future Farmers of America. He received county and state awards in FFA and if anybody was going to make it, boy, this young man was. He was the only child of a family that had been on the same land for three generations. And when he graduated from high school, his folks stuck their neck out and helped him start farming. Oops! He was born at the wrong time. Because in 1984 his operation fell apart, and his folks stood to lose that farm that had been in the family for three generations. And he took the blame on his shoulders for what was happening. He blamed himself. In fact, I think he took the blame for the whole rural crisis on his twenty-two-year-old shoulders. And one day, when his folks had gone to town on some errands, he walked out of the house and into the barn that his grandfather had helped to build, and he strung up a rope. When his folks came home, they had to cut down the lifeless body of their only child.

No, our kids were lucky. But our son, who was twelve at the time, still harbors resentment for that dream we lost. We discovered that last winter when Jason, who is now seventeen, had to give a speech in school. He chose to write about the rural crisis. And thank goodness! He gave that speech to Gary and I, practiced on us before he went to class. We were both shocked at his attitude. In his opinion, the only good lender is a dead lender, it was all their fault there was a rural crisis, and they didn't care about the farmer anyway.

Oh! We sat down with Jason and had a long talk with him, trying to explain that the crisis has been precipitated by low commodity prices, high interest, and falling land values. It's been in the making for over thirty years, as our government has formed national farm policies that favor large corporate farming. The crisis has just helped to speed up the takeover of the family farm by corporations and wealthy individuals. Every producer with which the farmer does business has the power to set their own prices, but the farmer does not. Our nation's cheap raw products policy has been helped along by governmental initiatives. The loss of the family farm is not the unfortunate result of policies that have failed, but rather, carefully developed and implemented policies to eventually eliminate the family farm.

Now, Jason did rewrite his speech, thank goodness. And I notice now that his friends will talk to him about how the crisis has affected them—when they sadly enough may not feel comfortable or be able to talk to their own family. And Jason himself has given a few talks about how he sees the rural crisis affect his peers.

The Day the Bank Died

ALVIN "JIM" KROEGER
Todd County, South Dakota

Jim Kroeger is a rancher who lives a few miles north of Cody, Nebraska, a small town in the midst of the Sandhills, an arid country largely inhabited by farmers who graze cattle. Cody's only bank failed in 1984. This chapter, unlike others in the book, is not based on a taped interview, but is a sparingly edited speech. A group of Sandhills ranchers attended a seminar in Des Moines on December 15, 1984, which farm credit attorney James Corum, from Minneapolis, was to present. Unfortunately, inclement weather prevented Corum from flying to Des Moines, and those attending, with the help of Prairiefine staff who had organized the seminar, held their own improvisational session to discuss farm credit problems. In the midst of a discussion of bank closings, Jim Kroeger came forward to give this talk.

WHAT happens when a bank goes broke? That door is shut. And I mean shut, period. They tell us a few words I want you to forget: "business as usual." Like hell. Pardon the language.

On a Wednesday morning, early, about daylight, before the bank was to be opened, the press started calling our banker, and wanted to know what was going on, if the bank was closed. Well, he didn't know anything about it. We didn't, either. But before the bank opened, before 8 o'clock, the FDIC people and the sheriff's department, seven strong, were sitting on the bank door. I don't know what kind of people they thought we were, what they needed all this law for, but they had to have two deputies in the bank all day long, plus they had a roadblock set up out on the highway checking traffic. Plus one of the deputies going north out of town, into South Dakota. Every fifteen minutes he made a round trip, six and a half miles out and back. What for, I don't know. But that's the way it went. And they closed. And when they walked into the bank, they just started throwing stuff in boxes. They had no idea what was going on. The people that were working in the bank didn't know what was going on, either. By 9 o'clock, there were two liquidators in there plus forty other FDIC employees. There were so many people in that bank, one had to move before another could.

And where do we stand today? I stand just like I did that day: with nothing. The banks were sold. There were two banks that went down at the same time: one in Kilgore, one in Cody. If you think this is a good deal, the bank in Kilgore was bought for $51,000. Nine million in deposits. The bank in Cody was bought for $303,000, with $9.2 million in deposits. Boy! And they don't want to write off 10 percent?

This is what we're getting. We're sitting there today; that territory is cold. I mean cold. I had a chance to sell heifers. I went into the bank and asked, "What should I do?" They said, "We suggest that you don't." What does that mean to you people? I had a fellow that called on Sunday. He was coming out to look at the heifers. He was an order buyer; he had a fellow that was interested. He called Saturday night. The banker told the fellow to stay away from us. Sounds familiar, doesn't it? The two banks that bought the closed banks, one of them was the Abbott Bank Corp., which has headquarters in Alliance, and has fifteen banks in the state of Nebraska, out in that territory. The other one was First National Bank of Valentine, which now has two banks that are right around there. It's 135 miles to a different bank, other than these two banks. Those banks are loaned up just as far as they dare go. If you go anywhere else, your federal and state banking officials say that you should stay within seventy-five miles of your bank. They discourage a bank from lending to anyone over seventy-five miles away. Where does that leave you? Where's that going to leave you people? We're gone. We're down here to try to keep it from happening to you. Now that's what happens when a bank goes.

Now we've got two PCAs in the same area that are closed. Same thing applies to them. Where do you go for refinancing? They moved the PCA from Valentine to Broken Bow. That's 150 miles from the office that was in Valentine. So where do you go for refinancing there? That PCA will refinance some of the loans, the better loans, as they call them. I can't see the difference in a lot of them. But they are charging them stock on top of stock.[1] The stock people have in the Valentine PCA is laying there; they are still paying interest on it. When you go to Broken Bow, you have to borrow your total of what you borrowed and your stock in the Valentine PCA, and then go from there with it. Did you figure out how much stock these people have purchased? They've got 20 percent stock purchased. You start adding this interest on there; they've got 30 percent stock purchased. When you can't make it on 10 percent stock, how are you gonna make it on 30 percent?

And we have a rate differential out there, too.[2] We have a Bank West in South Dakota, that runs down through a good share of the banks out there; they're to the north side of us. Their base interest is 15 percent. If you're borrowing less than 50 percent of your collateral, they will lower it one point; that's 14 percent. If you go over 50 percent, up to 60 percent, it's 15 percent. From there on up, there's no 16 percent interest, it goes to 17 to 20. If you can't make it on 13 percent, how are you going to make it on 15 or 14 or 17? There's no way. It's a sorry situation.

But we tried to tell people three years ago that this is down the road. They laughed at us. We had some people that were laughing at us when this bank closed. They've quit laughing. Your neighbor might be laughing at you, too, but, brother, I've got warnings for him: He's next.

The good bishop up north here told a story last year at the [Catholic] Rural Life conference here in Des Moines. He said two guys were out in the woods for a hike. They came upon a real hungry-looking bear. And one guy sat down and put on his track shoes. The other guy said, "That ain't gonna do no good. You can't outrun him." And he said, "I don't have to. All I gotta do is outrun you."

And the good bishop's closing remark was, "Yeah, but he forgot that tomorrow the bear's hungry again."

---

[1]See the section explaining the Farm Credit System in Appendix A for a definition of "stock" as used in the Production Credit Association.

[2]A rate differential is used by lending institutions to discriminate between customers of varying degrees of credit quality, according to various criteria they may choose to apply.

PART THREE
Main Street

The Banker

BRUCE SCHMAEDEKE
Cleghorn, Iowa

Schmaedeke, in his mid-thirties, is vice-president of the Cleghorn State Bank, a small single-office institution in a town of fewer than a thousand people. It has about $9 million in deposits, and 90 percent of its loan portfolio is invested in agriculture. He came to the bank in 1982 after working at other lending institutions. He talks with me about the change a farm crisis has imposed on small-town banking.

THERE'S not much security. As far as the people, it's kept pretty mum with me. Pastor Carlson says it's kept pretty mum with him, too. Farm families are proud.

But some people think it's people who spent too much money. Yeah, some people did spend too much money, but a lot of people are very conservative livers. You can go out on their farm place, and you can see an old kitchen, and they drive five-, six-, seven-year-old cars, and those people are also in danger of losing their farms. It's not necessarily people who are high livers that are getting caught into this. It's both ways. There are people who speculated hundreds of thousands of dollars and lost it on the commodities market. But there are also people who are very conservative and are not making it. I explain that especially to old, retired farmers. They just can't understand that these conservative people are also in danger of losing everything.

Economists say the best thing you can do is lock into a profit. Well, you haven't been able to lock into a profit with grain (since 1984). And very few chances with cattle. We have some opportunities to lock in a profit with hogs, however. But to lock into a profit, you have to have the facilities there. You can't buy 250 head of feeder pigs and expect to feed your family on them. We're talking big-volume hogs to lock into a profit. And to do that, in order for a banker to loan somebody money for a thousand head of hogs, you have to have. . . . We're not going to loan 100 percent on a thousand head of hogs, even though we know you can lock into a profit. Or lock into a price, I should say, because hogs can always die.

Our bank has always been fairly conservative. We did not want to take on real estate as collateral. Of course, now we're being forced to take on real estate as collateral. About every other bank is. We are looking at cash flow a lot more heavily than we did two or three years ago. We're taking statements twice a year instead of once a year.

Three years ago [1982], we actually refused large real estate loans. We've got a very few small housing loans. We didn't want to depend on second mortgages as collateral, and many institutions did. You go to a lot of them, you'll find they took a second loan, took a second mortgage on the land, and the land on the second mortgage is worthless in most of those cases on $3,000 [an acre] land.

I started three years ago. I'm told that up until two or three years ago, they had a chargeout of something like $20 to $30,000, and they never had that much charged out. An older guy's retired, worked there about fifteen years. In the whole fifteen years he worked there, they never charged out that much on any loans, and. . . .

Our bank's in good shape, and we will continue to charge out, to write off, as loss loans, I guess over the next two or three years. Five years ago, it was a real terrible thing to have to present to the board of directors. And now, it's a way of banking.

Collections are not fun. Maybe you read the article in the [Omaha] *World-Herald* Sunday about a bank real close here. Did you read that? Collections—it made it appear that this bank was having a good time collecting. Collections are not fun.

I've collected a loan on somebody that I've known for ten or eleven years. Good friends of my wife, and it's not fun. A banker in Nebraska called a month ago, and I mentioned that story, and he said, "Well, I've got a lot worse one. I'm foreclosing on my father-in-law."

I said, "Why don't you just quit?"

He said, "I would but my dad owns the bank, and I'm expected to manage his bank." So there's things like that going on.

I'm a country banker, I want to stay a country banker, and we have almost as many fears about our traditions as the farmer. A person walks in the door, I don't have to interview anybody for fifteen minutes to an hour. Ninety percent of the people that come to the door, I know I'm going to give them a loan before they even ask, before they even come to my office. We're afraid of our traditions changing just as the farmers are also afraid of it.

What sort of reactions have you gotten from people when you've been forced to call in the note?

A couple of cases, they didn't blame me, they didn't blame the bank. At that time, I had the pastor out to deal with them emotionally. They were on the brink of suicide, and they were talking about suicide. I'm a small bank. The president of the bank is really in charge of the ag loan portfolio. I'm the vice-president. If anybody's going to get more heat, he is. I haven't had anybody snub me or look away from me—and he has. He's had one or two threats on his life. So when you're talking to me, you're talking to the guy who's taking a lot less brunt of the situation. And realizing that the bank's in pretty good shape, too. Our problems are fairly minimal.

If I was a farmer living in a small town and had in the back of my mind that I've got to live in this town, I want to try to stay honest. It's hard to stay honest sometimes when your back's against the wall. I'm not so sure I would be honest if I got my back against the wall. Who knows? Some people who I never ever thought would be dishonest are. But their backs are against the wall. And I still think of them as good people. The main thing to stress to farmers is to stay honest. When somebody starts being dishonest, it makes it a lot easier for me to foreclose. When a guy is really honest, that's the hardest thing there is, when he's cooperating all the way.

You have to think about their families. It's easy to tell them the important things in the world aren't money, and it's easy to say, but at the time. . . . And your traditions are changing, all those fears are there.

How much of a problem are chain bank buyouts for rural banks and the tradition that you've been talking about?

That trend is slowing down because those big bank corporations have had a lot of bad buys. I have friends who work for big corporations, and they have told me that some of the banks wish they had never bought them. Of course, those banks were bought three, four years ago. And it's a bad buy. Buying a bank is a lot of work. A lot of work. And the smaller bank holding companies aren't all that willing to go through all that work. Buying a troubled bank is a lot of work, and you have a hard time generating sufficient income for the first three, four years. There's two banks in Odebolt, one failed, one was in better shape. I was very surprised to see the bank was sold. I didn't think anybody'd be interested in buying a failed bank in a town with another bank in it, of a thousand people. So far, we've had the willingness to buy. The farmland, there isn't that much willingness to buy farmland. They don't know what it's worth. There's not money around.

You probably wonder why I work for an independent bank. In this bank, I probably will never go up the ladder any more than what I am now. Vice-president in two years, with a president the same age I am. But I'm satisfied there. I want my daughter to grow up in a small-town tradition. And many other independent bankers will feel the same way. Any other country bankers will feel the same exact way. I enjoy banking. If I have to leave, I'll leave. If I'm forced to leave for a bank in Omaha or Des Moines, I guess I will. I'm very familiar with the big banks because we work closely with the big banks.

We used to have a lot of farmers coming in for $500 loans. What they called operating expenses. You don't see that anymore. They aren't taking vacations. We used to have a lot of small operating loans in our portfolio. They're coming in for crop expense, and that's about it. They're cutting back a lot. A lot of their sons are leaving, and they're going to Sioux City or Sioux Falls or somewhere like that to find a job.

The Appliance Dealer

CHERIE ROQUET
Jefferson, Iowa

The town could easily have been written about by Garrison Keillor. Jefferson is not a city on a hill, nor does it hug the banks of one of the myriad rivers that drain to the southeast across the gently rolling Iowa landscape, like the Wapsipinicon in Grant Wood's rendering of Stone City. Jefferson is simply there, *straddling the junction of two highways at its northern outskirts, but mostly just plunking itself down in the middle of an expanse of flat prairie covered with corn and soybean fields. The grain elevator tells you all you need to know about how it came to be.*

But it is more than that now. It is a county seat and retail center, with an obligatory coffee shop whose Saturday specials will get you breakfast for under $2. Its straight, tree-lined residential streets fill up a few blocks in either direction from downtown until they fade into the dominant countryside. That is as it should be. That is what makes towns like Jefferson.

The only thing missing from a Garrison Keillor story would be the Norwegian bachelor farmers. The bachelor farmers are there, but they have average American surnames that just don't sound ethnic, for the most part. David and Cherie Roquet, whose surname sounds like the great American mountain range despite its French spelling because David's grandfather wanted to Americanize its pronunciation, live in one of those postcard-neat brick homes that has the warmth one associates with Norman Rockwell paintings of classic American families in the 1950s.

They did not grow up here. They moved here to go into business

93

and left their secure jobs at the Land-o-Lakes dairy plant in Fort Dodge. David now works for a small company that tests electric meters for rural electric cooperatives.

WE'VE always wanted to be in business together. We started looking for something that we could afford and would be of interest. We wanted a smaller community for our kids. We were impressed with the people we met, and we bought an appliance and hardware store. Both of us like hardware. Appliances just happened to be the bigger part of our store.

We came in 1978, took a SBA [Small Business Administration] loan. 1978 was a very good year for our store. Greene County was recovering from the drouth of '77, but a lot of the farmers had been given disaster loans, and they were able to replace a lot of things that they were previously unable to. '79 was the year it started going down. We had been accustomed to having forty-eight to fifty appliances sitting either on the floor or in storage, which is a lot for a small town. So we were encouraged very strongly to use a floor plan. You go to the company and buy a large quantity of appliances at one time, and the bank guarantees it. Washers, dryers, refrigerators, stoves, deep freeze. You sign a note. As you sell your appliances, you pay the note. You do not have regular payments on the note. It's a form of inventory financing.

You have a certain number of months to pay it all off. You could get a loan for six months. Normally, in that period of time, you could pay it off. But as the farm economy started getting bad, they stopped purchasing like they were. We were told, as long as you pay the interest, no problems. Of course, we had to start paying interest plus the note, and they would just renew it. But they decided they were no longer going to renew. And we ran into problems of taking a payment over, and instead of it being applied on the oldest note, they'd apply it on the newer notes and let the old one pile up. Then they could come back and say, "Oh, but you owe this one plus this amount of interest. You haven't made payments on that one; you've made payments on this one." Of course, that was our fault because of lack of experience, lack of writing the note number on the check. We just took it on faith that they would apply it where we told them to apply it.

David is easier, softer-spoken, and mellower. I was never allowed in on any of the bank conversations. If I would call over and want to know something, "Well, he isn't here."

"Would you have him call me back?"

And they'd never call. They'd wait until David walked in, and say, "Oh, your wife called. Is there something we can help you with?" But they would not deal with me, and I'm sure it's because I am very outspoken. I may raise my voice.

We received a phone call from General Electric in June '82. "What are you going to do for financing?"

And we said, "What do you mean, what are we going to do? We've always used Brenton State Bank."

"Well, we have a letter here saying that they're no longer extending credit to you." We had no copy of the letter. I find out letters had been sent to all the companies we had dealt with, without our knowledge. And I don't think this is quite right.

Finally, David was called for a meeting, and we locked up the store, and I went with him. The branch bank president that day said, "I will see your store closed." David said, "You will not see our store closed." But he felt that the business was an unnecessary business; it was not an economically sound business; and he had chosen that this was going to be the one closed. There were three other hardware stores in town, and this one was not needed.

We realized at the time things were hard. We were affected because other people were not purchasing. But we also felt that with a little bit of support, and proper handling of finances, we could do it. Well, interestingly enough, the bank president turned to David, and said, "Your dad has money. Why don't you get the money from him?" Now, how he knew that, I don't know. [Dale Roquet lives in Fremont, Iowa, more than a hundred miles away.] But he did know that David's dad was quite well off, and he felt that we could turn to him if we wanted his support.

At that time, Dale had all of his money in one bank. It didn't matter how much he had, but it was a big sum. But a lot of people that we visited with, a lot of farmers, a lot of acquaintances of ours, at the meetings we went to, the ones that seemed to be picked on the most were ones that did have finances elsewhere that they could get their hands on. Now, this is at this particular moment. I'm not saying that that's the way it always is.

We had received a letter from a friend of ours who previously was in banking, asking if we had been notified by our bank that all Small Business Administration loans had been granted a period of paying only the interest and not paying any principal. We had not been. We went to the bank and asked about making new arrangements with this. Well, they hemhawed around and finally made new loan arrangements through the SBA.

We started doing that in 1982. Later in '82, David asked the SBA rep to call and make the final closing arrangements. An SBA rep came over to us, and we talked for a long time, and he did not feel, after visiting with us and seeing our records, that we were the type of business that he needed to close. So he called the bank and asked them to write a letter to him, asking for an immediate payoff. SBA pays 90 percent of the note at the time that the bank demands payment. We were to make payments to SBA and go on in our own way with what we were doing. He felt we were fine financially, that we knew our business, that we knew what we were doing.

'82 was our bad year. We had so much pressure put on us. Our daughter was being married the end of June. Of course, it had been in the newspaper, and the bank decided they were going to close the store the 25th of June. Right before the wedding. Good taste. They really didn't have SBA's permission. We wrote a letter to the bank, and a letter to SBA, telling them, because of this wedding, don't you think you could possibly wait until July?

But a bank director came over, and he said, "I don't understand why you feel that the bank is being unfair to you. You have these notes that are due, and all you pay is the interest. Granted, you've never missed an interest payment, but the notes are due. We have to call them." We were squabbling over $4,500. That was the total amount.

We had forty-eight appliances sitting on the floor, three-quarters or more paid for. . . . You can take an average of say $400, so that's ten, eleven, twelve appliances [to cover the note]. There was plenty of inventory. We had nothing to worry about. And he said, "We just feel that you do not have the financial stability to go on in business."

David's dad's attorney said, "They have nothing to stand on, don't worry about it." David's dad gave us an inheritance to pay the $4,500 off. We paid off everything we had at Brenton. From '82 forward, we had no loan with them. Even when we closed the store, we closed it out of choice, not of financial necessity. I know a lot of people don't believe that, but we felt that, with the farm economy still as bad as it is, and we had struggled so long and so hard, it was the opportunity for us to get out.

But you wonder how these officials who have encouraged people, buy more, buy more, buy more, keep your inventory up, get lots on the floor, we have money for you. . . . How can these people sleep at night? How can they go to bed after they have talked somebody into being so far in debt? It's just unbelievable to me. But they do it all the time.

I am told that you developed connections with a local farm survival committee that tried to help you out by putting pressure on Brenton Bank.

There was a group of us who met: Iowa Farm Unity Coalition. Basically, we were helping each other as well as saying, "Now this is what they did to me; don't let it happen to you."

We did go to some of the foreclosure activities. By this time, David and I were just running the store by ourselves. We found it very difficult getting away. David went to more meetings than I did during the day. It was not unusual for him to be out of the store. But it was really unusual if I would go out of the store. We felt it was better that I stay in and he go out and do some of this activity. Letters were written; requests were made; and it's not just Brenton. The Farm Credit Corporation used to have an office in town. Their name and Brenton seemed to come up more than any other.

We went to one meeting and were shown a list of demands the bank made on a farmer. But in those demands, there was not enough to live on. And if you had company drop in once, you couldn't ask that company to eat with you, or you're not going to be eating for the next three days. And there was one clause in there that if, at any time, you overspent on any of these areas, your loan would immediately be called in. And many, many, many people sign those without ever reading them. Because their banker was a good guy, he was their friend, and he was the one who said, "Hey, this is just another piece of paper, no big deal." As far as I'm concerned, that wasn't "no big deal." It was something very, very important.

It just seemed that we had so many farmers coming in who just cried on your shoulders. This director I mentioned, the following year, was hit by the same bank after his wife had received a large inheritance. He came to us and said, "Now I understand what you're talking about." He had felt that it was all done in pure honesty, and really doing the best for the bank. I think they did take part of this man's land. I have not visited with him as far as what actually happened because he had such an emotional reaction to it. I think he was probably the type that needed to talk to somebody confidentially, not on a friendship basis. But within the last three, four months, he's opened up a lot. And you see him in church, and he'll say, "Oh, I wish I had listened to you more. Why didn't the majority of us realize what was happening?"

One lady refused to come to town because she was ashamed that they were having financial problems. But the bank really played on her emotions. They knew she had a very vulnerable spot. The bank president said to her one day, "Aren't you ashamed that you've allowed this to happen?" And she says that, at the time, she really didn't realize what he was doing. She said, "You would think that I would because I have a degree in sociology."

But she was so down and so upset because she had three children in college. She was working full time. He was working full time, as well as running this acreage that they had just purchased. And there's just enough emotional stress there that this lady would not come to town. She refused to go to church any longer. She would go to her job; she wouldn't talk to anybody. We were fortunate because we had to work with the public. We continued on, but other people came in and asked, "Didn't you just feel like you wanted to crawl in a hole?" No, I didn't. Because I'm too headstrong.

This whole situation has been really sad. Not just for us, but for the entire economy. I know my ignorance now from having been in business. I look at what closing our store has already meant. We no longer have a franchise for Frigidaire appliances. If anybody wants Frigidaire appliances, they must go out of town to buy them. If they want Maytag appliances, they have to go out of town to buy them. If they want General Electric appliances, they go out of town. If they want Kelvinator, they go out of town. So, a lot of sales that we had are no longer in our town. It's hurting us. It has hurt the entire Main Street. It has hurt everyday middle citizens in town. And in return, it's also hurt the bank because we no longer would put one penny of savings, checking, or a note in that bank.

All this adds up to one thing: Every penny spent within your community will circulate. In closing a business, shutting down a farmer, shutting down any person in any type business, you're pushing that person's business, and all the business that that person would give, to another bank. It's a vicious circle.

One of the consumer magazines that we received had an analysis of spending the dollar. A group of us sat down one evening. We're all business people. We took one farm, and we did this because they were closing the farm down. We knew that they had financial problems. Anyway, we pretended. We took him and we said, okay, we'll call him George. He comes into the grocery store once a week. We broke down how many dollars he would spend there. How many dollars would go to the REC [rural electric cooperative] to pay electric service. How many dollars in gasoline. We did everything we can think of, and it got almost ridiculous how small we took this. Even down to ice cream. The ice cream shop is not going to get their ice cream sales. It was funny because this guy and his wife loved ice cream, so it was kind of a joke when we got to that part. But we were surprised what we found because we multiplied that by the number of farmers within Greene County: how many of those farmers would no longer be spending X number of dollars on appliances, on groceries, on electric services, on feed, on fertilizer, and it was really scary.

We should have probably taken it another step because, if I did not get a $500 appliance sale, I was not going to have that $100 from my appliance sale to buy my groceries for the month. It's quite interesting when you break down what happens when one person does not have the opportunity to spend.

But I think sometimes we forget that not only is it financially stressful, but it's also emotionally stressful. Now, we have been very fortunate in Greene County. Nobody took their lives. But we had a group that was very quiet, very behind-the-scenes. They were an emergency call group. There were several wives who called. "My husband has been in the barn far too long. He won't answer when I go out there." I think the community can handle this type of stress less than the financial stress. None of the people who called for help had ever heard their spouse say, "I'm going to kill myself." But it was just watching the pressure. And even though those people maybe would never say a thing when they were in town, just their attitude, the look on their face, if you're at all conscientious, you couldn't help but see it. And that type of depression and emotional repression will also kill a town. It's not only the finances.

I know that hurt our business. There would be days that I know I didn't smile a lot. But it was always during that time in 1982. After that, things began to look up. But I don't think David got over it. He's still bitter, still very angry, still very hurt.

The Minister

DELMAR CARLSON
Cherokee, Iowa

"How blessed can we be?" quips Bethlehem Lutheran Church's pastor as we talk about his community's double whammy. In June 1984, the Farmers National Bank in nearby Aurelia, Iowa, closed due to insolvency. In January 1985, the larger Steele State Bank in Cherokee followed.

For farmers and small business managers alike, dealing with the Federal Deposit Insurance Corporation concerning their outstanding loans from a failed bank is hardly fun. For farmers, it is probably more difficult, both in that their success or failure depends heavily on their ability to plant and harvest crops and feed livestock in a timely manner, and in that FDIC officials had little understanding of farming. In fact, liquidating rural banks was a relatively new phenomenon for most of them, and rules that had applied to urban bank failures often had disastrous consequences in the countryside. Farmers became guinea pigs for FDIC's learning experiences. But for farmers and small businesses alike, maddening months could go by while they waited in limbo for FDIC either to liquidate or to sell their loans to another bank. Lost opportunities abounded. But for those unfortunate few who survived the first local bank failure, only to find false respite at the second bank just before it closed, the ordeal was frequently more than their operation could withstand.

Ironically, Rev. Carlson points out, *"There was a tremendous trust by the community in both banks."* Both, he notes, had survived the Great Depression intact.

I T'S a feeling of a closing-in experience. People have had their credit cut off. Those who had investments in the banks certainly are still very uptight because they don't know what's going on. That's still in a legal process. But, beyond that, there was a body of people who had loans out—farmers, business people—and, all of a sudden, they woke up to the bank closing. They then were faced with the reality of either paying back those loans or scurrying to find where they could get refinanced from, or to see if the FDIC would finance them, or the FmHA, or whatever.

And so what we find throughout the parish and the community is a sudden feeling of panic. What's going to happen now? And there was an approach to our congressmen, our senators—What can be done legislatively to help us out? There are some who have lost their farms already. There are some who are in this process who were given one year. Loans through FmHA, then at the end of one year, they have to refinance them somehow. And are not in any better position than they were before.

Looking at this thing on a broader basis, it seems to me the churches here made a twofold approach to ministry in this situation. First of all, I would like to say it's kind of a prophetic approach: gathering people together in meetings—farm meetings, community meetings—where people can air their problems, their situation, their concern about getting loans to put the seed in, the fertilizer in for the next year, and to make this known to our people in Congress and to the president. And there were, of course, the rallies, the community meetings, the evening meetings gathering farm people together. So I think that that was the first approach that the churches made. And I think it was a rather prophetic call for help and also a uniting of the people together to say we've got a common problem here that's affecting us all.

Then, the second approach after the fields were planted was more of a pastoral approach. Okay, we've got a lot of people who are silently suffering and are crying. Now, they don't want to speak about it. They don't want to share their circumstances openly, although it's pretty well known through the community, and so it's been a compassionate outreach to one another. And a call to the congregation to unite in compassion and ministry to one another and to support one another.

And that's where we still are right now. We're in a process where we say we hope; we're counting on the farm economy to improve.

Because right now there isn't profitability in farming, and because there isn't that, the businesses are hard-pressed. It's a holding-on situation until, hopefully, a profitability will return to farming. If that would happen, then, of course, the businesses would begin to thrive, and communities would thrive, and churches would thrive.

I have not seen the sky falling in on the church. I have seen a more conservative giving to the church, although I am totally amazed at how well our congregation continues to support the work it is doing. I'm amazed that they can do it. But there's been some cutting back. There's had to be. So that's what I see has happened.

The churches in Cherokee have conducted joint food drives to provide for the needs of the needier members of the community through a food pantry. Many of Bethlehem's farmer members donated for slaughter animals with minor flaws, such as broken limbs, in order to put meat on such families' tables.

Rev. Carlson continues to commit himself to "drawing people out of themselves," for many have been slow to admit physical or emotional need. That fact, more than anything else, disturbs him. As he learns from friends and neighbors of such families, "I always ask myself, 'How many more?'"

The Editor

CHRIS NANNENGA
Thornton, Iowa

Small town editors and publishers are renowned for their civic boosterism. It is rooted both in practicality—after all, a prosperous town means a prosperous local newspaper—and in the fundamental pride that any natural civic leader feels. In the midst of hard times, that pride is put to a certain test of character. Optimism can either take an almost clownish "see no evil" form or it can deepen the convictions that underlie a discriminating determination to save the best of the local values and culture. Newspapers that either downplayed the farm crisis or refused outright to see the problem often embittered local farmers who were suffering in a supposed land of plenty. Chris Nannenga, editor of the Southern County News *in Thornton, Iowa, is not one of those because he has shared those farmers' experiences and added some others that have profoundly shaped his outlook. If his proposed remedies for local troubles in this interview seem a bit vague, it is most likely because his is a mind still in turmoil, formulating questions and seeking answers. But he will not write editorials that blithely suggest there are sunny days ahead. If anything, he sounds Churchillian in his call for struggle.*

His parents raised him, his brother, and a sister on a dairy farm outside nearby Clear Lake, Iowa. Their two farms, where they also raised hens, hogs, and beef cattle, lay in the planned path of Interstate 35 between Des Moines and Minneapolis. The bureaucracy, he says, "lies very well" despite public hearings, and retains the finest law firms beforehand so that resisting citizens "find a good country lawyer and put up a good fight and lose. When you have a war, you're going to have casualties. We are the casualties." Whatever the nature of the family's legal struggles to save the farms, his father, he says, ultimately suffered minor strokes over the matter.

He went to junior college and then to Vietnam for a year, where he served as machine gunner in the bush at Pleiku and Khontum. He returned to farm, married, and acquired his own farm. A banker, who he says later committed suicide, demanded immediate payment on notes that had shown no previous sign of difficulty. He had, he says, a fine dairy herd. But he and his wife sold out, paid off the note, and worked their way out of remaining debts over a few years. He bought a local restaurant, sold it later, became a farm building salesman who led his company in a fifteen-state area, and then had a falling-out over a disagreement when, he says, the company sought to cheapen the product. "I never cheated anybody in my life, and I'm not going to start now," Chris says he decided.

That was 1983. After a few months training with the former owner of the newspaper, who was anxious to sell out, he took over. That was spring of 1984.

I was at a meeting three years ago at the Red Fox Inn in Waverly, Iowa, put on by the Extension [Service]. They provided some very influential individuals, and one of them was a vice-chairman of the Federal Reserve Board. People from all over Iowa were at this two-day session. They could have just put an end to everything when this guy got done. He said, "First off, in the Midwest, we've got too many banks. Second off, in the Midwest, we've got too much farm debt. We are not going to expect the average taxpayer to absorb this debt. We are going to get rid of a good share of the Midwestern banks. We're going to get rid of a good share of this agricultural debt. And it's going to happen through attrition. There's not much that anybody is going to do about it, simply because there's too much for too many." And that's all he had to say, and he left.

And three years down the road, we see what's happened. We've seen banks close. We've seen farmers leave. We've seen debt written off in many cases. After everything has been gotten that could be gotten, it's business as usual. We're going to continue to ignore this problem out here for a number of years. And we're going to have a lot of forgotten people absorbed back into society, as best they can, to get on with other things. But what basically happened we're not going to talk about; it's going to be forgotten. In the meantime, thousands of farm families have suffered tremendously. Thousands of businesses have failed.

We keep saying we want to save this small farm family as a real live entity. But do we really want to save it? How can they save something they don't understand? How can they save something they don't perceive?

We seem to have several separate societies. There was a study done for the 1986 Senate on the farm crisis here in the Midwest. It said that we were in a tremendous danger of creating a two-level society. Something had to be done to save this fabric that we've got out here, but nothing's being done. If you wait long enough, you achieve the goal of a bipolar society.

I don't know how we convince the powers that be that what we have out here is worth saving. We keep saying that businesses hire Iowa people. Iowa people have no problem being hired because of the work ethic. Iowa people have no problem being hired outside of Iowa because of our high quality of education. And honesty. When you talk to business people, that's always been something Iowa has been able to pride itself in. And yet those three factors have been under tremendous siege in these last three years. It seems that there's a force intent on trying to pull us down to a nationwide norm, that we have to be like everyone else.

How do we change that?

We have to help ourselves. No one's going to help us. There are a lot of people that say they will, but they won't.

We got something started in our area, the first time in the state of Iowa it's ever been done. As a result, we've had several others do it, too. We have seven communities in this area, we call it the Area Community Commonwealth. Every one of those communities has, or will over the next three years, celebrated their centennial. Look at our Main Streets in any one of these towns, and we aren't any better off than when we started. We stayed right where we were. The farm crisis just tore us to pieces. And Mason City has come along and just devastated the retail of a lot of our smaller communities because discount buying is strong in Mason City. There are a lot of discount houses there. People aren't loyal to their home town Main Streets. By helping ourselves, I mean we have to rebuild our own economy. If we really want to save our Main Streets, if we really want to save this way of life we've had out here, we can't wait for federal farm programs.

We can't look to Des Moines to do that for us. We have to start helping ourselves.

(The aim of such a commonwealth, Chris later explained, was to pool the efforts of small towns too small to mount serious economic development efforts strictly with their own resources. Most of these towns are under a thousand population. One of his proposals to the legislature, which he lobbies for aggressively, is to require the Iowa lottery, whose proceeds are earmarked by law for economic development efforts, to return 20 cents per dollar of profits generated by these communities for their own local development initiatives through these area commonwealths. The groups are voluntary affiliations of the municipalities involved.)

We've got the mindset from the commercial side of our life-styles that we can't fix our own plumbing; we have to call a plumber to fix it. We can't fix our own car; we have to take it to a car mechanic and have him fix it. We can't put in our own windows; we have to call in a carpenter to put in our windows. We've turned into such a consumer-oriented people that we can't fix our problems. We have to call in a specialist to fix our problems. All of a sudden, the specialists don't understand our problems at all. We have to fix our own problems. We have to start over and rebuild. We can do that, but it's gonna take a lot of work and a lot of education.

That push for farm size to grow has been there for years. But now, all of a sudden, they're coming back and telling us that maybe this isn't a good idea. Maybe big isn't better. John Deere's suffered severe business downturns. When you had 220 acres, or something like that, everybody says, "You can't make a living off this." You can't make a living when the land is inflated to $4,000 an acre either. When John Deere was turning out tractors that would work on 220 acres, or each 160 acres, the land was farmed. Look at all the machines you had out there. You start pulling it up to 480 acres with still one tractor and one combine and one planter, it's half of the jobs created and half the people fixing it and half the parts being sold, and half the farming families out here in the country. So we have a problem with our school systems now: not enough kids. We've got problems on our Main Streets. Not enough dollars, not enough people spending money. Not enough disposable income. And it all goes back to big, efficient, corporate units. It doesn't work. It didn't work. That's what they've got in the Soviet Union. Why should it work here? They've tried it.

It's not working. So why do we have to do what they're doing? Why isn't our life-style unique enough to save out here? Why do we have to be New Yorkers? Why do we have to be Californians? Why can't we be Iowans, unique in our own ways?

But we have these powers that be that keep trying to mold us into their mindset. And yet they don't know who we are or what we are. A lot of that's our problem. We can't sit back because we're Iowans, because we're rural. We've been drawn into this extra-fast life-style. All of the farm wives had to have the new house that their stockbroker in Des Moines had. We've built the new ultramodern house because it wasn't socially acceptable to have the quaint farm house. The merchants up and down Main Street all of a sudden had to catch up with the larger metropolitan areas. We've got to change that.

Do you think there's anything particularly dangerous when you still have the same sort of relative political passivity that was in the culture for years, and you're dealing with different forces than you used to be? When you were passive before, you didn't have to deal with that heavy hammer of modern industry and modernization.

Very much so. All they want to do is farm and make a living. That's not acceptable. What's gonna happen? Is our Iowa life-style worth saving? Or do we just go with the flow? Or do we try to put some order into this thing?

Iowa has gotten into the development game and tried to do it in a big way. But it's so disjointed, it's not really helping us at the rural level. They [the Iowa legislature] keep thinking that we are rural and that rural is a problem. We've got something of an identity crisis. Do we really want to be another Michigan, Illinois, or Ohio? Somebody came along and told them Iowa is about like being black or Hispanic. You know, we got buffalo and Indians and all this other stuff out here, which is poppycock.

I've been to a lot of farm crisis meetings. The last farm crisis meeting I was at, I vowed I wasn't going to another one. They brought in an individual running for some office. On one side of me, I had a young couple in financial trouble. On the other side of me, I had an older, retired couple. The older couple mortgaged considerably to help their son get started, and that's when everything started to fall apart. The younger family bought in at the wrong time. Their world was falling apart. The Farm Credit System was lying to everybody through their teeth. And FmHA wasn't helping anybody out, either. The guy standing up in front of them was telling them all we have trouble with the deficit, and we have trouble with the exports, and we have trouble with farm commodity prices.

But what is this family going to do tomorrow morning when they get up without hope? Their world wasn't going to change one little bit. What were we going to do for those people? And I asked the guy, "What are you going to do for these people tomorrow morning?"

"Well, this takes time."

They don't have time. We out here in the Midwest, if we want to salvage anything, we don't have time. We've gotta go to work. So I didn't go to any more crisis meetings. Until somebody was going to do something for these people, I wasn't going. I told them that.

There hasn't been any progress the last three or four years. You see, this whole thing was set up in the first place. We had too many banks, and we had too much farm debt, and they were going to get rid of it. The ceiling was on, and that's as far as you're gonna go, folks. And we went through the pain out here. They got rid of the debt. They got rid of the banks. They accomplished what they wanted to. Now, the war's over, with the few survivors straggling back home to try to rebuild their lives, rebuild their families again.

The day after. That's what happened. This whole last three years, if they would have just said, "We're not gonna renew your note, all these banks are closed," if they'd have just done it, we'd be three years ahead of where we are right now, instead of making us limp along through all this thing, and make a lot of lawyers rich [from bankruptcy cases].

PART FOUR
Great Expectations

My Old Iowa Home

GEORGE NAYLOR
Churdan, Iowa

I arrive in Churdan, Iowa, on a Sunday night in June, lacking directions to George Naylor's farm, and visit a small tavern. It is the only establishment open. Four farmers occupy one table. I ask the waitress. Uncertain of the directions to Naylor's farm, she consults the men at the table.

"Is that the same Naylor that lived there a number of years back?" one asks.

"That's Leonard's boy," another answers him.

I get my directions after the pair reflect for a moment. Two miles east, two north, and another three-quarters east. When I pull into the driveway, George is waiting. My timing is impeccable. No sooner do I bring my bags into his modest one-floor house than a storm hits. In two hours of driving from Sheldon, Iowa, I had missed storm clouds on either side of me. Now they break loose in a windy torrent.

As he does with all his visitors, George frets to scrounge up a makeshift dinner, and we talk casually through the evening. The interview takes place the following morning—after chores.

I was raised on a farm, right in this house. My dad quit farming in 1962, and we moved to California. He got a job in aerospace. There seemed to be a point where he could see the economic handwriting on the wall in agriculture. He didn't want to expand and go into debt just to stay on the farm.

My family was able to rent its farm out to someone else. We were still sort of country bumpkins and still considered ourselves

111

Iowa farmers. We came back to the farm every summer.

I went to college and, as time went on, I became disillusioned with city life. The ecology movement had smashed dreams of owning a Corvette. I got interested in the back-to-the-land idea of homesteading and living on a commune. Also, I read stuff on organic gardening and farming.

Then, my goal was to give up the idea of a big job in the city and go back to the land. I investigated the counterculture and the back-to-the-land movement. It never seemed to work out because I never had money to buy land, and I never found the exact social situation that would be comfortable. I was always dependent on having a certain amount of land or money to get started, and I didn't have that. I thought about coming back to the family farm, and I investigated raising organic grain, particularly oats for small granola companies. It turned out that my uncle wasn't ready to retire, so I couldn't farm the family farm.

The cereal companies came out with their natural cereals laden with sugar and advertised to the hilt, so little granola companies went broke. There wouldn't have been no market for organic oats, anyway. Eventually, some years later, after I had worked for my uncle on the farm, and then for an electronics firm in California, my family decided I could go back to the farm and make a living because of the incredible boom in grain prices in '73 and '74. For once, it seemed like the expenses would be less than what I would get for the crop. Corn was $3.35 per bushel and beans over $10.00 per bushel.

George returned to Iowa with his wife, Marilyn Fedelchak. Marilyn later organized a three-day symposium at Iowa State University, "We Shall Not Be Moved: The Historical Roots of Agrarian Protest," in March 1980. They have since then been divorced, and George farms alone. Marilyn is rural program director in Chicago with the National Trust for Historic Preservation.

But it turned out that the tractor I figured I would buy for $10,000 actually cost $19,000. Other machinery was a similar situation. The price of corn had been $2.70 when planted the spring of the first year, in the spring of '76. In the fall of '76, it was $2.30 at harvest. It was $2.00 that winter. The bankers and elevator managers said to hang on because it's got to go higher. I bailed out in August and sold my first corn crop at $1.74 per bushel.

They couldn't guarantee it wasn't going lower, and it went down to

$1.50 at harvest for my second crop. This was when there was a widespread drought, one of the worst in Iowa history. Some fields in Greene County were totally abandoned. The Mississippi River reached its lowest level in 100 years, so it seemed very widespread.

Nevertheless, the price just kept going lower. So I was rather upset. Things were not working out as they had on paper, and something obviously had to be done. I guess Jimmy Carter's promises were nothing but lies. He'd been to the state fairgrounds in '76 and said farmers deserved at least the cost of production. I said we have got to get Jimmy Carter in there, but prices just kept getting lower. At first, I bought the whole agribusiness idea that we had to get more exports and find more uses for corn.

I ran for the Iowa Corn Promotion Board. This is a quasi-governmental thing to spend about $1 million in check-off money from corn producers in Iowa. I had to get signatures to run because they had people nominated through the normal process. I won, but by running around and talking to farmers, I found out most farmers didn't believe this was going to help at all. Some farmers were telling me that export promoters were saying that we couldn't have better farm prices or programs because it would hurt exports. Exports were the promoters' concerns, and not profits.

After I won, I would talk to elevator managers and business people about how to use that money wisely, and they had no ideas whatsoever. One idea was to teach Mexicans how to mix soybean meal into corn chips. This helped soybeans, maybe, but not corn.

The Iowa Corn Promotion Board was going to spend money without even consulting anybody about how it would be spent, or whether it would do any good. It was like a given, or an act of faith, that we would give money to these agencies that were already getting money from the government and agribusiness to promote exports and more uses of corn, and encourage more production of corn at the same time. It became clear to me that that whole idea was counter to farmers' best interests and an agribusiness scheme to divert people's attention from the real issue.

That issue is society's relationship to agricultural resources and to the producers. It is an economic relationship. At the same time, the American Agriculture Movement got going and they were demonstrating, and I found that they had captured the imagination of a lot of farmers. Talk of a good program based on parity made a lot of sense. At the same time, I had come across the *U.S. Farm News*.

I had picked up a copy of it at Stanford University, even before farming, when we had a peace demonstration against Gerald Ford. I investigated the AAM because of all the attention it was getting [in 1978]. I got involved in AAM and organized a tractorcade in the county and went to a lot of meetings.

But, I don't know, through all the activity of AAM, I saw the interest peak real early, and just gradually it fell apart because of a lot of extraneous issues being brought into the organization and a lot of personality conflicts. An awful lot of right-wing ideology that didn't lead anywhere and diverted attention from farm issues. So, gradually I decided to spend more time working with the U.S. Farmers Association [publishers of *U.S. Farm News*], whose motto is "Peace and Parity," and who's much more clear on the farm issue, in terms of who are the enemies of family farm agriculture and what were the solutions. What kind of policy would be good for family farmers and the rest of society? Trying to get a government that would provide for farmers would be the same as trying to get a government that would encourage justice for other people in the world and peaceful international relations.

Of course, all through this farm movement organizing, there've always been attempts to get different groups together and unified, but not always a lot of success for various reasons. A lot of us hadn't had any experience, and that's why a lot of our efforts failed.

In the fall of '81, the U.S. Farmers Association convention zeroed in on an action plan based on the theory that many farmers were at the end of their rope and what we had seen of a deteriorating farm economy was going to reach crisis proportions. We passed that action plan. One of its parts was to encourage farm unity groups around the country. A lot of us were active in Iowa and knew there were a lot of sincere groups around Iowa with people who could go beyond their own organization's concerns. Unity was important. There were advantages in working together with one voice.

So, we called those people together, plus anybody else we could that we thought could contribute new ideas, to a meeting in Atlantic.

In January 1982, George Naylor and Dixon Terry, a Greenfield, Iowa, dairy farmer also in the U.S. Farmers Association, played a major role in organizing a meeting in the basement of a bank in Atlantic, Iowa, attended by representatives of several major farm

114

groups. At this meeting, those attending agreed to the formation of the Iowa Farm Unity Coalition.

I gave a presentation there on the economic reality and how we were plunging into a worse crisis, and how government had an important role to play in changing this course. Everything worked out, so there were initial links made and people started meeting more regularly.

One thing that helped was Jim Riordan's[1] trying to organize a demonstration of farmers when Ronald Reagan came to Iowa. There were quite a few people in a bigger coalition protesting Reagan's economic policies. I realized poor third-world people are plagued by the same kind of economic problems that U.S. farmers are. They are raw materials producers whose product values are determined in big markets in New York and London, and their countries are going into debt trying to produce the damned stuff. Then they have austerity programs imposed by the International Monetary Fund to pay back their debt. Plus, land holdings in those countries are usually concentrated, so the great mass of people have to beg, borrow, and steal to make a subsistence living. There is not much chance for economic development in those countries.

Rural America is actually just a third-world country within our own borders. Coalition work is real important. A lot more people are beginning to understand the economic connections and the need to get involved politically, and to challenge the power of the wealthy and the corporations and the military-industrial complex.

We need to just move away from a narrow focus on the farm problem and tie it to what's happening on a global scale, and to get people involved in militant action. We have us an education thing to do.

Our biggest handicap is to get the word out and get people to understand. It takes skills a lot of us just barely have. Involvement takes so much time that farm work suffers and friendships suffer. It's hard to find time to talk to your neighbors. To try to find a balance between your political life and private life is very difficult.

One looks at George and does not automatically jump to the conclusion that this is an activist who is helping to challenge some of the most powerful assumptions of America's agricultural Establishment.

[1]Originally a Boone grain farmer, Jim Riordan challenged incumbent Republican Iowa Secretary of Agriculture Robert Lounsberry in the 1982 election. Narrowly defeated, Riordan later ran for and won a state senate seat.

He is quiet and presents himself in an "aw, shucks," self-deprecating manner.

Yet there are other signs of an activist at work. A copying machine in a crowded living room. Stacks of newspapers in his bedroom. Piles of clippings on his small kitchen table. His office is a veritable obstacle course.

Economic conditions have changed farmers' perceptions more than anything I ever did. I think there will be a time when a lot of the organizing, speaking, and writing we have done will pay off. Because farmers in particular have become so depoliticized with their faith in the marketplace, propaganda with pushing more exports is what we are working against. You can't expect dramatic changes in people's orientation toward politics. The time is coming when farmers will turn their backs on the notion that the market, which is dominated by large corporations, can do anything for them. They will become militant and demand a government that represents peace and justice and a brighter future for their children and grandchildren.

The Farmer's Wife

BARBARA WOODS
Carlisle, Pennsylvania

We meet and talk at the Midwest Academy Retreat in Chicago, in the summer of 1985. She has just participated as a panel member in a workshop on the problems of American farmers, having served as the vice-president of the Pennsylvania Farmers Union. Her farm is in jeopardy of foreclosure, but the axe has not fallen yet. She is not waiting. She is here as a new central regional director for the Pennsylvania Public Interest Coalition, a grass-roots citizens' lobby. But her second marriage (her first husband died) is headed for divorce. She had three children coming into the marriage; her husband, Bob, had five, plus five grandchildren. They were married ten years. They are, she says, still on friendly terms.

I met Bob and wanted to move my children onto this farm. I still believed the imagery, in all of my naiveté, that this is the way of life that you should raise your children in. Went into the marriage really quite blindly to the real facts about farming.

One of the first things I had to deal with was the poverty. I didn't like being poor, and I didn't understand why we weren't making money. I began to examine all of our business practices, how we ran our farm, our operation methods. I would talk to everybody that came into that farm. I would pick their brains about everything that I should know. I became active with the Extension, ended up on the Extension board, local-county level, finding why—Why are we in trouble? I couldn't understand this because I saw us get up, I saw us work hard, I saw us do all of the things that all of these experts were

117

telling me had to be done, and still we were losing our farm. We were losing money. And I knew that the debt would continue to the point where we are today, where we're actually losing the farm. And I thought, "What's wrong? Something's wrong here."

Because of that, I became very active in farm organizations. I found that I had no voice as a woman in Farm Bureau. Real enlightenment there, didn't take me long! My husband said to me at a caucus, an annual conference, "Sit down! You can't say that."

I said, "What?"

He said, "You're a woman."

I said, "I'm your what?" And I mean, that was the last Farm Bureau meeting I attended.

I had served on women's committees, local-level Farm Bureau and everything, and I was becoming more and more frustrated, but that was the final straw. I became active with Farmers Union, which was more progressive, and I came from a county secretary-treasurer to a county president to a state vice-president. And became part of what was called the American Farm Project, which was funded by the National Endowment for the Humanities. That worked with identifying the economic roots and values of the family farm, and that, in turn, politicized me. That began to answer the questions that I was really having a hard time dealing with, and the fact that the farmer was not a poor manager, and the fact that it was a political reality that we were being forced off the farm.

Then I went back to Pennsylvania, more and more just committed to making farmers realize that it's not your fault when you're losing your farm, and it's not something that you can no longer share with other people. We have to get some part of that education process because all of the academics and all of the experts are not going to tell the population the truth about what's happening in family farming. To me, it was a commitment that farmers are too small in number any more to make any real difference.

Farmers themselves are still so conservative, especially in Pennsylvania, that they're not ready to become political. Politics is dirty. And they still believe that, if it is right, government will make it right, and they believe that they're going to be protected regardless if they're losing their farms. When the first 50 cent milk tax came on, I went out all over the state, preaching to get letters out to stop the 50 cent tax. We were projecting, on the average-size farm in Pennsylvania, an $8,000 loss in income with that 50 cent milk deduction. And farmers were saying, "They'll never do that because our congressmen *know* that we can't afford that." The first 50 cents went on. The farmers never went to D.C., never lobbied against it because they believed that it would never happen.

And did most of those Pennsylvania congressmen from rural areas vote for it?

Absolutely. Absolutely. And so, when the second 50 cents came out, we went to those *same* farmers, and they said, "They saw what that 50 cents did to us; they'll never put the second on." And the second came through! And it's that kind of frustration that leads you to realize that this community base is that conservative, that tied to the desperation of not wanting to admit that they're in trouble because they'd be identified as poor managers, and not being able to break through and beyond to the real problems of why they are where they are; I was going to have to do more.

So Farmers Union in our state and in many others is working with building broad-based coalitions such as Citizen Action Network to educate those fellow steering committee and board members as to the real problems in farming, much as they then, in turn, educate those very conservative farmers to the reality of what's happening in labor and industry: that it's not labor that's gouging and losing industry for the United States.

It's kind of a slow process and frustrating, especially when we're at the point now where our debt ratio is $1,200 every ninety days added to the debt. Even with my husband and I both working, there's no way we could handle $1,200 every ninety days just in interest added to our debt. So we started chipping away. We sold the cows. That was the first that we had a drought. We didn't have the money to buy feed, so we really didn't have any choice. We had three years' drought in a row, the third year wiped us out.

We had a herd. We were milking sixty head, twice a day. And we liquidated everything. All of the cows, all of the livestock. Then we couldn't service any of the debt because we weren't having the income. And FmHA was saying that we couldn't get the feed money, that our debt had become large enough at that point that they were shutting off the funds, that it was just a pointless effort because we were then projecting a lower milk price and we couldn't service the debt we had. So, in a time of drought, in a time of a depressed market, we literally gave the cows away and it didn't impact greatly on the debt.

But we had one year's grace that we didn't have to worry about FmHA foreclosing. So we sold off a tract of mountain ground, over a hundred acres. Again, just chipping away and giving us only more time and never dealing with the real debt problem. All of that adding to the stresses within the whole family. With my job and my commitment, having different political views from a very conservative husband who was raised on the farm and raised with such conservative views, we became strangers to each other, and we ended up moving much further apart. It ended the marriage.

But also a lot of stress. A lot of which he's having a hard time dealing with, but I've been so committed that I can't ignore what's happening now. And I can't accept his inability to act. And that's kind of sad, because when two people have fought and worked so hard for ten years, side by side, and it gets to that point. . . . But that's real, and that's where it's at. And it's difficult for the children. Most of Bob's children are married, except for one, and that one's Carol, and she'll be a senior next year, so she stayed with her father. She felt as if she couldn't leave him alone. He was not dealing well with the problems. And I took my three children and left. Moved closer to Harrisburg, closer to my work, closer to the commitment that I have to build that progressive coalition network.

What are you doing now?

I came to PennPIC as a board member, as a leader, representing Farmers Union, and moved from the steering committee up to the state board level within a few months. I was on the state board, representing as vice-chair the chief spokesperson for the state board, and out of that, I got a job with the Public Interest Coalition as a seniors' project coordinator. When the central regional directorship opened up, it was a natural for me to move into that position.

What were you doing before you got married and went onto the farm?

I was raised in a small river town in Pennsylvania. Our school system was relatively small, though not nearly as small as the one at the farm. The farm's in Franklin County, in south central Pennsylvania, outside of Chambersburg. And there it's even more conservative because they're in a valley, and virtually no one leaves the valley. Extremely Republican. When our children—Bob's children—were old enough to vote, his uncle came and picked them up on their birthday and took them to the courthouse to register them Republican. And there was never a question asked. I came onto the farm as a Democrat, and Bob's uncle says, "Bob, what are you going to do about Barbara?"

And Bob says, "What about Barbara?"

"Well, she's a Democrat."

"Yeah, she sure is."

"Well, what are you going to do about it?"

He said, "I don't intend to do anything about it. If you think you can change her mind, you're welcome to try. But there's no way I'm going to do anything about it."

So when other kids came of age, it got to the point where I would say to them before their birthday, "I think you should think about registration, and I think you should think very seriously about what the parties represent and what you want to align yourselves with." And let them know that Uncle Andy will be coming on their birthday, and they have the right, if they feel that they would like to register Democrat, to do that. His daughter, when she graduated, registered Republican. But I was hoping that she would register Democrat. But just that upset Uncle Andy so bad. There I was, an outsider in the middle of the valley, not knowing anything about farms.

Basically, in my first marriage, before my first husband died, I had done anything from a borough secretary's job while I carried my children, and an optician at Sears Optical after he died, where I could get some training. My job with the optical department moved me to Baltimore, and I didn't like raising my children in a large city setting, so it was very easy for me to find the beautiful farm valley that Bob lived in very attractive.

The idyllic farm life.

Right! Gee, this is gorgeous. And it was! It's beautiful. And I loved that. I loved just getting up, and going out, and seeing the countryside. I liked milking the cows. I liked the smell of the barns. But I didn't like the helplessness of the situation. I was totally frustrated. And it just seemed that somebody had to start talking to other people because of the garbage coming out from the administration and all of the experts. They weren't using the real statistics. They weren't dealing with real lives. They were using statistics to build their positions just because of the political realities of who owns and buys

121

and controls political programs. But I think we have to deal with that.

What makes rural organizing different?

I once went to Chambersburg, in Franklin County, the county that I have the farm in, right? For a press conference on local measured service. And they wondered why a farmer would be concerned about phone costs. What? Wait! You know. I was talking about what Pennsylvania Public Interest Coalition was, and why farmers have become a part of it. Well, why would you care about utilities?

Right! I mean, we're impacted the worst because, when you get local measured service, you have less dialing availability. We have less population we can reach than anyone else when you're in rural Pennsylvania. In rural anyplace. You're really a targeted group because you have less power, and that's why they billed it that way. They know you're not going to get everybody organized to fight. It's virtually impossible to get these people together on stuff like that. You just don't have the time to do that, and there's nobody else going to do it. So they don't worry about it. That's why two rural areas in Pennsylvania get a *trial* local measured service option on their phone service for one year, and they have no options. They knew that rural population didn't have the organization to fight it, to kick it out and say, "This is absolutely impossible. We won't put up with this shit."

It's very much because of those rural valleys and areas. God, you have to go twenty miles to Chambersburg from the farm. Who has time after working all day on the farm to go in there for a meeting, and then get back in time to get to bed so you can get up early enough to start all over again? It just lends itself to denying the ability to get a broadened sense of what's real. So it's easier for the traditional Republican regime to keep that imagery and everything that they want, because these people are so nonquestioning. It's like a blind faith out there. It's like Uncle Andy: What do you mean, the kids wouldn't register Republican? They have for generations always registered Republican. Why is it different now? What is she saying to me?

What prospects do you see for altering that in Pennsylvania?

Part of that is to bind those conservative elements into the local steering committees of the coalitions, so that they have those Farmers Union presidents sitting on the steering committee of the coalition board, where he has to deal with labor people, and labor people

122

become people to him. They don't become statistics. They become real to him. That helps broaden. Then they go back and say, well, gosh, public employees are out on a strike against the administration because this is what the administration actually did, and this is what they got last year, and they can't even make this much, and here the garbage is coming out on the radio showing exploited figures for salary. This person knows these people aren't making that kind of money, and says we got to do something. Those farmers will end up going to a hearing or joining a picket line when they never did that before. It's a slow process. I particularly encourage the use of television and radio talk shows to discuss the loss of jobs because of the impact that agriculture has. That's a tremendous tool and grows very quickly, starts getting questions coming out of the consuming public. Well, my God, what's true now? You know, these farmers are desperate. If things are so funky, farmers are doing so good, and ripping off all the taxpayers' money, then why are farmers in trouble? And it becomes real, something that they have to deal with. It's the only way that I know that you can do it in the country.

In Pennsylvania, we hear all the time through the media we're not as bad off as other states in farming because we don't have the bankruptcy ratio. I said, "It's less evident in Pennsylvania because we weren't grain belt states and the grains were the first hit. Our farmers were more diversified. But if you look at our FmHA profile, right now, over a quarter of our farmers were in jeopardy of foreclosure. We're going to lose 50 percent of our dairy farms in Pennsylvania. Somebody's got to deal with that. But because it's not happening right now, and there are people like me, where we're not paying off the debt, the debt still continues to escalate, but we're not in a foreclosure yet because we keep selling equipment, cows, or whatever, just to hang on a little longer, we don't show up statistically. Within two years, we'll be those statistics."

Merle Hansen

Selmer and Phyllis Hodne (photo by Cynthia Vagnetti)

Gary Lamb

Hollis Petersen and Justice (photo by Cynthia Vagnetti)

Louise and Eugene Wuchter and sons Eric (seated) and Jake
(photo by Cynthia Vagnetti)

Ruthann and David Hughes (photo by Cynthia Vagnetti)

Reva and Francis Crooks, *above*
(photo by Cynthia Vagnetti)

David Jennings, *right* (photo by
Barb Grabner)

Mary Beth and Gary Janssen, *above*
(photo by Cynthia Vagnetti)

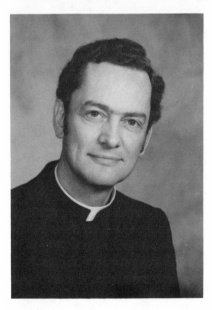

Delmar Carlson, *left*

Bruce Schmaedeke (photo by Cynthia Vagnetti)

Chris Nannenga and Elizabeth,
above
(photo by Cynthia Vagnetti)

Lou-Anne Kling, *left*

Anne Kanten

Fred Bentley

Pete Brent (photo by Bill Gillette)

Wanda and Bob Donahoo (photo by Cynthia Vagnetti)

Bobbi Polzine (photo by
Teresa Hieronimus)

Charlie Peniston (photo by Cynthia Vagnetti)

Dixon Terry, *above*

Wayne Cryts, *left*

Helen Waller (photo by Tom Kumpf)

Alan Libbra

PART FIVE
He Ain't Heavy,
He's My Neighbor

Back to the Basics

GARY JANSSEN
Rudd, Iowa

For those who have difficulty thinking and drinking at the same time, interviewing Gary Janssen could be a minor ordeal. No sooner had I found the Janssen farm on a gravel road just a couple miles south of Rockwell, Iowa, and been welcomed into the house by Mary Beth after making my way past Bosley, the furry, friendly sheepdog on the porch, than I was offered a beer. We sat down in the living room. (Since the June 1984 interview, they have moved three times.) The interview was, in the end, conducted over at least four beers apiece, supplemented later by some good ham and escalloped pota- toes served by Mary Beth, all of which was topped off by strawberries with cream.

To simplify what turned into a very long story that night, the Janssens began to farm the Rockwell land in 1974, and through various circumstances, including the death of Mary Beth's father, their operation grew in two years from 160 to 906 acres. Gary teamed up with an old schoolmate to form a fertilizer and spraying business. The farm remained 906 acres until 1981, but the rise in interest rates was already taking a toll on the young business by 1979, when one banker "told us that we just had too much borrowed capital . . . [but] his bank wasn't big enough to extend us any more credit anyway."

By April 1980, Gary received "the first sign that there was any trouble. The bank wouldn't give us the money to make a farm payment." But he found people he had done business with who would extend credit. The bank put its name on his checks, allowing it to collect its payments but preventing the Janssens from paying back

127

*the people who had extended credit. Predictably, the telephone
began to ring. By the spring of 1981, the downhill slide was accel-
erating. Gary claims that the banker sat at his kitchen table one night
and advised him to bankrupt the corporation, but told him at the
time that he would deny it later—and did. The two were the only
participants in the conversation. But one day that spring, while
Mary Beth was in the hospital, Gary came home to a stack of letters
four inches thick in the mailbox. "All from the bank. All individual
letters. Half addressed to me, half addressed to Mary Beth: notices
to cure on every one of our notes. Every stinking one of them. I
took them up to the attorney; he said you've got twenty days to file
bankruptcy."*

*The 1981 planting season, undertaken beneath the sword of
bankruptcy, was a trying one. "We didn't have any money. The next
year, in '82, was even tougher because the bank allotted us $800 a
month, and that had to buy all our gas, all our food, all our health
insurance, which was $260 a month and which we ended up dropping."*

*Finally, by 1983, they were able to get $20,000 in operating money
from the Farmers Home Administration, with some advice from Dan
Levitas, a staff member of Rural America (now Prairiefire) in Des
Moines. As the bankruptcy court proceedings went on, the Janssen
farm shrank through sale and receivership. By the time of this
interview in June 1984, the farm was down to four hundred acres, and
Gary was working part time in the maintenance department of North
Iowa Area Community College. The bankruptcy case was already
closed, and the Janssens were beginning to gain some perspective on
the affair and develop a new life-style based on their new realities.
Their children, Jason, now at Iowa State University, and Jennifer,
still in high school, were also adapting comparatively well to their
parents' new realities.*

M ARY BETH: When we started farming, Gary was very . . .
idealistic. Everything will work out, do it right, it'll work right.
Even before we started farming, he had a job when we first married,
at $8,000 a year.

Gary: That was in 1970. That wasn't too bad wages.

Mary Beth: His attitude was, well, I haven't gotten a raise, but I
don't ask because they'll realize how good I am and they'll give me a
raise. He was very idealistic, and he learned the hard way that people
don't always do what the right thing is. And I sat back and watched a

128

lot of the things that bothered me, that he was so sure would work out. . . . We both learned some things the hard way.

Gary: Well, once you swallow that initial shot of pride, the second time is not near as hard. And that's where a lot of farmers, I think, have problems. They were like I was, wrong.

Mary Beth: Do it right, work hard, everything'll work out.

Gary: The farmer lives on hope. You put the crop in in the spring, and you know a 150-bushel yield is good, but you hope you get 175. That's just the way a farmer is; he lives on hope. And when that sucker goes down, it's awful hard for him to swallow that pride.

Mary Beth: I came into it just the opposite. I was very . . . not trusting of people and had to look things over first. And we have pulled through this, plus some things that have happened to me again.

Gary: Yeah, we're both about at where we can look at something, and we can see it coming the same way. Where we didn't use to. Mary Beth would say, "Watch that guy." Then I'd say, "He's all right."

Mary Beth: And then, when he screwed Gary . . . [laughs].

How did you come to be an activist with the Iowa Farm Unity Coalition?

Gary: I was like a lot of the other people. I called the hotline and I wanted answers. And I didn't get those answers. I got help, yes. . . . But it doesn't come easy. It's hard for anyone down at Des Moines in the coalition office, the people that answer the telephone, to know your situation on a first phone call. They just can't do that. And/or the first meeting.

People don't like to tell you face to face, one on one, let alone over the telephone, to somebody they don't even know. I've always felt that you needed someone else to talk to besides your spouse. Or your family. I've always felt that way, because you need to have someone to bang an idea or two off of. In your own family, you've got them instilled into the way you live, and the way you're thinking. Lots of times so much that they'll agree with you, and it might be the wrong way to go. So I started banging things off of Dan [Levitas] and Dave [Ostendorf] down at Des Moines. And, of course, this formed a relationship, nothing serious, and then they had a rally on the west steps of the capitol, and I went down to it. Well, I was still trying to get into FmHA up here, and this was in. . . .

Gosh, it was colder than the dickens, must have been February of '83. And, of course, I met a lot of other people there. But back to how I got connected with the hotline, this one night I was desperate and needed somebody to talk to, so I just called information. And I said I knew there was a farm crisis or some hotline number or some number in Des Moines I could call and talk to, and she gave me both the farm crisis number at the [Iowa Citizens for Community Improvement] headquarters, and also the hotline number at Rural America.

I called the farm crisis number first and talked to Joe Fagan of ICCI. He said that the fellows down at Rural America were more involved with the farm thing than he was, but they had their number and tried to do what they could. So I ended up down there helping make posters at ICCI headquarters and met some of the people from Rural America at that time, and we went over to the state capitol and stood on the steps.

I can't remember whether it was that time or the next time I went down, we lobbied the legislators and met with Governor Branstad, and I was one of eight or ten farmers who got in to see Governor Branstad at that time.

That first time I was down there in February, when we were on the capitol steps, I kind of stood in the background because I hadn't got my financing with FmHA yet. I know how these farmers feel, well, I couldn't say I know how they feel, I know how I felt and I'm sure that they feel somewhat the same way I did. I was down there on the capitol steps, the reporters were all around, TV cameras, newspapers taking pictures of everyone in the crowd, and I'm thinking, well, hey, what if the FmHA office in Mason City sees my picture? I'm one of these militants out here, radicals, you know. And we're out here singing songs and trying to get people's attention that there's a problem. Well, then, when I came back up here to get into the FmHA office, I literally, and I mean, literally, beat my fist on the county supervisor's desk, and I told him, "Hey, I want to prove to you that Gary Janssen is not the bad-ass that everybody's telling you I am." And I said I guess I'm gonna have to start right here. And that's when our relationship between the FmHA county supervisor and myself started. Which, at least to today, is a good relationship, as far as we're both concerned, I'm sure.

This relationship came out of the fact that I stood up for myself. I had ground to stand on. And that I was a member of the Iowa Farm Unity Coalition. He threw up his hands in the air at about our third meeting and told me that I totally intimidated him because of the

130

handbook that they print out of Walthill, Nebraska [at the Center for Rural Affairs], that I had read cover to cover. And I'm not a reader. I wasn't a reader, but I am now. I read that book cover to cover at least three times. So I knew his obligations. I knew my obligations.

So, when he told me that I totally intimidated him, I said, "No, I shouldn't intimidate you. We should respect each other. . . . we understand each other. We knew what our duties were, what our obligations were. And from then on, it's been fantastic, I've lived by that book, I've lived by the rules. If you get a good supervisor, they're rules you can live with. A lot of other guys aren't gonna believe this because they don't have a good county supervisor, but I built my credit reputation more by dealing through FmHA and having them countersign my checks, and then being able to get off that countersignature on my loan. That does more for your credit than trying to hang in there with a bank that's got its name on all your checks. So I've got a good working relationship.

My county supervisor wants to know what the Iowa Farm Unity Coalition is doing. And he wants me to tell him. Well, I do, and then again, he doesn't get all the information. He's not telling me everything that's coming down from Des Moines or Washington, D.C., so why should I tell him everything we're doing? I told him last fall, the day we signed our notes, the day he took us over, I've only begun with the Iowa Farm Unity Coalition. I said, "You're going to hear a lot about me." And I said, "I may talk against FmHA; I may talk against banks; I may talk against PCA," but I said, "If I'm gonna talk against this FmHA office, I will come to you and tell you first what I disagree with." I said, "You know as well as I do, you're telling me we have farmers out there who are having problems, and I'm telling you that you have FmHA supervisors that are having problems. And you people go to your meetings and talk about the farmers; I'm gonna talk about the problems we see in the supervisors' offices." And so, he wants to know what's going on. He knows I'm out doing this. I have no problem talking with the papers. I have no problem talking with TV. I was on TV up here. I'm comfortable with the position.

Why am I there? I'm there because when I grew up, I was the type of person that would help, or liked to help other people. And not for money, not always for money. I guess that's maybe one reason why we went through the situation we went through. A little bit of it could've been that we didn't overcharge. If we had a job that demanded some special work or some special attention, yes, we charged more for it. But I don't think we overcharged. We charged with the rest of the people, as far as the application of chemicals, and I've given a lot of free advice on chemicals to people, and they bought someplace else. I've always been interested in agriculture, so I guess I grew up with that idea that you needed to do something for somebody besides yourself. So it was kind of natural for me after Dan had helped me get in up here at FmHA, and took a load off my shoulders, that I felt that I needed to give them something back. . . .

The one thing I learned is to try to listen. A certain guy might have a problem. It may be ever so small. But then, if you can solve that little problem, or help him solve it, or even at least have some success in easing that tension, why, then, you can use what you learn because, as you said earlier, there's a pattern to every one of these. . . .

One man, he's got a beef cow/calf operation. What I learned from working for him, I took and used in another operation, which is a purebred operation, where you're talking a $25,000 bull. Another man maybe only spends a thousand for his bulls and has a different operation. But I could take what I'd learned from him and plug it into another operation and it helps. And then before that, it was a dairy farmer. And I interrelated the stuff that I'd learned from the dairy farmer.

There's one thing that a farmer has to do when he loses his paycheck or way of life that most other people don't have to do. Now, I'm not saying all other people. When a farmer loses his way of life, 95 to 100 percent of the time, he not only loses his job and his occupation, and all his savings, but he has to move. He has to uproot his family, and in all these rural communities, in very few of them can a farmer go to town and find a job. Now just think about this. He's taking his kids out of a school that's probably small, he's moving them to a school that's maybe ten to twenty times as big as what they're accustomed to. . . . When you foreclose, you just about guarantee that every one of those guys is gonna have to move. And moving is something that very few people like to do, unless it's for a promotion. But when you sell somebody out, you're not promoting him. . . . And lots of times he can't afford to buy a house, he has nothing left, and he's got kids. . . .

When you're first married, the excitement makes it easy to relocate, you know, that's part of getting married, you move in together, but with most of the farmers that are going through the problem with small kids, they have to explain why this is happening to them. And when they are emotionally strained, how can you explain it to a kid? How can you explain it to your son and daughter that you have lost this occupation, you've got to go into a different one, we have to move? That's what I think is morally wrong with the way things are right now.

Oh, there's something else. The good fortune we had was we invested about $3,000 in a computer program that we do use to help some of these farmers. I'll run their cash flows on it for them, try to get a cash flow that'll work for them. You know, it may be selling some cows or selling some hogs, maybe changing the operation. But I can do that on the computer in four or five hours, where I can't do it by pencil in four or five hours. We've taken what used to be our old living room and converted it into a computer room.

Gary became one of the volunteer counselor/advocates to whom the Prairiefire hotline refers farmers for assistance, usually from his own area. Prairiefire has a network of such people, some farmers, some ex-lenders, throughout Iowa, all working for free.

Later in 1984, the farm management firm managing the property they lived on terminated their lease. The Janssens moved to a new home three miles west of Nora Springs, Iowa, in early 1985. There they farmed only 114 acres nearby, plus 10 on the homestead, and Mary Beth found a job in Mason City with the United Way office. Gary, through new FmHA arrangements, began to raise hogs while keeping his community college job.

That location also became temporary. Finally forced to abandon farming, the Janssens relocated to Rock Falls, Iowa, just east of Mason City, in a two-story home overlooking the Shell Rock River. Prairiefire sought to hire him through grant funds, and Gary credits an article I wrote, profiling his activities in the December 1985 issue of The Episcopalian, *with facilitating a grant from the Episcopal Church, of which the Janssens are members. Whether or not that is true, Gary became a full-time Prairiefire field-staffer, and in the summer of 1986 coordinated many Iowa shipments of hay to drought-stricken southern farmers in what became popularly known as "the haylift."*

In the spring of 1987, Gary was confronted with misdemeanor charges from the U.S. Attorney's office in northern Iowa stemming from alleged conversion of sealed grain during his financial difficulties in the early 1980s. Because confused and even chaotic bookkeep-

ing often accompany farm financial stress, such charges have been a touchy matter in farm country during the 1980s' farm crisis. Difficulties in feeding livestock, as in the Crookses' case, have put many farmers in legal jeopardy. In bank-closing cases, farmers' difficulties in getting timely approval of necessary expenditures by Federal Deposit Insurance Corporation officials overseeing a bank's liquidation have been the source of ongoing strife, as the Rev. Carlson notes. The line between dishonesty and mere sloppiness under stress can be hard to define, and agricultural officials tend to be aware that the number of farmers vulnerable to such accusations often far exceeds the number prosecuted. In any event, after some tough legal wrestling, Gary ultimately chose to plead guilty to a minor charge in order to avert Mary Beth's potential involvement in the case. The result of that plea was fifteen days in jail in Cedar Rapids, served on weekends in the summer of 1987. The ordeal seems not to have diminished the local respect he has garnered from his farm counseling and advocacy activities. He now works as general manager in a new small business based in Rudd, their new home. The firm, which he shares with a partner, manufactures small livestock trailers. Mary Beth also works with the firm as its office manager.

Farmer Helping Farmer

LOU-ANNE KLING
Granite Falls, Minnesota

Among Minnesota farmers, Lou-Anne Kling is known as the driving force behind a statewide, state-funded network of trained farmer advocates who respond to calls for assistance from financially distressed fellow farmers. Her unique initiative in first establishing such a network on a volunteer basis and then selling state officials on backing it financially when the need outstripped her volunteer resources has blazed a trail now being followed by a number of states and by privately supported farm organizations, as well.

Kling is not without other things to do. At forty-eight, she and her husband, Wayne, farm 160 acres of their own near Granite Falls, the area where she grew up. They grow soybeans, corn, and wheat, and run a farrow-to-finish hog operation. Wayne farms another three hundred acres with his father. The Klings have four sons and three daughters, ranging in age from fourteen to thirty. The two eldest daughters are themselves married to farmers, while two sons are in the military. One is in the Marine Corps, Lou-Anne says, because they could neither provide him a job on the farm, nor the money for college. "He had no other options," she says matter-of-factly. Two sons are still on the farm and, says Kling, help with some of the chores, including "dish washing and pig feeding."

Kling ran for the Minnesota House of Representatives in 1982. She met with me in late 1984 to discuss the growth of the Farm Advocates program to that date. It has continued since then.

135

I campaigned on farm issues [in 1982] and talked about the farm crisis we were in. A lot of people weren't acknowledging it: farmers going broke, foreclosures, needing a price, everything else was band-aids.

When I came off the campaign, a neighboring farmer came over and said, "You talked about farm problems, we've got a problem. Farmers Home is going to sell us out. Will you help us?"

I knew nothing about Farmers Home. The only thing I knew about Farmers Home at that time was from when I had been a county chair of the Democratic party. I got a call from Farmers Home, saying, "You haven't gotten any names in here for county committee [the FmHA body that determines eligibility for FmHA loans]." And I didn't have the foggiest notion of what they were talking about. I asked them to explain it, and they said, "Your party holds the presidency [Carter] and so, therefore, you get to put the people on county committee." And I asked some questions. It wasn't cut-and-dried like that, but what names I put in made it to the county committee. And that was the extent of my knowledge of Farmers Home.

When I started going through this farmer's records, I found out how he had been *just* taken to the cleaners. The garbage they were using on him, to intimidate him. . . . They told him they were going to prosecute him for conversion of security. Well, when we went through his records, we found where the [FmHA county] supervisor said, yes, you may sell the silo. There was a letter to the bank handling the transactions.

So, when we were in the hearing and got this all down, I went through it step by step, and said, "Did the farmer not bring you the check and you signed it and gave it back to him, and told him to go pay his operating expenses? And the next day you realized what you had done? And then you had to cover your tracks?"

"No, no, no, that wasn't the way it happened."

And I said, "Well, why, then, would you trust a farmer with $26,000 that should have went on a loan, and for ten years you've never trusted the man with $50?"

So they wanted to go on to the next item in the hearing. Well, I realized then what I had stumbled into and what was happening. And, of course, this farmer told his neighbor and the neighbor came over, and that's how the program started.

I plugged along out here, helping people that would call, and ran into some other people that were doing the same kinds of things. Bob

Smith [a farmer from Murdock] and I got to talking about how we've got to get this information out to farmers. You know, we weren't able to get the information out to everybody, so we decided to do an informational tour, and we took two weeks, and we had people we had helped in different areas of the state set up meetings, and we went around. They did the advertising, and we went in and we did an informational [program] on Farmers Home and what their rights were. Farmers didn't know what kinds of loans they could get, what kind of interest, they didn't know anything. And it was just amazing when you stood up there and talked to these farmers and watched them as you talked, and you saw the light bulbs going on in their heads, like "That's. . . . That's my situation!" And . . . after we did that tour, then the calls just started coming more and more and more. . . .

And it was getting to the point where I was gone seven days a week. I was on the road helping farmers, and it got more than I could handle. And I ended up going in the fall of '83 into northwestern Minnesota, and I was walking into an absolute time bomb. I started bringing all this information back to Anne [Kanten] at the department, [the Minnesota Department of Agriculture] and telling her I needed more help. You know, we *had* to do something. The farmers couldn't afford to pay me, I couldn't afford to go, and we needed help out there for the farmers, and just kind of got bounced back and forth. Then when I got connected with the crew up in the northwest, I got some of them to come on down to the department to explain what was happening. After all, who was I, just some radical farm woman out there, getting hysterical over some small little items. But I started bringing in farmers with me, and they were laying out the story and showing records. So we finally convinced the department that we needed a program.

Then I took a map of the state of Minnesota, and just for my own curiosity, I started putting dots of where I had been, and I amazed myself when I saw where all I had been in Minnesota. I took that and met with some of the heads of the legislature. I think that was the best tool that we ever used because we'd talk and talk to 'em, and they'd be kind of "yeah, yeah, yeah," and I'd lay the map out and say, "This is where I've spent my last year. You know, this is only the tip of the iceberg. There's thousands of farmers out there in trouble. We need to get some people out there to start helping them." That's kind of where the program kicked off. Most of the thirty-five advocates were people that I at one time had worked with, so I guess that's what was exciting to me, that the farmers that I had come in and helped got involved helping their neighbors and wanted to do this. So we put out a call for people that were interested in becoming an advocate and brought 'em into St. Paul, into the training session, and that's how the advocate program was born.

This training session took place at the Minnesota Department of Agriculture building in St. Paul, March 12–13, 1984. While the legislature was being sold on a $50,000, one-year appropriation for Farm Advocates, the program was temporarily funded with money within the existing departmental budget until the next fiscal year started on July 1. The $102,000 used was sufficient to train and field thirty-five advocates. The appropriation was enough to retain only ten after that date.

We started getting calls from these other states because we got some publicity out of it. At the meeting in Crookston [in mid-August 1984], the bankers were in agreement that the advocate program was a good program. In fact, the state legislators are fighting to keep it now.

I would say of the thirty-five, there was probably twenty-five that worked this thing seven days a week. Ten, twelve, fifteen hours a day. I was amazed when I looked at the work sheets coming back, at what these people had put into it. They were so committed to it. And so committed to not turning down a farmer, to be able to help that farmer. No matter what time of day or night it was. Or how many miles they had to drive. We had farmers driving 150 miles to sit down with a farmer, if they were in an area, you know, where they didn't have a close advocate. The funding ended June 30. We've still got people working like you wouldn't believe, and there's no assurance they're ever gonna get paid back for these expenses. And they're putting in forty, fifty, sixty hours a week at it.

So they're people really committed to it, once it gets in their blood. I met with some of the advocates and we talked about, you know, if funding comes, and it's not retroactive, there's no way you guys are going to get paid for this time. They said, well, the farmers need us. The farmer's got to have somebody.

So, even after the program was cut from thirty-five to ten advocates, some of the other twenty-five continued to. . . .

Oh, they're still working. . . .

Even though they don't have any funds at all. . . .

138

Right. It doesn't even seem to matter that maybe only ten are going back on a payroll. The rest of them are still doing their work out here.

You know, it just amazes me, I get these calls from people that know they're probably not going back on a payroll if we don't get more funding, and they've got a whole week's schedule set up to work with farmers. And they said, well, we started with this guy, we can't let him down, we can't let him hang, we started with him, we've got to finish. They've given a real commitment.

How do some of these people survive when they've got their own farm to work?

A lot of the advocates are women. Something way over half are women. Up in the northwest, those women work out in the fields, so they work in the field during the day and do this work at night.

In the rest of the state, you know, they cushion them in between. I get calls from them at midnight. They're working out somebody's Farm and Home Plan [a loan form for FmHA] and they've got a question. Or 6 o'clock in the morning, they call, they're working on a Farm and Home Plan, they've got a question to ask. You know, if they're running their own farms plus putting this in on the sideline, some of the spouses and families find themselves equally involved, because it seems like when someone gets into this program, they just go 100 percent into it, and it becomes a driving force. I think they see that by helping a farmer, it may be one of the ways of turning that situation around, to educate fellow farmers on what the real problem is, what needs to be done, what has to change.

Is there any danger of their being taken advantage of if the legislature sees so much volunteer work in spite of low funding?

I'm worried about that. Although, when we met with some of the legislators, we kind of laid it pretty heavy on them, saying, we're broke, too. And we can't continue. The farmers don't have money to pay us. You know, we'll talk to them if they call us, if they come to our house, we'll help them, but we can't be going to hearings and we can't be going to their houses and everything, because we're broke, too.

And it's real easy to burn somebody out. . . . I worry about that, if they're gonna get bitter, and bitter toward the wrong things . . . and just become inactive and hide out, rather than do the things that normally should be done.

139

We're working on some other kinds of funding that will come up quick. We're also working on some funding that might come through in December [1984], and then we're coming in for a two-year program. It would have to be passed in the next session, so we don't lose time.

We've lost two months this summer when we should have been out there working with the farmers, getting their financial picture put together for the fall, and how to handle dollars coming in this fall and where to go, and we could've had some more training sessions this summer on stress and depression, and how to handle all that.

We could plan for two years, where we need our training, where we need to improve, where we need to recruit more advocates, because we have certain areas of the state that we don't have advocates, that we need to recruit more people into. We need to have informational meetings around the state for this disaster program: what it can be used for, how the farmers qualify. I've been trying to set these up, but if there's no budget, I can't afford to drive around the state to eighty-seven counties and have these informational meetings. There's no way I can put the gas in my car and drive out and do it.

Assuming that you had the money to do what you needed to do, what kinds of training sessions and meetings would you put into the program for the advocates themselves?

We need much more training in the legal field. How to advise farmers, where to go for the right kinds of legal help, how to be able to spot whether they should seek legal help. We need to get into the whole mental health section of it. Stress and depression, family problems. When a farmer comes into financial problems, the first people he takes it out on is his family. We need to get into the whole welfare system, making sure a farmer has food on his table, how he can qualify for food stamps and medical help, so his family's health doesn't go down the tubes when he's in this financial situation. Because the first thing they do is cancel their hospital insurance, stop going to see the dentist, stop going to see the doctor, and then that in the end brings out a whole new realm of financial problems, because it becomes a point where they got to spend twice as many dollars. And we also need to do more training with the lender's rules and regulations, how to negotiate. We need a big session on how to be a good negotiator. There's lots of areas we need to cover yet. . . .

We're lucky the program went as well as it did, with the quick

140

training we did. We had some people that were sharp and caught on quick. We could've fallen flat on our face on this thing.

So, for Minnesota to be the role model that we've become, and had the other states coming in, following us, I think it's a responsibility we have to hold up now, for the rest of the states. . . .

Instead of just letting it fall.

In the spring of 1985, the Minnesota legislature approved a $210,000 annual appropriation for the state department of agriculture to continue the Farm Advocates program with a paid staff of twenty. As before, they would receive a half-time salary that equaled $5 per hour. As before, they continued in most cases to work longer hours. In addition, according to Kling, some forty to forty-five advocates were actually in the field, the remainder working without state funding, sometimes being paid for expenses directly by the farmer they helped. The department also received a Bremer Foundation grant to cover training expenses for all the advocates, salaried or otherwise.

But the stress of the task took its toll on Lou-Anne, who suffered a heart attack in early 1986 and has been forced to slow her pace to some degree since recovering. One major adjustment has been the transfer of her advocate telephone number to an office in town, leaving her with reasonable hours and a reasonable opportunity to enjoy a home life once again. She bristles at suggestions that the farm crisis is over, noting that in January 1988 the office was still receiving 25 to 30 calls per day for assistance. She continues to travel, doing training for new advocates across the country. By early 1988, sixteen states had advocacy programs whose advocates had been trained by Lou-Anne Kling, the most recent including Vermont, Louisiana, and Mississippi.

The Farmer Goes to St. Paul

ANNE KANTEN
Milan, Minnesota

A farmer involved in the American Agriculture Movement and the tractorcade to Washington, D.C., in 1979, Anne Kanten is now Minnesota's assistant commissioner of agriculture, working directly under the state's commissioner, Jim Nichols. Both came into their posts with the election of Governor Rudy Perpich, a Democrat who first won the office in 1982. Anne and her husband, Charles, own a farm in Milan, where they raise sugar beets and other crops. After learning of the Farm Advocates program while doing farm credit research for the Iowa legislature, I interviewed her in her office in August 1984.

I came here as a farmer a year and a half ago. I spent a number of years before that soapboxing for stewardship and salvation of the land and people who work on it, basically in terms of a price structure more than anything else.

Since coming here, I have been absolutely deluged with telephone calls from farmers about what we can do about credit problems. My first year here, we put together a governor's commission on the farm crisis. We looked at what government could do and what resources existed, and found it was pretty meager. The governor plunked the minimum price bill[1] on my desk, which was very controversial. We

[1]Minimum price is a proposal for state legislation to set a floor on the price of certain agricultural commodities, similar to minimum wage. It would be pegged to parity in some percentage fashion, depending on the law passed, and would go into effect when states producing 60 percent of a given commodity had passed the same

142

saw more people hurting and more problems this year. I have a friend [Lou-Anne Kling] out in western Minnesota, who one day just got a call from her neighbor who said, "I've really got some problems with FmHA and don't know what to do." She went over and sat with him and looked at records and cash flow, and said she didn't know what to do to help but offered to be a friend.

That farmer told another neighbor one day that Lou-Anne helped him, and she got another call. She figured she'd best get the regulations and familiarize herself with the statutes. She talked with me about the needs farmers have and the kinds of ways it was helpful to have another farmer walk through the process with them. It was burdensome for Lou-Anne just to maintain the telephone calls on this thing.

Last year, at a Christmas party at our home, Bruce Roberts, head of the psychology department at Saint Olaf College in Northfield, talked about the need and value of people helping each other. I came back and thought about that in January. We were bothered by our inability to help farmers out of the Agriculture Department. Jim Nichols wanted to think about that. One day, I talked to State Senator Stumph about an advocacy program. He was from a part of Minnesota that had suffered flooding. Jim Massey, an attorney, was urging department involvement in lawsuits in other states.[2] We had a meeting with all these people on how to get something going on the advocate program, with some real initiatives by some Legal Aid people, such as Jim.

We knew we needed money, so we put together a special supplemental budget request to the legislature of $50,000 with the approval of the governor.

We very quickly talked to and screened thirty-five applicants as advocates, based on geographical placement and familiarity with the system and ability to deal with all parties, especially FmHA. We invited these thirty-five to come to the Agriculture Department for leadership training, with Jim Massey and Lou-Anne Kling having mastered all the details and laws. We had two days of training, March

---

legislation. In 1983, the Minnesota senate passed the bill, but it lost by one vote in the house agriculture committee. In both Iowa and South Dakota in 1984, the legislature passed it, but the governor vetoed it.

[2]Massey has represented several class action suits by farm borrowers against lending institutions. In 1986, he became executive director of the Farmers Legal Action Group in St. Paul.

11 and 12 [1984], and saw a positive impact on people in this building, from seeing that room jampacked full of people learning and sharing. With [department staff members] Mark Ritchies's and Martha Ballou's help, after two days of training we sent them forth. In the attorney general's office, there was an established hotline for home mortgage foreclosure problems, which was expanded to include farm debts. This was called Hotline FARM [Farmers Advocacy for Rural Minnesota]. Roger Culhane, who sat at the hotline desk and referred farmers and kept referral data, was absolutely overwhelmed by the stress he discovered. The advocates were overwhelmed, too. Several months later, we brought them together for sharing and an update of their problems. My only reaction walking out of that meeting was, "We've asked too much of these people."

The budget paid their telephone bill and put some gas in their tanks, and paid them $100 per week. Some were working sixty or seventy hours per week.

I think it has been a tremendously powerful program because suddenly we got calls from North Dakota, Wisconsin, Arkansas, Arizona, Vermont, and other places that have heard about it, like Illinois and Montana.

I think that FmHA was very nervous about it [at first] and wondered if we'd sent a bunch of radicals out there, but those who really cared about farmers saw it helped the paperwork get expedited, and in many ways helped the FmHA offices. FmHA borrowing has increased from 12 percent to 25 percent [of Minnesota farmers] between January and July of this year.

The Attorney

FRED BENTLEY
Whiting, Kansas

Now in his late thirties, Bentley works with the Kansas Rural Center, a nonprofit organization working on agricultural issues whose modest office is in a house in tiny Whiting (population not listed in the 1986 atlas). It grew out of the Kansas Organic Producers in the mid-1970s, but incorporated separately in 1979. Along the way, it acquired four VISTA volunteers who worked on a variety of projects, including a study of land and water use in southwest Kansas by Mary Fund and Elise Watkins Clement, who have stayed on since their VISTA service. Foundation grants have facilitated ongoing research, public education, and advocacy efforts. Primarily, in this June 1985 conversation, Bentley spoke about the center's advocacy efforts.

W E'VE had a telephone service providing referrals to attorneys, credit counselors, and information on rights, what can be done, what you should do, figuring out what their options are, just providing a lot of moral support.

As you're probably aware, *Farm Journal* ran an article,[1] and our name was in there, and immediately we probably got two hundred telephone calls from people who said they had read the *Farm Journal.* It was so bad we had to get another phone line.

Well, one thing that's happened is we got some legislation passed which originated here about three years ago. We tried to convince

---

[1]A January 1985 article by Elizabeth Curry Williams concerning farm counseling hotlines, with a sidebar listing their telephone numbers.

the lawmakers to pass a legal aid bill for farmers. Ed Reznicek, who was working for Legal Services at the time, was the one that more or less proposed it the first time. In the '84 sessions he got heard, got it passed through one house, and it got killed when it got to the other. But then, a year ago, the governor started to support it. He came up with a more extensive program which gives Extension about $190,000.

The new thing is that it's the first time the state legislature has actually appropriated money directly for a legal services program to farmers. Minnesota has had a program funded by the Department of Agriculture. So we do feel that we've had some impact in terms of getting this passed.

We're a little concerned about what Extension is actually going to do with it, given their track record, so we're kind of waiting. We are working pretty closely with Legal Services in terms of trying to help them develop a program. We've done one training session with them, and Ed's doing another in July [1985].

We hope that we can transfer these calls to the state program; that's what it's there for. We've got a pretty good opportunity to have some impact on Extension because I think they're going to be under the gun to an extent to be helpful. They're kind of willing to treat it like they've always treated things. They just don't have a very good grasp of the grass roots. I don't think the grass roots really completely trust Extension. These guys [the state university Extension staff] come out in their white shirts and trousers and ties—I don't say this negatively necessarily because Extension has a lot of good people— but I think there's something about a person who has spent his life at the university that is different, and people can sense that. The university person can tell there is a difference. So there is a gap, and I think Extension has that problem. I think it's just something you should expect.

They very studiously ignored us in terms of communicating with us, but we feel we may have had a little impact on what they're doing. Last winter, we started a series of seminars around the state on legal rights for farm borrowers, bankruptcy options, Farmers Home rules and regulations. Well, this winter they started doing something fairly similar. I think, in that sense, we have the opportunity to play the role of someone that's maybe a little bit closer to the grass roots, understands maybe a little better just exactly what's going on out here and what people want. That's one of our longer-term goals, I guess, that Extension is very well capable and very well organized and

146

situated and financed to be providing a lot of help out here, but. . . .

They bought off on industrial agriculture. They bought off on the idea that you have to be big to be successful and to be efficient, and that pretty much runs counter not only to the evidence but what we can all sense is right for us out here.

I guess it's the problem with any institution. The bigger you get, any organization is going to feel it has certain things it should represent and defend.

We're working right now on developing a network of farmers. We've had all these calls from farmers in the last six months, several hundred, and we've talked to several hundred others just at our seminars and workshops and identified a lot of resources out there. We've identified a lot of farmers who would like to be doing more; they just need a little encouragement and a little help to do it. So we're going to bring about twenty to thirty-five of them into a meeting, which Pioneer Seed Company's giving us some money for. We're going to bring them in about noon one day and have a one-day meeting in two days; bring them in, pay for their meals, pay for their lodging. We're going to make some presentations, have an attorney talk on bankruptcy, try to give them some information they can use, and make them a little more knowledgeable about what's going on and how they can be of help. Lou-Anne Kling is going to come down from Minnesota and talk about what they've done up there. We'll have a pretty full schedule for the day, but we hope at the end to be able to set up a network of exchange.

We're going to give everybody a manual free—a pretty thick manual with a lot of information which they can use: names of attorneys, information on the different Farmers Home loan programs, articles on how you should deal with somebody and how you should respond to somebody when they have a problem and they come to you— some of the stuff that the Iowa people [Prairiefire and the Iowa Farm Unity Coalition] put out. It will be things like a list of what you can exempt in bankruptcy, just a lot of basic information that we feel they should have if they're going to try and give anybody advice or help. We envision that they can use this manual if somebody comes to them and wants them to help. If they can't help them, if they don't have the information, they can call one of the other people in the network—they will have a list of the names and telephone numbers of the network members—or they can call us.

We'll pick up information from them. They will be a great source of information in terms of telling us what's happening. We'd like to know more about what's happening at the local level, especially unusual things. Are there people being written off or some unjust things happening; are people getting ripped off here? We need to know more things like that, so that we can try to better inform ourselves.

How, as an attorney, did you get involved in all this?

I grew up on a farm in western Kansas, along the Smoky Hill River, real beautiful country, quite different from the flatlands. I went to Kansas State, got a history degree there, and then went to Washburn Law School in Topeka to fulfill some vague dream of becoming a lawyer.

I started looking around for a job. I became an abstractor of land titles and sold title insurance for about eight years in Holton. I got involved in some political things and became more aware to the need to do something out here in the country. I'd joined this Kansas Organic Producers group and had been to China and had seen what they were doing to their agriculture. I just had done a lot of thinking about the changes and where everything was headed, which didn't seem to be very good. The organic people made me more aware of how we were using the soil and the land, and that we were putting these high-dollar petro-inputs into agriculture. We don't know very well what the long-term impact of a lot of chemical usage is.

The credit thing was more us responding to what we felt was a real need. We do have this dual part of our organization, which I think is a real good balance. We're developing a very strong research base on the one hand. The research has had some pretty good direct contacts with our local conservation officials and local watershed district people. That, combined with all the other feedback we're getting from farmers, has given us a pretty good view of what farmers are really thinking and what they're experiencing.

I would have to cite that as probably the unique thing about our organization. We feel that we are very close to the grass-roots opinion. We want to represent that opinion, which we don't feel is getting represented very well, very often, or very accurately in the media. Our small-town newspapers hardly ever print anything that challenges what we're doing, the way we're practicing agriculture, or the kinds of problems we're having with foreclosures. There's just no way you can really get that information out, it seems. They're all afraid of stepping on somebody's toes. The Farm Bureau is a big advertiser. The banks are big, big advertisers. They don't want to alienate those people.

So, in that sense, we're fulfilling a much needed role, I think, and the feedback that we're getting from farmers has been very positive.

Our funding levels are increasing, and we're getting more and more support now from national lending sources, and things are going very well. It's sort of ironic that things could be going so bad for farmers while it's probably indicative that things are going so bad for farmers that there's increasing recognition for the kind of work we're doing. Traditionally, the kind of work we're doing hasn't really been done in the rural areas.

Taking Control

KITTY and REG PITYER
Viroqua, Wisconsin

The Pityers, who initially became active in farm issues because of their own difficulties, are now recognized leaders in a program of farm counseling initiated by the Wisconsin Farm Unity Alliance, which also engages in a good deal of lobbying, direct action protest, and public education on farm issues and, like similar grass-roots coalitions in other Midwest states, supports the family farm reform legislation promoted by U.S. Senator Tom Harkin. The Alliance has been prominent in numerous meetings and conferences at which movement leaders have ironed out their collective and national strategies.

K ITTY: We got involved basically because of our own situation. We were faced with a foreclosure. My dad happened to see an article in the *Milwaukee Sentinel*—just three lines—talking about Wisconsin Farm Unity Alliance and how they had taken over either a PCA office or an FmHA office. It sounded like the kind of thing we might be interested in, so we tried to track it down and found out that they were having a meeting up in Mondovi, and we went up there and happened to meet some people that lived just forty miles away from us in Viroqua.[1] And they were as impressed with what the farmers were doing, helping themselves become more educated, as we were.

So we got a chapter going down here. And our activity in our

---

[1] At the time, the Pityers were farming in Elroy, Wisconsin.

community increased. I think in all these farm situations, you know, at *some* point you get to the point where you just *die* enough, just bad news after bad news, and having friends in Farm Unity really helped us get through. Even when you get bad news, if you've got a friend to share it with, it helps. And because there was so much that we had learned subsequent to our own situation that could have helped us had we known it, but we didn't know it in time—you know, there were so many things in our situation we just had to carry through on its own course, because we didn't get smart soon enough, so we thought—rather than just sit around and be angry about it, you know, we would get our satisfaction out of helping other farmers avoid those pitfalls.

Farm Unity was basically responsible in getting the Wisconsin Department of Agriculture training program going. We had known a lot of people in Minnesota and had attended their program, must have been last March [1984], and realized that something like that was needed in Wisconsin as well. So Tom Quinn and Doug Harsh, a director and our president, started talking to the people at the Department of Agriculture to see what we could get going. And we had a training session then in May of last year, and then again in December.

We were finding out that what they call their training program is farm credit advisors, which is somewhat mild. When we got involved in this, our whole interest has been to be advocates, 100 percent on the farmer's side, and we will fight with that farmer for survival.

So in January of this year, we kind of broke away from the state training program and became involved in what we call the Farm Credit Advocacy Project, which is sponsored by Farm Unity, and we have a two-tiered program. We have some certified advocates like Reggie and myself, and Doug and Carol Harsh, who have been doing it for a long time, that are paid a nominal hourly wage by the farmer in addition to actual telephone charges and mileage. Because we're quite literally doing it seven days a week. The phone starts ringing very early in the morning and rings til late at night. We were getting stuck with phone bills that we just couldn't pay. Our relationship with the phone company was pull the plug first and ask questions later. Our credit was not very good.

When we found ourselves unable to meet our own expenses, we realized we had to structure the advocacy program differently. At our January [1985] board meeting, we decided to start charging a

151

nominal fee for the certified advocates, and it's been working out real well. All the farmers that we're working with understand that we've got to have something to keep our own cash flow going, and I'm coordinator of the advocacy project. All the money is channeled through the Farm Credit Advocacy Project checkbook.

It's quite a name, I do think we could have come up with something a little more catchy. And then at the end of the month, the advocates send in a list of their expenses on each farm, and I write out a check to them, and we do that with our certified advocates who get paid an hourly rate, and also those advocates who are working towards certification. They're going to be doing it with farmers, but just on a phone call and mileage basis. So they're volunteering their time until they gain enough experience to become certified. At least this way, they're able to do it without robbing their own family budget.

So it's working very well, but the need for the advocates is overwhelming. You know, we're to the point where we're saturated, you know, you can't give any more. We don't have the time to do it, and right now we're looking at putting our crops in, and in the summer you want to spend time in the garden, doing your own daily chores around the place, but we're shorting ourselves in order to do the advocacy. So we recognized about a month ago that we need help. We just can't carry the burden that we're carrying, and that's true of many of the other advocates throughout the state, so we're going to get more people involved. And we run into people who've been willing to help. People that we had worked with and had helped want to turn around and share what they've learned with somebody else, so it's turning out to be a long-range, very neighborly type thing, where you take the knowledge and pass it on.

One of the things we're trying to stress to the advocates is that you don't have to do it full-time. We're able to just because of our circumstances. What is a minus on one side turned out to be a plus as far as the advocacy. But if you can only help five people, fine. Help those five people. That's better than not helping anybody. Your situation changes, maybe you do have time to help a few more people, do it. But you can structure your own schedule. One of the things people have to guard against is not being able to say no, because quite frankly, you can overextend to the point where you're robbing your own family of your time.

Reg: We've had to tell some farmers we've been working with that we've had it, there's nothing more we can take on. And they come back and say, gee, give some phone numbers to us, we'll take calls. These people that we've been working with, now that they know so much more than the person who's coming in cold, can help the people a lot in the beginning. A lot of this stuff, after you do it for a while, is so simple, cut, and dried. We've got these people to that stage now, where they know how to handle their own situation, so they can be a big help to somebody that's new, having a problem. And we find that that gives them a lift because they can help somebody else.

You know all this stuff. Where did you learn that? They learned it by doing it themselves. And by working with us. But that gives them a lift that they can help somebody where they thought they were down and out, and now they can help somebody else. That's what's really good about the situation. We don't want to hold all this information in and sell it out. We run into too many people that do that. We want to share it, so they can share it with other people, and those people can share it. Nobody's got the big bucks, you know.

Kitty: These advocates that are working towards certification, we put them on a consulting basis. If they run into a problem and they don't know the answer, they can call us. You know, I'm working with Farmer Brown and this is the situation, what should we do? And do a little brainstorming over the telephone. That saves everybody time, traveling, and things like that. We'll be able through those other advocates to help out more people.

We're finding that a lot of times when people sit around our kitchen table here and tell us what they've been through, we know, I mean, we know for real, we're not just saying, "Yeah, I know how it is." Because we lived it! That's very true that you're halfway there, you've got an automatic bond just because you know exactly what you're talking about. By going through it, you learn a lot. You may have made wrong decisions along the way, and that's how you learned it. Most of the advocates that we're working with are farmers who are either going through it or have gone through it themselves. And we're all on various rungs of the ladder as far as how many years the trouble has gone back. The key thing is that everybody wants to help.

One of the most important things is you've got to retain control of your own situation. We went to a lawyer and, not having had a whole lot of experience with attorneys, we didn't know what to expect, but basically we listened and took their advice, even when it maybe

153

didn't feel quite right. That was a mistake. We should have done a lot more of the work ourselves. Believed in ourselves, to do our own negotiating. Rather than having to pay somebody else. And I don't know if we would have been extremely successful doing our own negotiating back then because we wouldn't have had this knowledge that we have now, but what is very dangerous is just to go into an attorney and say, "Here, solve my problems, tell me how it comes out." You've got to be involved with the attorney, so when he's going to court, you know exactly where you are, and you know how you want it to come out, or if he's negotiating for you, you know what you want him to negotiate. He's doing what you want, rather than you doing what he suggests.

We've run into so many farmers that, because they listened to this person and this person and this person, they're really in a mess, and they can't get out of it. At least if *you* make a decision, if you're wrong, you've got only yourself to blame, but it's really frustrating when somebody else made the decisions, and you just went along with it, playing a passive role, because then you can kick yourself in the butt.

I think, too, we're learning more recently that lenders are willing to negotiate. They're more willing today to re-amortize a loan, or to do something on the interest, lower it or somehow take interest-only payments. You can go in and work something out. And it's helpful, if you or an advocate goes in, because when you get your attorney involved, your attorney has to talk to their attorney, and pretty soon the two attorneys are talking to each other, and the farmer and the lender don't know what's going on anymore. And again, you're in a situation of somebody else deciding your life. We've run into situations where the attorneys have made deals that sound fine on paper, but it was something the farmer couldn't live with.

Another important thing along the same lines, so often people find themselves pressured to make a decision now. Either their lender is telling them this, their attorney is telling them this, somebody is. We learned a long time ago nothing is immediate. If you don't sign that paper today or make that decision today, it's not going to be a big deal. You can do it tomorrow. If you're going to be signing something or agreeing to something very important, you should take a day or so to think about it. Because a decision made on the spur of the moment may not be a good one. You may regret it. You've got to recognize that what's a good deal today will still be around tomorrow.

TAKING CONTROL: Reg and Kitty Pityer

Eventually, the Pityers lost their own farm and moved to Viroqua, where they still use a fifteen-acre lot for organic gardening. Reg continues to field calls for assistance, which he says escalated after a bill to bail out the Farm Credit System passed in December 1987. He is also working to develop a local marketing cooperative for producers of organically grown produce.

PART SIX
Fighting Back

Three Generations and Out

PERRY WILSON, JR.
Kidder, Missouri

A slightly chilly but sunny March day in 1985. Nearly a thousand farmers and labor activists, black and white, gather outside the Clinton County courthouse in Plattsburgh, Missouri. They await a scheduled sheriff's sale of seven hundred acres of the Wilson family farm, foreclosed by the St. Louis Federal Land Bank. Three genera- tions of the Wilson family are in the downtown streets.

They want to avert the sale through organized mass protest. The state patrol has come to assist sheriff's deputies and the Plattsburgh police. More than a dozen speakers address the crowd during the hour before the sale is to begin.

"We're hoping for no violence," Sheriff Bob DeFreece says in his office inside the courthouse. "At 2 p.m., the attorney will conduct the sale, and the sheriff's department will provide security. I expect any problem to be from people outside the county. Local farmers are not endorsing the rally."

But this is a sheriff who is uneasy about his task. When pressed, he thinks the rally "is all right." Farmers, however, should take their problem "higher up," and the government "should give them more time and more help." And he has "worked all week to get this sale called off," but the Federal Land Bank "stood firm." The rally con- tinues outside. The sheriff braces himself.

The trustee who is to conduct the sale finally emerges from the courthouse onto a narrow concrete apron under an overhang. Televi- sion cameramen and news photographers are crowded into a bare flowerbed to his right, about two feet above the street. Little work is

159

getting done inside the courthouse; everyone is looking out. On a narrow front lawn stand several crosses planted in the ground to represent foreclosed farmers. A few signs carry messages like "Export John Block."

Within seconds, the crowd presses in on the trustee and the officers accompanying him. For nearly twenty minutes, they shout in unison, "No sale! No sale!" A few people are roughed up, some are arrested and dragged forcibly through the front doors into the building. The crowd's anger builds until a cheer erupts as the sheriff's men retreat into the building.

Outside, the protesters exchange stories about what they saw, about how this shouldn't happen to working people in Plattsburgh. One of the Wilsons' teen-age girls complains of being jostled by the police, whom she will "never trust again." Perry Wilson, Jr., begins to address the media representatives who crowd around him. One is missing: Police arrested a member of the ABC crew in the scuffling by the front door.

I eventually corner Wilson to ask my own questions.

D AD started farming over fifty-two years ago. Us boys started farming, we've been through all the drouths. And he succeeded. I mean, we're being put out of our farm by controlled low prices and high interest rates.

And all at once they said he was a bad manager. How stupid can people be to even believe such a thing, the garbage that Washington puts out, or the politicians?

I've been farming all my life. Ever since I was old enough. I'm forty-two years old.

You have seven hundred acres, I understand.

Well, we farmed 820 acres. Seven hundred is going on the block today, and April 8th the rest of it goes on the block.

Roughly $300,000 of the debt was the second mortgage through the Land Bank. Was it last fall, then, that you missed the payment?

About a year and a half ago.

And what had happened after that?

Well, we just couldn't make the payment. We kept trying to, we did put in another crop, but the.... There's no way of paying

160

someone when you're operating under the cost of production.

That was the first time you had missed the payment?

Right. Like I said, we had weathered everything. He's lost money on the cattle at different times, and we always were able to make it back up. But you can't make it back up when they've got the prices way down so low. One of the things people don't understand, it wouldn't be a cost to them to get the farmer a price for his product. It wouldn't affect it on the other end. You could double the price of wheat, and it wouldn't cost them but another 3 cents for a loaf of bread. And it would make the economy just boom!

They know it. They know it. They're controlling the things. They want to do away with private ownership in this country. That's all there is to it. They're taking away what our forefathers fought for and our freedom in this country. It's no accident. And the people are getting tired of it. They're getting tired of it.

So, then, over that past year and a half, you had borrowed more money to make. . . .

No, I couldn't borrow any money! No, I couldn't borrow any money.

I was lucky enough that the seed man give me the money to put in a crop last year even though they knew. I mean, that man stuck with me, he trusted me. And he stuck his neck out for better than $20,000 for me. $24,000, I believe it was. He didn't think I was no mismanager.

The rest of them's familiar with what I'd done, too. They knew we wasn't mismanagers. Like I say, it's a controlled deal.

I tell you, the way things are going right now, I don't know where I'm going. Come back out later, and I'll tell you where I'm going tomorrow.

Nobody, none of these farmers are asking for a forgiveness of this debt. But we do need a price. If they would give these farmers a price that isn't controlled so they can make a dime, every one of these farmers would pay these debts off. They know how to farm. They're the best producers in the world.

Do you put the blame on Reagan?

You bet. Every bit of it comes from Washington. Our farm policy hasn't been to help the farmer, it's been to screw him right into the ground off his land.

161

Did you ever feel that way about Reagan in the past?

I never did like the man.

Some people did and changed their minds.

I never did.

When he can help, and people are losing their homes and farms, and the way things are going out here in rural America, rural towns are disposed of one by one, there's something wrong with that man. He's got a heart of stone.

Did things go off pretty much like you thought they would today?

We were successful.

But it didn't. . . .

I didn't want any violence. The state patrol kept telling me to call it off. I said, tell the Federal Land Bank to call it off. They were the ones that had the sale. I didn't have the sale.

All it woulda took was that trustee of Federal Land Bank to call it off. And the state patrol and the sheriff to call it off, say the potential of trouble was there. Nobody wanted to call it off. It looks to me like it was all bought and paid for. People don't mean anything to them. We do what they tell us to do.

Did you have any trouble with negotiations with Federal Land Bank the last few months?

I sure did. Not in the last few months. We sent a letter to Federal Land Bank last week, though. We found that we had more rights that we hadn't been told about. Appeal rights, negotiations, and what not, restructure of our debts whenever we couldn't make a payment due to things beyond our control. With the interest you couldn't do that. No, no, you couldn't do that. They hadn't heard from that letter, but the last time we had negotiations with them, he said, "I will determine the interest we have in your land." Well, that's the attitude they have.

They don't want us to unite like this. They want us to go down divided. And they work so hard at that. They infiltrate, they get one organization fightin' agin' the other. They're scared to death of the people being united. It's like this thing over here. There's all kinds of stories that went out before it even got off the ground. That I belong to this, member of this organization or this organization. I'm not even going to say anything, I don't want to say anything.

They wanted to raise a question in people's minds as to whether this was a legitimate cause to come out for?

Right, right.

Are there other organizations that you've been active in, like the American Agriculture Movement?

AAM, I have been in, yeah, NFO. We were in NFO.

Your father was. You also have been in the National Farmers Organization?

Right.

Traditionally, a lot of the attack was the red-baiting of folks. Have they turned to that sort of thing around here?

Red-baiting?

Calling you a communist. . . .

Yeah, sure. Sure. That's what I'm talking about. Right. Right. We've got all kinds of rights, that's what our forefathers died in the Revolutionary War for, freedom, and it's special today, and anyone who stands up for the rights that we have, they'll be called all kinds of things. The people in this country have made the biggest mistake. They elect George up there to take care of their business. Let's let George do it, and we'll lose her right out from under our noses. Believe me, George ain't taking care of it up there right now. We're about to pay for it through the nose again.

The crowd gradually disperses after learning that the courthouse has been sealed off to the public for the rest of the afternoon. I wander around to interview people and take a few photographs. At the curb about two blocks from the rally site, some men passing out literature hover near a pickup truck loaded with bundles of their publications.

One of them sees me with my tape recorder, note pad, and camera. He eyes me as they eye everyone: They are anxious to pass out their newspapers, but visibly suspicious of all passersby, particularly newspeople.

"You a journalist?" he yells to me.
I nod.
"Why don't you guys tell the real story of what's going on?"
"Which is?"
"About our money being controlled by Kissinger, the Jewish bankers, and the IMF." He hands me a copy of a Lyndon LaRouche-sponsored magazine.[1]
I easily show my hard-to-hide disdain.
"You're not a socialist, are you?" he asks.
I walk away.

Postscript: Three weeks later, there was less physical confrontation. At Perry Wilson, Sr.'s invitation, the Rev. Jesse Jackson led the protest, both as a speaker and in a march around the outskirts of town back to the town square. This time, it was the local bank's sale, but a technical error was committed in conducting the nonauction. This, says Jackson, is the bank's way of conceding the point without "losing face."

The Wilson family eventually lost the entire farm. Perry Wilson, Sr., is now living in an area nursing home. Perry Wilson, Jr., worked for awhile for a construction firm building railroad yards. He now works for another local farmer, Marvin Porter, who organized most of the first rally.

[1]Later examination of the magazine, *Executive Intelligence Review,* found an elaborate organizational chart of an alleged conspiracy controlling the "radical farm protest movement," headed by the Benedictine order and "subordinate religious operations": the Russian Orthodox Church, the Lutheran Church of America, the World Council of Churches, and the Society of Jesus. Alleged coconspirators included groups that had organized the rally.

Taking a Message to Washington

PETE BRENT
West Des Moines, Iowa

"When I was growing up," says Pete Brent, "Oak Lawn was still at the edge of the Chicago area. My dad raised chickens. When I met my wife, she was a farmer's daughter, and I always wanted to be a farmer."

Maybe so, but Chicago left its mark on his tough, slightly wise-guy speech mannerisms. His career had a few detours while he worked as an insurance claims adjuster and an armored car guard before leaving the big city to plow fields and slop hogs.

That was in 1960, but he and his wife, Ardith, quit in 1966 and returned to Chicago. "I wasn't smart enough once, I had to do it twice," he says, and after continued career detours, he "knew I'd made a big mistake. And in '74 I had a chance to come back and rent a fair size farm without the investment in machinery." They farmed roughly five hundred acres, "basically corn, soybeans, hay, oats, and I was feeding cattle, somewhere between two to four hundred head a year."

In 1979, with a Farmers Home Administration Loan, he purchased 320 acres on a land contract, at $850 an acre at 8.5 percent interest. "I don't think we had the ink dry on the contract before the interest went right up, all the input costs went up, and the price of everything I had to sell went the other way. And obviously you can't sell stuff for less than it costs to produce it." The first year, he says, "we were short of making all the payments by $20,000, and it was just downhill from there."

Eventually, FmHA decided not to continue making Brent's payments

165

on the land contract because of the growing indebtedness (he had operating loans as well). This exposed position meant that the landlord could, with thirty days' notice, evict them from the farm. This prospect was imminent as Brent prepared for a trip to Washington with a friend, Tony Bos, in the spring of 1984 to protest the farm crisis.

"I could see my poor wife, who was working in Des Moines, getting home at 6:30 and finding all her personal possessions sitting out in the road, which would be perfectly legal. So to protect her from this situation, we entered into bankruptcy." The story below represents a turning point, for Pete already knew that his days as a farmer were over—but fought back anyway.

THE church Tony went to, they had a little coffee group after church, and they'd go to somebody's house. Tony thought there was a real emergency, and he was going to take a saddle horse and ride to Washington and bring the news that there was a crisis in the countryside. And as he thought about that, saddle horses didn't quite epitomize modern-day agriculture. Saddle horses are for recreation, more or less.

But one of the guys in his church coffee club said what you need to do is take an old tractor—and he drew a picture on a napkin of an old tractor—and then they were joking around, and he said you ought to put an outhouse on it, I mean a manure spreader, because that's all that's coming out of Washington anyhow is b.s. So they drew this picture with a manure spreader, and then somebody came up with the idea of an outhouse. So that all transpired on a napkin, and they all had a good laugh.

On the 16th of March, we had a protest on the state capitol about having a moratorium on farm foreclosures. We were both there, and we had both testified at some legislative hearings. This rally happened fifty years and three days after the rally they had in 1934 for the same damn deal, for a moratorium on foreclosures: it wasn't planned that way, it just turned out that way. They had like 3,000 farmers storm the statehouse then; we had about 150, but, I mean, there's less farmers today, right? Anyhow, after the deal was over, there was a bunch of us that went over to a pizza place here in Des Moines, and we were having pizza and watching ourselves on the TV.

Anyhow, as we're eating pizza and we'd had a few more beers, Tony says to me, "Brent, how would you like to go to Washington on a tractor and a manure spreader?" And I thought, well, I don't know, that's kind of wild, number one, and I wonder how much of that is beer talking. So I said, "Why don't I meet you on Friday (this was Wednesday) at Rural America and we'll talk about it." Well, in my own mind I just thought that was a fantastic idea, so we'll figure this all out, but I didn't make a commitment til Friday.

Then I met Tony, and we sat down. And we said, "Okay, do you really want to do this? Okay, *how* are we going to do this?" We ain't got any money, two broke farmers, Tony lost his farm in '82, and I'm sitting there about to lose mine, really hadn't lost it yet, but I could see the handwriting was on the wall.

But, anyhow, we said we're going to do this thing, so we started to make the plans. But like all ideas, originally you have a lot of enthusiasm, and as it progressed, we had people falling by the wayside. We had some folks that were going to drive our pickup for us so we'd have a way in case we broke down. First thing that happens, "Well, we can't go, we're committed to do something else." I mean, one day they were free to do it, and the next day it got to be a little different deal. Basically ended up as Rural America people and the Farmers Union, and that was our support plus whatever Tony and I could find on our own, and American Ag was somewhat involved.

So anyhow, we got the thing lined up as best we could. We decided we would leave on the 7th of April at 10:00. We had to have a starting time just like a train leaving from a depot. Then we called, got our stuff together. Basically, we just took a couple of suitcases, we ended up with some extra baggage as we went because we had to have some file cabinets. Plus a bag for dirty clothes. We had a regular traveling show going on, and we had to make phone calls back to different people.

We had places to stay along the way. We took sleeping bags just in case we got trapped, but I don't think we ever used them. So we started out from Des Moines at 10:00 in the morning, did a big press conference and got a lot of pictures.

My wife painted the slogan on the outhouse. She also thought up the little slogan we had, "If your debts are free and clear, you can stand right up and cheer. But if like us you've lost your rear, toss your shorts right in here." And we had a barrel that you could throw shorts in, and we were asking people to mail their shorts to President Reagan. That was our entourage.

The folks that were going to drive our pickup couldn't or wouldn't do it, so I said, "Look, you drive the pickup following us from here to Davenport. We'll be there Saturday, and we'll find somebody from

167

Davenport to drive east," and that's how we ended up doing it. We had people driving that pickup we never even met, seen, or nothing else. The pickup would be someplace, and next thing it would be down wherever we needed it. So, anyhow, we started out, and the first day we drove from Des Moines to Brooklyn, Iowa, and we stayed with a farmer there. One of the things that we found was that to get our feel of what was really going on in the countryside, we'd have to stop a lot. Plus, my kidneys wouldn't allow me to go too far: no springs in a manure spreader.

So we just made it a practice to stop in coffee shops, taverns, sale barns, union halls, anyplace where we could find somebody. I probably drank more coffee. . . . And we had a regular show deal. We'd go in a place and set up our shop, put up our sign and the barrel for the shorts, hang our flags up, and we'd put on the back of the outhouse "White House." When we'd stop in a place, Tony and I'd get to talking. We'd start joking with the waitress: "Did you see the 'White House' out there?" Pretty soon somebody'd go out and just laugh and carry on. Everybody would have to go out and look, and then the conversation would just really flow. Folks realized that here was a couple of guys, crazy or otherwise, that at least were serving some purpose.

We did that for thirty-five days, and we talked with probably close to four thousand people. One of the things we tried to ask was, "If you could see the president, what would you ask him or tell him?" I had all kinds of comments, and most of them are unprintable, but there was a guy near eastern Iowa who said one thing that still sticks in my mind: "Just tell him to make things fair." One thing that seems to be lacking in this administration is being fair or evenhanded. I mean, there's obviously some people doing very well, and people that are already well-to-do, and the people who are finding themselves on the low end of the totem pole aren't really getting any advantages whatsoever. I guess President Reagan just figures that those who have ought to have more and those that don't have, well, that's all right, we don't need you.

But anyhow, from Brooklyn we went to Iowa City. We didn't have anybody lined up in Iowa City, and we stopped. There's a big co-op elevator there. The manager lined us up in a motel, and he also let us park our tractor. He paid for our motel, really a super gentleman, and that set the tone for the whole trip. That was on a Friday morning, and I had to laugh because we got up and it was just snowing. This was the 9th of April, snowing to beat hell, big flakes, combination of rain and snow. Tony said, "You ought to ride in the pickup with your wife, and I'll just tool down the road. Nobody's going to be out on a Saturday."

My wife said, "I think the Lord's testing you guys, you better ride in that." Well, I ride for a little while to see what happens. I said, "I don't think anybody will be out," and this was like 7:30 to 8:00 in the morning. So we get in the thing, put on our rain gear, and the tractor had a heat houser on it, canvas job but no roof over it, I didn't have nothing on the seating chair on the outhouse. We didn't go four blocks, by gosh, there was a guy out there in a ditch just clicking to beat heck. We knew then, if we were going to be really honest, then we best ride that machine. There was two miles out of the thousand or so to Washington that I didn't ride in that manure spreader. The only reason was that we couldn't find a road to get from where we were to where we needed to be because the state of Ohio shut down part of old Highway 40 for the interstate. They never put any sideroads in, and we couldn't ride the thing on the highway, so we put it on a dolly and dollied it for two miles. We tried to use gravel roads and everything else, but there was just that one stretch that we couldn't find a way. Other than that we drove and rode that thing the whole way.

We got to Davenport that day. Just on the outside edge of Davenport, a highway patrolman stopped my wife in the pickup and said, "Them guys are going in the wrong direction. This road will take you out to the interstate, and they don't want out there." So she told us to turn around and where to go because the highway patrolman had told her. When we got to the west end of Davenport, a TV crew was sitting right there, and we said, "How did you guys know that we were going to be here at this time, anyhow?"

"Oh, we just called the highway patrolmen. They knew where you were, they told us exactly when you'd be here." The highway patrol had us all plotted out; they knew how the heck we were going to get where we were going.

And so a guy that's president of AFL–CIO in the Quad Cities, Leonard Davis, and an old farmer by the name of Elmer Geotsch, they took care of putting us up and feeding us. Then Elmer drove the pickup to Rock Falls, Illinois. The Catholic Church there lined us up with a family that had nine or ten kids, and some of them were off to college, so they had an extra bed. As it turns out, that was the one place that Tony and I had to sleep in the same bed together. We decided after that that one guy would sleep on the floor, and the other guy would sleep in the bed, and then we'd reverse.

Then we had a guy that was in the American Ag Movement, and he drove our pickup from Rock Falls, Illinois, over to Plymouth, Indiana. From Rock Falls, we went to Aurora [Illinois]. A Congregational minister put us up in his house. He had laid out going to the Caterpillar plant. Them guys were on strike then, going out on the picket lines, radio and TV and newspaper media people, so we had good coverage. He was really a super fellow, and his mother was staying with him. She had to be in her eighties. I forget what she donated, but she gave us a nice donation to buy fuel for the tractor.

From there we got to South Holland, Illinois, on the south side of Chicago. Tony's got some relatives there, and they checked us into a motel.

From there we were going to South Bend. We got to Chesterton, Indiana, and we were going by a U.S. Steel Workers union hall. It was cold, and I had my parka and all that. I was just looking up, and I seen this United Steel Workers sign, and I hollered at Tony, "Let's turn this thing around and go back over there." We turned around and just whipped right in there. We walked into this union hall, and I mean, people looked like, "Who the hell are you two guys?" You know?

"Well, we're on the traveling 'White House'."

"Traveling White House?"

"Yeah, go on out there and look!"

Man, them guys came in there and couldn't do enough for us. Then we found out them people are having the same damn problem the farmers are having. They're economically getting their throats cut, they're losing their houses, they're losing their cars. I mean, it's the same damn thing. Obviously, one of the reasons that they're not working is, farmers ain't buying machinery which is made out of steel. They understand that. It seems awfully strange to me that on a one-on-one basis, they have no trouble understanding why we don't sell tractors or why we don't sell steel if you guys ain't out there making money or buying it anyhow. But it seems like leadership can't get that across to each other—I got my turf to worry about and you worry about yours—but the poor working stiffs in this country all have a little different slant, especially on a one-on-one basis.

The members that were working, which weren't very many, had a regular payroll deduction to buy groceries for their fellow brothers that weren't working, and they were sacking groceries in the back of

170

the union hall to make sure their members still had something to eat. I tell you, when you see that in this country, you've got to say to yourself, something's really wrong.

We left that place, and we were supposed to stop at a cookie factory because there were going to be some media people there. So we whip into this cookie factory. They give us cookies and coffee. It's like 30 degrees out and rainy and snowy, so it was all worthwhile. Anyhow, the guy that was driving our pickup, when he left the union hall, they gave him a sack of groceries. I didn't know it at the time. It's got like macaroni, dried beans, and just staple foods. Tony and I don't have no pots, we ain't got no place to cook nothing, and we didn't need it. Somebody was feeding us all the time. This made me so incensed that I'd like to kill that guy that was driving our pickup. Tony finally cooled me off, and I said, "We'll take that back." And it was like forty miles back down the road.

He said, "No, we'll find a church." We stopped at a Catholic Church and gave them a sack of groceries, and we said, "Look, there's got to be somebody in your community that needs some groceries. The union donated these groceries to you." Why would you take a sack of groceries from people that obviously need them to give them to two fools that are getting somebody else to buy their food all the time? It just made me mad, it was wrong.

He indicates that he had some "religious experience," and that he and Tony had discussed some ground rules about the trip that dealt with his religious convictions.

Tony had said we wouldn't drive on Sunday. I said that's fine, and then I decided that what we really ought to do is we ought to tithe, so I said everything we collect, we'll give 10 percent back to whatever church we go to on Sunday.

Well, Tony thought I was crazy. His contention was that's fine but you don't tithe until you know you have enough money for the next week. In this case, we didn't know the next day if we would have any money. You know you hear that phrase many, many times: "The Lord works in mysterious ways." There was one church that we stopped at and we tithed. I think for the week we got donations for $400, so I put $40 in the church collection plate. Before we left the church after church services, visiting with the folks in the church, we walked out of there with over $90, so I mean you talk about increase!

We started to do some speaking at meetings. We found that was good for us. We learned what was really happening out there. There were pockets of bad stuff, but some of the people really weren't in terrible shape yet. This guy in Illinois was still doing fairly well, but he knew there were serious problems because some of his neighbors were already starting to go down the tubes. Over in Indiana, they seemed to think everything was pretty decent yet, but we got over on the border of Indiana and Ohio, and there's a pocket right through there all the way into Columbus. They had some bad weather, and the high interest was just killing them. In Columbus, they had a rally for us right on the State House steps, and they had a bunch of their state senators and legislators out there. And we had a deal for a moratorium because they were trying to get a moratorium in Ohio, which we were trying to do at the same time in Iowa.

We had a young guy who was going broke that lived up in northern Ohio. He drove our pickup from Columbus to Pittsburgh. We went to Wheeling and got put up in the diocese complex, and they had kind of a hospital type of thing for you with rooms and beds. The guy that was in charge of this, a social worker, had a farm. He had some good land on that farm—fifty acres. If you've been to West Virginia, there ain't much good land. "I want you to meet some of my friends and neighbors." I'll tell you what, the hill folks of West Virginia, wonderful folks, but they're some tough hombres. Needless to say, we probably imbibed a little too much of the spirit, but we had a good time and they treated us well.

From there we went to Pittsburgh, right outside of Pittsburgh, a place called 84 PA. I thought it was a milepost or something. We stayed with some folks there over the weekend, and we were supposed to eat Sunday dinner at this one place. So we showed up for Sunday dinner, and we'd ate breakfast like at 8:00 and went to church. So at noon or 1:30, we were going to eat lunch or some dinner. Anyhow, we ate dinner—the whole thing: meat, potatoes, all Dutch cooking, loaded us up. We're sitting around, and there's quite a rap. And the folks start coming from all over. These folks were Farmers Union members, but these people kept coming in the house, and we got to talking and we never moved away from the table. Then, after a while, somebody pulled out a bottle of whisky, and we had to have a little of that and a little beer chaser, and we kept talking. Kept talking, kidneys about to kill you. Get up and take care of that business, come back, sit down, and about 6:00, Frances [our hostess] said, "Time for supper, just a light supper." And they brought out twenty

172

yards of spaghetti! I mean, there was spaghetti, so we just never got away from the table for about seven and a half hours. It was just one of them situations. Folks wanted to talk, I mean, they had basically the same concerns. They were having a tremendous amount of house foreclosures because the steel mills were obviously not working. The sheriff decided he wouldn't foreclose on any more, and I think they took away his badge. I guess obviously just a real depressed part of the economy.

So, as we were doing this trip, we had come to one conclusion, and that is, even though the guy in Pittsburgh don't understand why that steel isn't selling, if you talk to him on a one-on-one basis and make him understand that farmers are one of the biggest consumers of steel, and the reason you're not selling it is that farmers don't have the money or the capability to pay for it, he can understand it.

From there through the rest of Pennsylvania is like a blur in my mind because if you've ever been to Pennsylvania, there's no roads that run straight east, west, north, or south. They run zigzag and around and sideways. And so, anyhow, we had a field man from the Farmers Union in Pennsylvania, and I thank the good Lord for them, there were two of them, and one guy took us through the western end of the state and the other guy through the eastern part. Without them guys, Tony and I would still be two lost souls in the middle of Pennsylvania, trying to figure out where we were. It was fun, though. They found us good places and good folks.

We had on the front of the tractor a sign that said, "They are coming." When we got to Washington, we wanted to turn that sign around on the back side, but we didn't have it painted. We wanted to put, "They are here," so these high school kids painted that sign for us. We put it back on, "They are coming," and when we got to Washington, we obviously just took the bolts loose, turned it around, "We are here." So from there we went to Harrisburg, Pennsylvania, and from Harrisburg, we went over to Lancaster, and then we had to go back. We were going to go to Philadelphia, but time was becoming somewhat of a problem because my father-in-law was terminally ill, and I needed to be thinking about getting back. We went to York, Pennsylvania, and from there we dropped into Maryland and then into Washington.

We got to Washington the 4th or 5th of May. Took us thirty days, and Rural America had set up the whole thing, and we had parade permit, police permit, we had to have a public gathering permit, police escort, the whole thing. In the meantime, even before we'd left home, we had wrote the president for an appointment at his convenience during this week. The last night before we got into Washington proper, we stayed in a motel in Silver Spring, Maryland, for one night, a Friday, I think, and then we stayed the rest of the time we were in Washington at a student seminary house. Basically, what it is is an order working with rural social problems, wonderful bunch of young gentlemen, they were really super to us. And then this guy, Elmer Geotsch from Davenport, Iowa, shows up there. He had so much fun the two days that he hung around with us, he drove all the way to Washington, D.C., from Davenport. He's like seventy, but he just wanted to be with us, I can't hardly believe it, so anyhow Elmer stayed with us.

On Monday, we retrieved our tractor out of the motel parking lot. We were supposed to meet our police escort right on the edge of the District. So we pulled up. I jumped out, and one of my tricks was to stick my hand out, "Hi, I'm Pete Brent." I thought the cop was going to draw his gun. He wasn't sure what the heck was going on. I mean, people just don't walk around in Washington sticking their hand out at you. So, anyhow, we introduced ourselves. One of the cops said to us, "Where's the rest of your guys?" and we said, "This is it—just one tractor and an outhouse and a manure spreader."

"You guys are crazy."

"No, this is us."

We said, "We want to go by the White House." We had all these shorts we had collected, and we were going to leave them at the White House. Well, obviously, the president ain't going to talk to us. They had told us that one of us could take the shorts and bring them into the Executive Office. We had done this whole trip together like Siamese twins connected by this tractor. If we couldn't do this together, then we wouldn't do it, and we'd mail the rest of them shorts to him also, and that's what we ended up doing. So we just tooled by very slowly. We wanted to stop, and they said, "No, you can't stop, can't stop. You'll block traffic."

They take us to a place all roped off for us right in front of the U.S.D.A. building. They'd contacted all the media. We get there and pile out, set up our little can and sign and flags, beautiful kind of day, probably 65 or so. Pretty soon they've got me on one side, asking me a bunch of questions, and I look over and they've got Tony on the other side, doing the same thing to him, and I know what's going to happen now. We'll just change media people, and we'll be telling the same story nine thousand times. So I said to Tony, "They're going to do this just like they do a regular Washington press conference. We'll have answers and the whole thing just like they always do." So we said, "That's it, we ain't answering no more questions, look, we'll have a regular Washington-style press conference. Where would you like the tractor and the manure spreader?"

"Well, if you move it over this way the sunlight is better," so we moved it over two feet, and they set up their microphone stands. Pretty soon people were taping mikes on there. It looked like there were fifty. I mean, there was just all these microphones and scads of people, TV vans and radios, everybody was there. And so we started. We told them about what we were and who we saw and what was really happening out in the countryside. We had decided previously that we would not go in the U.S.D.A. building because we felt that U.S.D.A. is nothing more than a policeman. They don't make the rules; they just enforce whatever rules are dictated to them. As I was answering some questions, a young lady came up to Tony and said, "Who are you going to see in the U.S.D.A.?"

Tony said, "We're not going to see anybody," and he went through this whole thing about policemen. When he got all through, he said, "Unless Pete says we're going to go in there."

I was standing back and I had my hands behind my back. Somebody stuck a piece of paper in my pocket. It was a note that Mr. Lyng,[1] who was the number two man in the U.S.D.A., would like an appointment with us at our convenience. Now, I mean, the number-two man in the U.S.D.A. wants an appointment with Tony Bos and Pete Brent, who are two broke farmers—very strange, man. When we got through, I said to Tony, "We've got to go in there."

We were going to be done at noon, so I said, "How's 12:15 or whatever?" That's fine, and so we got through with the press conference and everybody's asking where are you going. "We're going in there." So a bunch of them followed us with the TV cameras. Well, one of the seminary students had rode his bicycle and followed us down there. He wanted to see what it was all about, and so he asked me if he could go in with us to Lyng's office. I said, sure, I have no problem with that. This is no big secret deal.

So we go in there and get introduced to Mr. Lyng and introduce

[1]Richard Lyng became Secretary of Agriculture in 1985.

175

the seminary student. Now the TV crew leaves, and two big muscle men are going to hustle this young seminary student out. He says, "I'm with them." I say, "Leave him here," so they look at Lyng and he says, okay. We're sitting at a conference table, and that sucker's got to be half a mile long. I mean, it's the biggest table I ever seen but it's long, polished, so there's Lyng at the end, Tony and I sitting across from each other, and the seminary student is way down at the other end. I think he'd need a big hearing device to hear what was going on, but he wanted to sit down there.

The first thing, Lyng says, "What do you guys really want?"

We said, "Look, you've got $600 million in emergency money[2] sitting here that you ought to be putting out in the country because there are people that need that very bad." There's no $600 million, he tells us. Well, now we'd heard for months that the $600 million was there. We're on the rope, we really don't know any more, we don't have the firm commitment that there is $600 million in emergency money. We went through a few more things. We thought that we need a longer-term food and fiber policy. We both know you've got to have some lead time if you're producing food, so I'm convinced that we need a long-term program that maybe runs for ten years, fifteen years, and let's start thinking about where we're going in the future.

Lyng told us, "The problem with you guys is you're in the wrong time frame, you just did things at the wrong time," and then he proceeded to tell us how he bought a walnut ranch in California in '39 or '38 for a little bit of nothing, and then he sold it all after the war for a high price. That's how the man made his. Then he showed us [Secretary of Agriculture] John Block's office. Big deal, who cares, you've seen one office, you've seen them all, right? Then he showed us this picture on Block's wall and said, "You see, John Block's a hog farmer, this is how he raises his hogs." Come on, man, John Block ain't out there shoveling no shit! He got some hired flunky who's out there doing it. Don't give me how great a hog farmer John Block is.

We left there, and we went outside. Our police escort finally showed up. It was one guy, and he was a big, tough-looking D.C. cop. In the meantime, while we were standing around waiting for him, there was a gentleman who looked like a farmer. He was looking our rig over real close, so we asked him who he was and where he was from. He was a farmer from South Africa, and things there are no

[2]An emergency loan fund for Farmers Home Administration.

different than things here. Over in South Africa, people trying to make a living off the land have the same kinds of problems: poor prices, quotas, and all kinds of things, so we visited with him. Anyhow, this cop shows up, so he asks us, "Is there anything you guys would like to see or do?"

"Well, the one thing the media wanted us to do was to stop in front of the White House."

"Okay, we can manage that."

"Those guys this morning said we couldn't do that."

"Don't worry about it. Whenever you're ready, I've got all day."

"We're ready."

So we got in the thing, and just before we pull away from the curb, a young man comes running down the steps. He reached over and said to me, "Hey, I work in there, but I want to tell you I don't agree with all their policy, and a lot of us don't. Is there anything I can do for you?"

Tony says, "If you know any TV stations, call them and tell them we're going to go by the White House."

So we follow the cop. We get over in front of the White House. The cop stops right up against the curb, so Tony stops. The cop comes walking back and says, "Shut her off."

Tony says, "If I shut her off, it might not start."

"Don't worry about it, shut it off." So we shut the darn thing off.

So as we were standing around visiting, an old woman come up who's out there picketing, and she wanted us to sign this petition for protesters to be able to picket out in front of the White House. I said, "Hell, I guess I'm a protester, I ought to sign it." So I signed it, and Tony signed it. Man, we didn't hardly get through with signing that thing, out come a White House policeman. He wanted to know who we were. I said, "I'm Pete Brent." Stuck out my hand and the guy, I swear, almost did pull his pistol. He had his hand right on his gun—very touchy kind of people. So, anyhow, I said, "I'm Pete Brent, that's Tony Bos, and that guy's Mr. Hollingsworth." And obviously he's a cop, there's no mistaking cops, he had his uniform on, and he had a motorcycle, what the hell, says D.C. police. So he said, "How long are you going to be here?"

Tony says, "How long do you want us to be here? We'll be here for an hour, two hours, two days, a week, a month. How long do you think it will be that we'll do some good? We'll stay that long."

Well, the cop can see he's really got some smart asses. And he said, "Okay, who all's involved in this protest?"

I said, "Me, Pete Brent, Tony Bos and, I guess, Mr. Hollingsworth." So he writes down all three names, see?

Then they get into where's your parade permit, so Hollingsworth pulls out all this paperwork he's got, and the guy says, "Well, you guys got to move."

"Can't move."

White House policeman says, "You've got to move."

Hollingsworth says, "I can't move, don't you see? There's supposed to be two of us here." And he hadn't even called for the second guy, see?

So then the White House policeman says, "Geeze, it's almost quitting time." So when he walked back to his little guard shack, Hollingsworth then called the dispatcher. So we were there for about forty minutes right in front of the White House.

Then we took the tractor and the manure spreader over to the seminary, and it sat there from May to September on their little parking lot, not in the real ghetto but in the fringe area, and nobody ever bothered it.

The rest of the week we spent lobbying Congress. Probably the one guy that most impressed me was de la Garza, head of the House Ag Committee, because he said, let us have a meeting at 3:45. At 3:45 he was there, and he wanted to know what we had to say, and what we thought, and you know, in a lot of cases you can tell they're listening in one ear and it's going out the other. Tom Harkin's staff was really good to us. Tom and I had argued for ten years. I'm a Republican, and he's a Democrat, and some things I obviously don't agree with, but I have to say he's trying to help people. He does a pretty good job, I think.

Went to see Mr. Jepsen[3]—myself and Tony and Elmer Geotsch— so they were going to have a photographer come in and take pictures and all the things that they normally do with constituents. I flat just told him, "Look, things just don't turn around. I don't think you and Reagan could get elected dog catcher." Shows you how much I know because Reagan got elected. Man, he's conned so many people I can't believe it, but that's besides the point. I'm a Republican and just made no bones about it. I felt that if they didn't do something to

[3]U.S. Senator from Iowa, 1979–85.

178

change, that at least through the Midwest they couldn't win the election. Tony is talking about people who are committing suicide in the country and beating their wives and all the bad things that go along with this problem. The senator is sitting in this big plush chair, basically sleeping. The photographer never did show up, because once I laid into him about not getting reelected, I guess he decided he didn't need to waste the money for photography. We proceeded to get ready to leave, and the senator sort of shook himself and said, "I'm not going to get on my soapbox, but this administration has done more for the family farm through the inheritance tax. . . . "

And Tony looked right in his eye and told him, "Look, I don't have a farm to leave to anybody any more, what good is this inheritance tax?" It was just that type of stupidity. So I knew when I walked out of there that if at all possible, whatever I could possibly do to get him defeated, I was going to do. So this last campaign I was basically a Democrat. I knew that Senator Jepsen really didn't represent the vast majority of people in this state.

We came back, and my father-in-law was terminally ill. I got back on Saturday, and on Monday morning, 5:00 to 5:30, he died. So we had a funeral that week, and the following Monday after we'd been home a week, we called a press conference down at the state house, just where we left from—the state house steps on the west side—we laid out the story about Jepsen.

About the middle of summer, this would have been in '84, we offered Tom Harkin and Jepsen both a weekend ride in the manure spreader and talk to folks. Harkin, he was really for it—we could never get the logistics—and never even got an answer back one kind or another from Jepsen's people or from Jepsen himself. Then one night I got a call, and someone said, "Did you see you guys on TV? You're on a Harkin commercial. Two Iowa farmers drove their tractor to Washington, and Jepsen went to sleep." So Harkin made it part of one of his commercials with Tony and I, and it made me feel good. It made me feel like maybe the system still works, for all its shortcomings. Obviously, with 220 million folks, it's awful tough for one guy to make a huge wave, but one guy with a combination of other folks can make some changes. You see it every once in a while, but you have to be committed to that.

You guys also brought that manure spreader to the showing of Country *in Des Moines.*

179

I have to back up just a little bit. See, actually the movie *Country* is a composite of a lot of folks, but the basic thrust of the thing is Tony's and my deals combined. The farm numbers, the cash money deal and all that, was numbers right out of my farm, the price, the interest, the whole thing. You got to have someone who's been bankrupt to have the numbers to make it work, so that part came off of my farming operation, and we were involved in that part of the writing of the movie. But the guy that had the sheep in the middle of the night was Tony. That's where it all came from and the sheep, some of the sheep in the movie actually are Tony's sheep. So anyhow, him and I were involved, and Jessica Lange spent the week with us, tooling around and visiting different folks.

We said that when they made the movie, we had decided that all the premieres we had ever seen, people always went with formal attire. So we said what we will do is we will wear coats or tails and white gloves and top hats, and the women in formals. So anyhow, they did premiere in Washington and New York a couple of days or a week before we had the first showing here in Des Moines. Or the second showing, I guess, because the first showing ended up going for a benefit for Johnny Gosch and this Martin kid.[4]

So we rented the tuxedos and we got top hats, white gloves and the whole thing, and we drove that rascal to it. We had picked up the women also in their formals, and we had my kid out there with a red carpet.

But bad movie, I don't recommend it to anybody that's went through or is going through that process of economic disillusionment. Shouldn't go see that movie, it's just like somebody opened up a big sore. Just about the time you think you're over the thing, some movie like that is just too tough on your emotions. Just like somebody pulled a big scab off a sore.

It's a good movie, I don't have complaints; as far as technicalities, there's a few discrepancies, but when you make a movie, you can't have everything fit exactly right to make it flow. It's a good movie, but it's not a movie that a guy that's either going broke or is broke off the farm should go see because the worst part about it, when you get all said and done, is the very tail end. Makes you really think that they're going to be able to save that farm and, in all, actually that's false. Eventually, the numbers are going to win, and you're going to lose.

---

[4]The Des Moines premiere was a benefit for two missing children.

180

Obviously, there are a lot of folks that I wish I could really feel good that they're going to get saved, but there are so many of them I had talked to on that damn highway that there ain't going to be no saving them, I don't care what they do, the numbers are too big. You know, when you start talking about $100,000 or better interest a year, $100,000 is a lot of produce. I don't care what the hell you sell, that's a lot of stuff you have to sell just to make the interest. It's real tough.

The Gang of Five

HOLLIS PETERSEN
Sutherland, Iowa

and BOB DONAHOO
Peterson, Iowa

Bob Donahoo is a farmer and a member of the Storm Lake [Iowa] Production Credit Association. In the aftermath of this story, he has been involved with a delegation of farmers in ongoing discussions and negotiations with Omaha Farm Credit Banks officials concerning borrowers' rights.

HOLLIS: Back several years ago, I had the opportunity to rent some land. I could see that I probably wouldn't be making a career out of the Farm Credit System.

My philosophies and the philosophies of the system were not going to be that compatible, and I felt that there was a lot of turnover. I had seen a lot of friends of mine leave the system. I decided I better have something to fall back on, so that maybe I could have a little more independence and not be as concerned about leaving the system as some of the other workers. So I started renting some land around here.

My personality, or my philosophy, I guess, wasn't compatible with the president's, and I think he just took a dislike for me. I always treated him with respect, but I guess he just didn't especially like me, and there was a branch manager I worked with when I first started in Storm Lake, and I think Jim probably defended me as best he could. He left Storm Lake and took another position in a different district in

'82. Then there was a new branch manager hired in August of '82. I could see that we didn't have a branch manager that was going to represent the employees of that particular branch. In '83, I was given a reprimand for putting on a loan. It was a loan that I picked up from the Spencer branch, which is part of the Emmetsburg association. I received a reprimand from the board of directors, and I think probably on the advice, or on the information, given to them by the president at a board meeting. I was never even given the opportunity to defend myself, and I felt that at least I should have the opportunity to talk to those directors who are farmers and explain the process I went through. I told the branch manager that "I can see what you're doing. These things were in writing." And I had seen what happened to other people that they started documenting things. They're preparing you for termination down the road. Then, in August, I was told to sign a letter of awareness. They were outlining certain weaknesses that they felt I had. I felt I didn't have these weaknesses, and I hadn't done these things that they were trying to accuse me of, and I said I can't sign something like that. When I sign it, that's my accepting it and agreeing that I have these weaknesses. And I was told, well, if you're not going to sign this letter of awareness, you're going to be placed on probation.

And so then I was placed on probation. They said some of the reasons were that, over the past several years, I was handling quite a few problem loans and that I was not following a plan of action. I could prove that I had followed a plan of action. And I told them: "Which loans are you referring to? I want to see a list. Show me." They never would provide me with any specifics because I think they knew that I could counter any of the criticisms that they would make if they would recite a certain loan.

But I think they already had the intention of terminating me. One of the statements in the letter was that none of this is to be brought to the members. The members should not have any knowledge of what was happening to me, and I could see in the office that there was no one that would take my side and at least give me a fair hearing, including the branch manager. I was threatened with termination the day I refused to sign the letter of awareness. He brought it to me one day in September, I guess. He said here it is for you to sign, and I told him, "Well, Ken, I told you I can't sign that. You can put it in my file, but I'm not going to sign it."

And he said, "Well, you're terminated." That morning, he told me that. I thought it was serious enough then that I should talk to someone, so I called one of the members who I was quite close with. I guess the reason I called him, I wasn't able to reach the director, one of the board members, who was in Buena Vista County. I went out and I talked to this board member, who lives in B.V. County.

I just thought I would confide in this man and tell him that I was concerned about what was going on in the association. I even had several farmers who went out and talked to him. They were accusing me of not having a plan of action, so I decided I'm going to bring out one of the farmers I had worked with who had what was called a problem loan, have him talk to this director. I showed how I had approached the loan and just how accurate I had been in working with this particular farmer. The next day I was told I was terminated. But there was never any reason for my termination. I was kind of expedited out of the office. I mean, I left in a hurry after being there about six years. I'd never been treated like that before.

Bob: But we got concerned, you know. We wanted to know why. We talked it over, and we got about three carloads of farmers, drove down to the president, John Holst in Ida Grove, he's the president of the board, and I made arrangements to visit.

We wanted to discuss why Hollis was terminated. And he said, "Well, I can't talk about it. Hollis is going to sue us. Pending litigation, I've been advised not to say anything." So, what else could you say? We then questioned him about a few things, and one of the things was we would like a set of the bylaws.

Were you in fact going to sue them?

Hollis: No, I hadn't made any mention of suing.

Bob: And he says, "You can't have a set of bylaws. I can't even have a set of the bylaws." What kind of association is this, you know? We were just dumb farmers. What have we got ourselves into here? We all got thinking about it. Anyway, we contacted Omaha, and they gave us a runaround. If you want your own set of the bylaws, you can go down and look at 'em. We couldn't get a set of bylaws.

They sent some public relations material. Finally, then, we went to Clayton Hodgson, an aide of [Congressman] Berkley Bedell, and he put some pressure on. And finally, we got a set of bylaws. I'm talking about months' runaround, to let us have a set of the bylaws. Well, then we did see in the bylaws that there is a provision that 10 percent of the patrons can sign a petition for a special meeting. Then we

184

went back to them. We said we want a list of patrons in the five-county area. Then we got about a month's runaround on that. Finally, Mr. Hodgson, Berkley Bedell's aide, put enough pressure on them, we finally, reluctantly, got the list.

Oh, forgot! I'm leaving out one important thing in there. In the meantime, we asked for a hearing. Five farmers asked for a hearing in front of the board of directors. And they said, reluctantly, "We usually don't do this, but we'll listen to you." So we went down and we met with the five board members.

We got Clayton Hodgson to come in, too. We had questions on past policies and what happened to Hollis, and the president said, "Hollis has been a bad boy for a long time." Fortunately, Hollis had kept some of his performance records, how he had been rated by Production Credit. They were all good to excellent, and, in fact, their last one was dated in what?

Hollis: August or September of '82.

Bob: "And he's been a bad boy for a long time." We said, "Well, if he's been a bad boy for a long time, how come these performance records in '82 give him good to excellent? On everything?"

"How did you get them?"

"Hollis gave them to us, you know."

Then they had to look at them. I don't really even think they'd ever seen them! So we had about a 3½-hour discussion with the gentlemen. And we did finally get them to agree that they would let Hollis come in and talk to them. And they answered no questions that we asked them on policy or anything. They tried to lecture to us on different things, that we were fighting a losing battle, that once a man is terminated, they're terminated. But anyway we got Hollis a hearing. But Hollis didn't get a hearing. The next morning, we got a call from Mr. Holst, the president of the board of directors. "Our legal counsel says. . . . We got a real chewing out by our legal counsel; we can't have a hearing with Hollis."

Now we can't figure out whether the president of the association went to a lawyer and got him to say this, or whether this was in truth. I don't know. But there was no hearing for Hollis.

Hollis: So it contradicted. Then I was going to have a hearing, like Bob said, with the directors. And I also was going to be given the opportunity to look at my personnel file, which I never, ever looked at before. They denied me that option, too, I guess on the advice of legal counsel. I really feel that they felt that they might have libeled themselves to some extent. So I've never seen my file.

Bob: Then we got the lists of the members. We sent a letter of invite to every member of the association, we made up a letter, to come to Storm Lake to the Stevens Center. We were a group of concerned farmers. We were all welcome, we paid for the postage out of our pocket, the rent for the building out of the five farmers' pockets. We made all the rent arrangements and got the letter out. I think we mailed it on Friday, a few got it on Saturday, and the bulk of them on Monday. And we were having the meeting Tuesday.

In the meantime, the Storm Lake association president put out a letter to the effect that this was a clandestine meeting, that we had no authority, that none of the board members would be there, just a few farmers that had a gripe. Sort of downplayed this. But we had our meeting, and there was about what—eighty people there?

Hollis: Probably eighty to a hundred.

Bob: We presented our case, and we said that we would like to have a special board meeting, that we were going to present a petition. And we heard a lot of gripes about people, some sad things that day, some of the economic problems that these farmers had been facing. But anyway, the paper said there was thirty-five people there. They downplayed it some more in the letter.

We had TV coverage. Most journalists we talked to thought it was a good meeting. So then we proceeded with the petition to have a special board meeting, to get the board to answer some of these questions, and then, you see, we could've put forth a motion that day to have a special election. If the board was to mandate a special meeting like we wanted, then we could've put forth a motion to reelect the board members. But we never got that 10 percent. And so, that's pretty well what happened to the gang of five.

But there's a lot of questions. As Melvin Schneider[1] says, why the change in philosophy, all of a sudden? We're pressured, you know. Myself, I was put under quite a bit of pressure by my new loan officer. I went to a specialist in agriculture. We laid out a plan for my operation. My paydown will not be great this year; my net worth will increase about $100,000. And they're still questioning my loan.

Not many people will go up in net worth this year, from what I've seen.

---

[1] A retired PCA loan officer and volunteer farm credit counselor.

Bob: Well, we're a large grain operation, livestock primarily. And hogs. And the increase we've done in our hogs. We've used realistic views, and I have met every one of my goals set forth in my operation this year up through the first part of September. I will have marketed x amount of hogs, I have lived behind my budget, I'm not using as much money as I anticipated, been fortunate. We've got a reasonably good crop, by the grace of God barring bad weather, but still they're putting pressure, you know. All they can talk to me about is: Get us some cash, get us a bunch of cash in a hurry.

Castles in the Sandhills

LAURETTA and GARTH BARNES
Todd County, South Dakota

JOHN BUSH and DON NELSEN
Valentine, Nebraska

and RAY KICKEN
Ainsworth, Nebraska

The Sandhills aren't like most of the rural Midwest—they are the first really convincing sign in Nebraska that you are entering a different part of the United States. The soil is not hard under your feet. It squishes, even when it's dry. It's like a beach without the water.

The hills roll, but it's not really desert yet. There are constant signs of vegetation: scrub pines, silkweed, grass that pops up in spots. Cattle roam ranches that commonly encompass three to five thousand acres. A congressional study that once included Cherry County, Nebraska, as a case study mysteriously found a shrinkage of average size of farms with the advent of corporate farming. The reason was simple, although seemingly not obvious to the authors: The corporate operations were not grazing cattle. They were trying to convert the Sandhills into irrigated cropland, primarily corn.

I had heard and read about the experiments with center-pivot irrigation in the Sandhills before I ever visited the area. Critics charged it was ecologically destructive. The sandy soil would blow away with the first high winds once exposed to the elements after plowing and planting. The soil wastes much of the irrigation water because its absorption capacity is so limited. To old-timers in the area who know the environment's limitations, it seemed a case of technology gone mad.

But such operations also need capital, and, if they are ecologically risky, they can also prove financially risky, as well. Those capital costs make the operators who invested in them even more subject to the whims of the declining grain market than farmers in general, who have found farming to be increasingly capital-intensive over time. A few of those investors were, it turns out, looking to "farm the tax code," as some have put it, rather than to earn money from farming itself.

What amazes me as I drive across Nebraska's Highway 20, to Cody, where I will turn north on a country road over the South Dakota border to the Barnes ranch, is the idea that anyone ever really thought such land could be used this way. Longtime ranchers have raised a little corn on dry ground for nearly a century, it is true—but only to feed their own cattle, not as an end in itself.

In retrospect, it should have amazed some people who were managing the Valentine and O'Neill Production Credit Associations in Nebraska. On November 9, 1984, the boards of both associations voted to enter into voluntary liquidation following a presentation concerning their condition by officials of the Omaha FICB. Among the large loans that put the association at risk was one to Gerald Kirwan, who filed bankruptcy in February 1983, and $4 million of whose outstanding obligations to the Valentine PCA were unsecured. In 1985, he was still farming more than three thousand acres in Rock County by center-pivot irrigation.[1]

It would be an understatement to say that the liquidation of the PCAs was a powerful blow to the longtime members of the two PCAs. To say that their perception of the events that followed is widely at variance with that presented to the public by local and district Farm Credit System officials is to belabor the obvious. But it is worth considering their perception of the meetings that ultimately ensued in early 1985 with FICB and PCA officials.

G ARTH: This FICB meeting in Valentine on the 25th of February came off a challenge I made to them down there the 2d of February.

I asked them to get a professional outside audit and come up here

---

[1]"Kirwan's Multi-Million Dollar Debt," Center for Rural Affairs newsletter, October 1985, p. 1.

and explain the situation. And I told him at that time I'd guarantee a civilized meeting for him. And then Hanser[2] called and wanted us to hold a meeting where we would submit, what, six or eight questions?

Lauretta: No, you'd have six on your panel and six on theirs. And you had to submit your questions ahead of time.

Garth: And then they would review those questions—and then they'd meet with us.

Lauretta: They wouldn't have an attorney on their side, but they'd have one in the audience.

Don: Garth says, "I don't believe we're interested in that."

Garth: We turned it down; Ainsworth people turned it down; nobody wanted it. And then they came out and put together this other meeting.

Lauretta: And they did take questions from the floor then.

John: And it was all a dog and pony show. They evaded the questions. They just said, hey, boys, times are tough, and we're just working for you, we're trying to help you, you know.

Garth: But I wanted them to come out with an audit so they could explain the situation, and bring the CPA that done the auditing with them, so they could explain the whole situation to the people. We didn't get that in the end.

Lauretta: And you ask questions like stockholder lists and right to read the minutes, and things. First, they'd say, well, there's rights of privacy. Well, then we said, will you mail letters? Well, we'll have to turn that over to our attorney to look it up, you know. And then we asked for the minutes of the board, and he said, well, there's rights of privacy. There might be individual loans in the minutes. And I said, well, block those out. We're not interested in that. We want to see how our association got to the point where it's at: in liquidation. Well, he said, "Send me a letter and ask, and we'll review it." And I said, "I'm asking you right now." So the attorney stood up then, and he said they would review it. But they turned it down. They said we can have anything in the minutes that pertains to our loans, but other than that, we can't have the minutes.

John: Well, see, I pushed him, after you got done on him, and I said, "To me, you said 'no.' What did you really say?"

"What do you mean?"

"I mean, your saying you'll take it under advisement means 'no.' "

2Vice-president for public affairs, Omaha Farm Credit Banks.

190

Lauretta: And that's what they did.

John: "I want to know what you're gonna do. What will you do if we send this letter?" And he finally said at that point, as I remember, "Well, we would probably mail the letters for you." And then I told him, "Well, I'm going to count on you." You [Lauretta] mailed the letter, and we know what we got back.

The whole thing was covered up. I don't know where the news broke that there was financial trouble in the Valentine PCA, but immediately after that, we got the letter from the chairman of the board, and they did call a little meeting. They did call a special meeting. It was just an informational meeting. It wasn't that annual meeting. And Gary Connot.[3] . . . Everybody talks about how Gary Connot talked throughout the meeting and wanted to know just what the heck was going on. And after that, it was all covered up. They talked merger; they said we're going to merge because it will be best for the system. And this thing is going to work. And the letter we got from the chairman said, "This in no way means your PCA is failing financially." Rest assured. And they hit us with a media blitz.

They were stonewalling. They somehow thought they'd come out with this huge media blitz, and nobody would question them. And they advertised in our local papers and on our radio that they're the farmers' and ranchers' friend, we've been in business for years and we're going to be here for many years to come. . . .

Lauretta: Go the last mile. . . .

Don: Go the last mile, and then they liquidated.

I'm talking about our local ads. They were designed to take the heat off. They were designed to lull everybody to sleep that things are all right. Don't question anything. And nobody did. If we had seen the financial statements, somebody would have surely said, "My goodness, we've dropped from $69 million in loan volume down to $40-some million, whatever it was, this doesn't look right." But we didn't have the opportunity to do that, and, as borrowers, we didn't have the opportunity to question what was going on.

John: According to the bylaws, we're supposed to have that right.

Don: We didn't have the opportunity to make a decision: whether we wanted as an association to sell down those bad loans, if that was our problem at that time, or recapitalize, or pull out of the system entirely, or anything. There was a lot of different options we may

[3]A PCA member farming in Sparks, Nebraska.

191

have had, had our employees been responsible. What do you call it, fiduciary responsibility? If they had exercised that, then we may have had an option to make things different. But we didn't have, we were not counseled at all. And by law, it's my understanding they are required to do that for you. If you're the owner, they're acting in your behalf. But they covered that up. We didn't have anything to do with it. Other than being lulled to sleep.

Garth: At the office meeting, we had those FICB people in Valentine. There was only what, three, four, five at the most, individual people that stood up and asked questions that were not, say, on the board of directors. So their intimidation pretty well worked.

Ray: What they did is if you stand, give your name, and how long you've been [with PCA], and don't ask any personal confidence. So you couldn't talk about your personal deals.

John: I was dumb. I didn't realize what they were doing. They were sitting up there writing down the names of who all talked. . . .

Don: The liquidator was sitting up there right beside them. And they said, "Give your name and how many years you've been in PCA." And the liquidator was right there with his pen and his piece of paper and made it very obvious. If you didn't catch it, you were about the only one in the place that didn't. As soon as you raised your hand and asked a question, he was up there, wrote your name down, what your question was, and everything else.

Lauretta: Of course, it could have been legitimate, you know, he could have been thinking, well, maybe I can solve this or something, but it was very intimidating. It really looked very intimidating because you're sitting back there thinking, boy, I've got to go get my loan settled, and I don't want to say anything that's gonna shake that up.

Don: At this meeting, we overwhelmed them so bad, didn't we?

Garth: They came in there and they expected half a dozen questions and to be able to give their pitch, pack up and go drink coffee until it's time to go to O'Neill. They finally had to shut it off so they could have time to get to O'Neill.

John: We actually backed off. The tempers flared a little bit, and we were asking questions that they couldn't answer. They had to dodge them, and they would move to Paul Parliament[4] to come up and take the mike, and he would fast-talk his way around it. And it was really a dog and pony show. And you couldn't nail 'em down hard

[4]President of the Valentine PCA prior to liquidation.

192

on anything. I sat there and somebody asked them a question, they didn't answer it very well, and I wrote down another question to ask them, and then a follow-up question and baited them, and then they fell into the trap, you know, when they answered the question after I asked the first one. I said, well, how come you said a little bit ago this. And they went around the whole thing. Garth and I, I think, were the ones that stood up and said, "Let's keep this meeting civil. Let's calm down, people. We've got nothing against these guys up there, let's try to work with them." And now, I don't feel like we should've done that. I wish we hadn't. I wish we'd let it get out of hand. Because they just put on a little show for us, kept telling us, we're just working for you, boys. And then they left the meeting, and the stockholders, so many people left, saying, well, gee, we had our meeting. There's this whole relief that you actually went face to face with them. And they walked down and gave the newspaper and the radio press releases as to what the meeting was all about. And it really made it sound like they had come from Omaha and *saved* us when it was really the other way around. They really hadn't said anything.

Lauretta: And any question of substance which you wanted an answer to, they said they had to review it and they'd send you a letter. They circumvented the whole crowd getting an answer that way.

Don: Nobody really caught on to what we were digging them about: that is, a possible illegal liquidation, and what was really going on. And stockholders' rights. Then they used the press, and they've learned how to do this, because they are the system. They hand out press releases and, bingo, we've been had.

Lauretta: We had one paper in Valentine that wrote a few of the questions down and everything, but it wasn't. . . .

Don: What I'm getting at is the whole system. We're at such a disadvantage with the media because we don't know how to use the media. I guess we're learning, but they use it to make things happen.

Garth: I had been to those two previous meetings in Council Bluffs.[5] I intentionally had the board lined up with questions. And I had trouble keeping quiet a couple of times, but I pretty well did til right at the end.

Lauretta: Garth didn't have to give his name. They said, "Well, hello, Garth."

---

[5]A stockholder delegation had a series of meetings with Omaha Farm Credit Bank's officials concerning their grievances as members.

Garth: I stood up; everybody else almost had to laugh. Everybody else had to stand up and give their name. I stood up, and Dean Raber[6] said, "What do you want, now, Garth?" I tell you, that's one time I didn't feel privileged to be known.

Lauretta: I forgot to give my name, and they asked me. They wouldn't let me talk. I just started asking my question.

Garth: Well, you asked about stockholders' rights.

Don: The questions that we asked were all pertaining to the liquidation of the stockholders' rights. We did get halfway organized, and we sat down and thought up questions so that we could have something legitimate to ask. We didn't want to be asking a bunch of off-the-wall questions. We wanted to have questions that were pertaining to what had happened, pertaining to our bylaws and our rights.

Lauretta: Well, we had had that seminar with Jim Corum,[7] too. And that opened our eyes to some things that we didn't know about.

Garth: We sat down for an hour or two before that meeting, and we all had a long list of questions, and John and the rest of them added a few, and we more or less assigned questions. Otherwise, we'd have had their questions at the meeting and. . . .

Don: That's all it would have amounted to was their questions.

Garth: But there were these people getting up all over the crowd, asking questions.

John: One point I'd make: Ken Jasperson[8] was being questioned: "How long did you know before you liquidated the Valentine PCA that you were going to liquidate it?"

Don: He's the statistician, I think. The one that has all the numbers. Well, how did he say that? He said. . . .

Lauretta: It was an ongoing thing. . . . There were problems, but we didn't know. . . .

John: Yeah. Then finally he said, "Well, I knew thirty days ahead of time."

Lauretta: But there was no other viable option, he said.

Don: And boy, he got some looks from the rest of them, and. . . . they tried to talk back around it, and make it sound like he didn't

---

[6]A vice-president of the Omaha Farm Credit Banks.

[7]Former general counsel for the St. Paul FICB who was fired over a major policy disagreement and went on to represent dissident farmers against the Farm Credit System and conducted numerous seminars on the rights of Farm Credit System stockholders across the country.

[8]The senior vice-president of FICB in Omaha.

know thirty days in advance. Well, he appears to be a pretty honest guy; he didn't realize he had to be deceitful about the whole thing. And they were actually loaning money that thirty days. Now if he knew that thirty days in advance, what the hell were they doing making loans? And selling stock?

Lauretta: And not telling them the stock was at risk?

Garth: We've got a member that they loaned money to the day before.

Don: The day before.

Lauretta: And they didn't tell us anything about the stock being at risk.

John: These are things that are stockholders' rights. We should've had the right to know what was happening in there. And they kept that away from us. And, you know, on the whole thing, we were never counseled. We were never counseled on the risk of the stock when you took out the loan and you were told it was an accounting procedure, don't worry about it. Now everything you read coming out of the FICB or the Farm Credit System states this is venture capital. You know, my God, it's like buying uranium shares in Montana or something. But they were never counseled as to that. And it is— and Don Blasingame[9] has pointed that out. He said it is venture capital. He said it is at risk. It always has been.

Although Valentine and O'Neill were the first PCAs in the Omaha district to be liquidated, they turned out to be only the tip of the iceberg. The stock in many others was frozen in the spring and summer of 1985, not only in Omaha, but also in other districts. Ultimately, individual PCAs were merged into single, multistate district PCAs.

In the spring of 1986, Lincoln attorney David Hahn filed suit on behalf of eighty plaintiffs, all stockholders in the Valentine PCA, against the Federal Intermediate Credit Bank of Omaha, its liquidator, James C. Larson, and five former directors of the Valentine PCA. The somewhat complex suit sought $670,823 in collective damages for the lost value of the plaintiffs' "B" stock, which they had to purchase as their member ownership of the association, equal to 10 percent of their outstanding loans.

The primary allegations were: that the FICB had "special and unique knowledge of the Valentine PCA's financial conditions prior

---

[9]Retired chief executive officer of the Tyler, Texas, Federal Land Bank.

195

to liquidation, yet reassured the members that there was no need for concern, and that such reassurances were false"; that, in various ways, including "failure to obtain adequate and sufficient appraisals for collateral," the FICB had violated its duty to deal with members in good faith; that the FICB had prevented the PCA from taking advantage of loss-sharing agreements with other PCAs; and that the FICB had misrepresented the stock borrowers were required to buy. The suit also charged the former directors with negligence in their own fiduciary duties and charged the liquidator with allowing the FICB an unfair advantage against the plaintiffs' claims against the PCA.

The defendants paid a bond to remove the case from state district court in Cherry County, Nebraska, where it was filed, to federal district court in Omaha. Meanwhile, the FICB made withdrawal from the suit a requirement for any plaintiffs to settle their debts with its liquidator. A few plaintiffs did drop out, including the Barneses. The plaintiffs later succeeded in transferring the case back to Cherry County. In early 1988, they were expecting a trial date to be set within a few months.

We Shall not Be Moved

ALICIA KOHNEN
Roscoe, Minnesota

First State Bank of Paynesville was the scene of a farmer sit-in August 7, 1984, but not because Gerald and Alicia Kohnen, on whose behalf the protest was mounted, had arranged it. Their award-winning dairy farm was the target of a foreclosure action by the bank, a branch of the First Bank system based in Minneapolis, despite the fact that the Kohnens had never missed or been late on a payment. The bank merely claimed that declines in local farmland values had devalued the collateral and jeopardized the security on the loan. Paynesville bank president Martin Dietrich then exercised the bank's rights under a "payable on demand" clause. Under the pressure, however, the Kohnens had been trying to arrange for start-up credit at 5 percent interest for their son, Donald, through the Farmers Home Administration, in the hope that he could then continue the operation of the farm. But that would take time—the amount of which they could not come to terms on, apparently, with the bank.

The Kohnens say that Dietrich did offer them ninety days to arrange Donald's finances with the Farmers Home Administration, but that "it takes a whole year at minimum to get worked in." If they could get him in, they could then use that refinancing to pay off the bank. But, they say, when Dietrich insisted that he had offered sufficient time and refused to offer more, the Kohnens took $15,500 they say they had been willing to give to the bank and used part of it to pay their attorney to file Chapter 11 (reorganization) bankruptcy. Alicia Kohnen says she told Dietrich, "I'm not gonna sign nothing, and you aren't gonna get this money unless we have a year." And they

197

walked out. That night, the Kohnens came home to a sizeable gathering of their neighbors.

It was their neighbors who decided not only that enough was enough in their increasingly difficult dealings with First Bank, which they suspected wanted to withdraw from agricultural lending generally, but that the Kohnens' case made a perfect example for such a protest. Many of them were members of COACT, a Minnesota citizens' group that has taken a leading role in the state in organizing farmers.

A LICIA: The guys said, "You want to have a meeting out to your place Friday night after you meet at the bank? If he signs the thing, you get what you want, we'll just have a party. If it doesn't work, then we'll plan what we're gonna do."

They had called a few neighbors, and I didn't even know who they had asked to come in. When I came home, there was people here that half of them I didn't even know. And Father Torberg came. I had met him at a distance; I had never talked to him before. He sat there, and he said to me, "How can you have a smile on your face when you're facing this?"

I said, "Well, Father, I came from a family of ten. I guess we were fortunate. My mother taught us to work and stick up for our rights and fight for what we thought was ours. I've been stepped on many times. You just bounce back and start over again. What would it do me any good to go sit in the corner and cry? That don't accomplish a darned thing. The only thing we have is we know that we've worked hard. We haven't gone out and spent money foolishly. Sure, we've taken a vacation and we drive these old Cadillacs but we could sell all our cars, the whole works that we have, and we couldn't even replace it with a new car of any kind." We've got the cars as a hobby for my husband.

These guys said that they just couldn't believe that the man [Dietrich] could be doing this, because we got our payments made up, and we had given the bank $40,000 out of our milk check in one year. They took 29 for interest, but still, that's $11,000 off the principal, which is almost $1,000 a month.

I just didn't feel as though he had really any gripe. Til we had the auction, we still had all our property. And the only thing we sold was those cows, and we didn't down our herd that much, because in '82 we had sixty-five heifer calves born. And we knew those were all coming into replacements in '84. They're still coming in, and I imagine we've got up to eighty cows in the barn now, and there's quite a few that are heifers. So we weren't afraid of not being able to get back into the thing.

These guys just decided this would be a typical case to go up there and do a thing on the bank. They said to call up the ones that we wanted in on it. I didn't know who to call, who not to call. While we were down to his [Gerald's] dad's . . . Warren Reeck's wife called, and the kids thought it was the wife of one of the trustees at the bank calling. So they wouldn't give her any information. When we called home from where his dad lives, they said this Caroline had called, and she wanted to know what was going on out here because Channel 2 was called to come out here on Friday night. Her daughter works for Channel 2, and her future son-in-law came out here on Friday night.

As soon as I got home, I called her and told her what the deal was, and she just couldn't believe it. She says, "I know what this farm situation is doing," and she would just as soon come and put her 2 cents into it. They were at retirement age, too, and they can't afford to retire because they're too much in debt. This year they figure they've lost up to $1 a bushel on all their corn. This fellow is sixty-two years old. The bank has told them that he shouldn't fatten all his beef. He should sell those cattle and sell his crop. He'd make more money on it. But he's got these cattle, and you sell these cattle right now, when they're half fed out, they're not going to bring nothing. The other bank had told him he should go out and look for something to do at sixty-two years old. I think the fellow has some education, and he probably could get a job, but where? She came over that night, and I think her son came. There were several people that we didn't expect. And there were people here from American Ag Movement, NFO, and Farmers Union. And, of course, we belong to NFO and Farmers Union, and COACT. And we're paid-up members of Farmers Union for twenty-five years. We're a little behind now [laughing].

The sit-in was scheduled to go on Monday. Over the weekend, we were supposed to call as many people as we thought could come. And they had a task force meeting on Saturday. They wanted me to come, and I said, "Hey, I can't leave the place here." They said, "Okay, but we're gonna line up this thing for Monday, and we're gonna have people come in."

Members had contacted KSTP. There was Channel 11, and every newspaper from all the surrounding areas—Willmar, St. Cloud,

Paynesville, every newspaper, they were all represented. And I think there was at least three or four sets of TV cameras that followed us right to the bank, and Channel 4 flew in with a helicopter. When we got to the bank, of course, everybody just drove in and parked their cars. The whole mess was in the bank before anybody knew what was going on. The bank was filled.

There was Mike Laidlaw and the priest, and Gerry and I, and some of the kids and the lawyer, and this Bill and his son, Chad. And a couple of these other farmers that he's [Dietrich's] driven out of business, they were there. Of course, they don't like Dietrich anyway, and they just sat there. And then he says, "I can't talk to you guys with all these people in here." A few weeded out, and he said he'd talk to us. And then he says, "I've gotta call somebody," and we had to leave the office. Then he calls the cops and his lawyer.

This was about 1 or 1:15, and we were in there for a while. We went out, and about 1:30, quarter to 2, he called us back in the office, and we started talking again. One of the families that he had sold out a year or so ago, her brother was a cop. Of course, when he walked into the bank and saw his sister and her son standing there, he just about choked. When he figured that there was going to be arrests, he told his nephew to get his mother out of there because, he said, "I really don't want to arrest your mother."

During the day, as time went on, these women from Duluth went out and they brought in groceries. And this Paul Wellstone, he got up on a chair, on a desk, and he talks with his whole body. He is a terrific speaker; it comes right off the top of his head. There was all kinds of talk. Heads of the different farm groups were there. Of course, I didn't know a lot of these fellows then.

It was kind of funny. When we couldn't get anyplace with the bank, the guys said, "Now, if anybody wants to be arrested, you do it on your own." I said, "You guys, don't get arrested on account of a deal like this. This is ridiculous." But they went ahead, and I didn't realize what they were doing until the priest and my lawyer called me out of there [the bank] at five minutes to 4, and wanted me to come up and file for some papers. I really don't think that's what they wanted. They just didn't want me to get arrested. Gerry didn't get arrested because he had to come home and do the chores. When I came back to the bank, all these cops started coming in.

They're putting these people in these cars, and all the ones arrested had grins on their faces, and it was just hilarious. I looked into a car, and I saw all these people in there. It just reminded me of when you put these chicks in a cage before you butcher them. They all stand there with their tongue hanging out with the saliva. Then they headed for St. Cloud. Karen, our daughter, said they had almost had three accidents on the way into town, they were going that fast. She said she was really upset about that, but they were having fun. She said that was the most fun they had in a long time. They didn't have the keys to unlock one of the fellows' handcuffs. . . . We were listening to some scanner, and they said they had a traffic jam on the way to Paynesville with all these cop cars going in.

The kids said, when all the cops had cleared off the lot [at the bank], here are two big tractors sitting there, and one of them wouldn't start. And that was one we were paying for through the bank. So they got another tractor, and pulled that one off the lot. We didn't dare to just leave it on the bank parking lot. Nobody was there. They pulled it along the street and left it setting, and they went back later on and started it. They were going around the bank the wrong way. The cops came out and told them, you can go around as often as you want, but turn around and go the other way!

And they had all these signs on the tractors [during the demonstration], "First Foreclosure Bank," and with real cute sayings on them. And they had these signs all over, picking on them. When the people were arrested, they had passed out these red armbands, and whoever wanted to be arrested had a red band on. There was a baby about two months or two and a half months old. They even had a red armband on her. But they didn't take her fingerprints 'cause they said she was too young to be arrested. Tom [the Kohnens' lawyer] says, "Let's go fly to St. Cloud and see what's going on." Gerry says, "I got to go home and milk cows," so Tom and I took his plane and flew to St. Cloud.

That night we had a bunch of people here [at the farm] again. They planned what we were going to do next. This Bill decided we should have something here on Saturday [after the sit-in]. He said, "There's more people in trouble than you realize, and when this hits the paper, there's gonna be people who're gonna understand what's going on. And they're gonna want to know what's going on. They're gonna want to come out." I went on several radio stations during the week and told people we were going to have open house for anybody that wanted to come and discuss what was going on, and anybody that wanted to come and see the farm or anybody that had any

201

problems. I don't know how many we had. I suppose, during the day, there was a hundred people that came in and out.

Archbishop Speltz was here. Father Torberg had called on Saturday, and he said, "Would you mind getting a couple of the neighbors in? Archbishop Speltz wants to come out and see your farm and just see what's going on." And I says, "We don't mind." Then I was in a dilemma because we hadn't told the ones that Gerry is the closest to. We figured we'll just file Chapter 11, and when people find out, they'll find out. No big deal. We just hadn't said nothing to them. We hadn't even told them we were having this deal at the bank because we just thought you don't advertise your business. And then, all of a sudden, here it was, Father Torberg wanted us to get a couple of our closest neighbors in. I just didn't know who the devil to call. So finally I got bold, and I went to the phone and I called Rosie and Andrew Kelsen, and I said, "Would you mind coming down and sitting in Sunday? We're having trouble with the bank, and Archbishop Speltz and Father Torberg want to come out. They're going to pick up Father Tim, our parish priest, and come out on Sunday, and they want to just talk to the neighbors, and look the farm over and see what's going on."

And they said, "Oh, no." They just couldn't believe what was going on. And I had to explain a few things. I thought, oh, heck, I'll just break down and call Swensons, tell them that we're having problems. I'm sure they weren't aware of anything going on. So, of course, I had to explain to them, and they were glad to come down.

Father Torberg and Father Tim and Archbishop Speltz came out. We all went into the living room, and Archbishop Speltz asked a bunch of questions. He did ask about a few things about us. He satisfied his curiosity that the farmer's getting a bad end of the deal. Whatever went on that Father Torberg wanted to sit in on or do, he could.

There was another celebration at the Kohnens' farm, on September 20, 1986. Stalled in its foreclosure efforts by the Kohnens' Chapter 11 (reorganization) bankruptcy, First Bank finally renegotiated the loan by settling for a $50,000 buyout on a $137,000 obligation. The Kohnens then refinanced their operation through the First National Bank of St. Martin. From throughout the state, friends, neighbors, and COACT and other farm group supporters gathered at the farm. They claimed it as their own, as well as the Kohnens', victory.

With a Car and a Placard

BOBBI POLZINE
Brewster, Minnesota

In the aftermath of the well-known 1960s' NFO protests in which she participated, "my own activism quieted down," Polzine admits. "It was limited to working politically, keeping track of the voting records of legislators, going to the polls."

But early in 1982, she says, "I was at a Democratic-Farmer-Labor state convention in Duluth. I'm listening to farmers trying to explain to legislators what the root causes of our problems are on the farm. The legislators just couldn't quite understand what the problem was." With Norm Larson, a friend who was Nobles County DFL chairman, and Burt Henningson, a professor of agriculture history at the University of Minnesota at Morris, she conceived the idea of initiating a series of raw materials economics seminars to educate DFL candidates and officials. She began to call these people off the lists, around the state, and arranging times and places, with Henningson and Larson to conduct the seminars. A number of the seminars took place with good attendance until, finally, the opportunity arose to conduct a private seminar with DFL gubernatorial candidate Rudy Perpich, who was then challenging incumbent Republican Governor Albert Quie. It was to take place in St. Cloud.

WHEN we met in the St. Cloud hotel, I told him I had an idea for marching on the governor's mansion. I said we should march on the governor's mansion and demand a moratorium on farm and home foreclosures. He kinda chuckled and thought that was a great idea.

I called COACT one day, and they were planning a protest down at the capitol in the rotunda. I said, "Why don't we march on the governor's mansion and demand a moratorium?" The idea grew. By the following Monday morning, they called up and said, "Hey, we've arranged a bunch of MCT buses to come down and pick us up at the capitol and take us to the governor's mansion. And guess who's going to stand up there and be the spokesman and demand the moratorium?" I was scared to death. I'd never done anything like that before.

So, with COACT leadership on one side and Dr. Henningson on the other side to hold me up, I'm standing there screaming at the governor's mansion: "We demand a moratorium on farm and home foreclosures!" And they dramatically took the red bandana off my arm and tied it on his gate. The governor was not in his mansion, and he was not even in the state. We didn't care. The media had picked up on it, and the ball really started rolling. We went from there to a bank in Minneapolis. They were the largest holders of farm loans in the state. We marched in the building and demanded to see the president of the bank. Of course, he wasn't in, and if he was, he wasn't about to come out and talk with us. So I left another calling card—another bandana. Pretty soon, they all started giving me their bandanas, so that any place I could go I could leave a calling card. We started pushing really hard on the moratorium and coupled it with minimum price because moratorium was only going to be a stall tactic. It wouldn't bring any long-term relief.

After the election, I started pounding on Governor Perpich again, telling him the farmers are going down in great numbers. He had called on the agriculture commissioner, Jim Nichols, to put together a study. The governor came down here to Worthington. I was driving him around, and every time we'd get in the car, I'd say we need a moratorium because all these farmers are being foreclosed. He said, "Now, that isn't true. I got the results of Jim's report, and he said there were only four foreclosures in the whole state last year."

I said, "That's in the report?"

"That's in the report if you want to see it."

I said, "If Jim Nichols said there were only four foreclosures in the whole state of Minnesota last year, he's a goddamn liar." At this point, we're in the airport, and Norm Larson is standing there. He kind of went into shock: "You can't talk to the governor that way!"

And the governor said, "The hell she can't." This brought it down to a humorous level.

COACT decided that they would help in this, and this led to further protest actions. I went to a COACT meeting up in Lincoln County. They called a crisis meeting. There were several being held across the state. These crisis meetings were bearing out more and more what I knew had to be the truth: that the gravity of this situation was just overwhelming. The strange thing about these was finding a way of drawing the people out, and they really had gotten it down to a science. If you had a crisis meeting, you would start advertising that there was going to be a farm crisis meeting at 8 on Monday night at the township hall. The speaker would be Joe Blow, and we would be addressing moratoriums on foreclosures, bankruptcies, pricing structure of commodities, etc. Well, about six people would show up at the meeting. You would have a second meeting on a Monday night, one week later, in the same town hall. Same featured speakers, same issues. Sixty-six people would show up. At the first one, those weren't local people. They came from fifty or a hundred miles away when they heard about the meeting. They got down there and all six people looked at each other and said, "My God, Joe, if I'd known you were coming down here, we coulda rode together." He says, "I know, Herman, but I thought I was the only farmer in trouble." Word got around town, and at the next meeting there would be sixty-six people.

We had a very fine example at a meeting in southwest Minnesota. I had asked, "How many of you are dairy people?" Almost all hands went up. "How many of you are financially distraught?" The same hands went up. They were all in trouble.

Lincoln County happened to be the home county of the commissioner of agriculture. At the first meeting, the sheriff, Abe Thompson, got up and gave a short talk. He was pleading with these people. "Now, you have to be sensible about this. There's a lot of trouble out in the countryside, and we don't want any violence, and I don't like to be called out at night when a wife is calling and saying, 'John went out to the barn, and he....' I never know if John's going to come back from the barn."

I got together with Sheriff Thompson. He happened to be the person in charge of serving foreclosure papers and notices on the people in his county, and I asked him to put together some numbers, and he did. There had been fifteen just in his county the year before, so I knew the commissioner's figures had to be off in his report.

Governor Perpich did get my message that there were terrible things happening out here. He went ahead and put together a farm crisis commission in March of 1983, and I was notified that I was going to be appointed. One of the first things I did was to challenge the report for lack of credibility and offered some documentation, some of it coming from Jim's home area.

After the workings of the crisis commission, I started getting invited to many political functions, speaking engagements, all kinds of protest groups and farm organizations.

In April 1983, the North American Farm Alliance was organized as a loose confederation of many major state and national farm groups seeking reform of farm policy. By that fall, it was getting its feet wet as an activist force and organized some rallies, including one in Waterloo, Iowa, where farmers donated sausage to the unemployed. NAFA also sought to develop an alliance with iron workers in northeast Minnesota.

It was decided that someone should be sent to the Iron Range to see if we could get support from some of the strong unions there. Lou-Anne Kling and I were volunteered by NAFA to go to the Iron Range. We had a very good contact up there with the unions and set up all the meetings with the union heads and union membership. If we could agree on a few basic principles, we could issue a unity statement that would be signed by farmers and labor. The union people only knew that there were two farmers from southwest Minnesota coming to the Iron Range. They were looking for two men, and I think they were caught off guard when two women walked in. In starting the dialogue with the people up there, I think there was probably more disinformation or misinformation than lack of information, and this I credit a lot to our major newspapers here in Minnesota. Perhaps farmers around here think iron miners and steel workers are highly paid workers. I do not care what their wages have been. I only know, in a way, I feel responsible for the fact that these people no longer have their jobs, that the mines are closed, and shipping is shut down, and the plants have cut way back, steel mills have closed and turned out their working people, tractor plants have closed. The farmers are the largest customers for iron and steel. When the farmer lost his purchasing power and couldn't buy tractors and machinery, it backed up all the way to the iron mills and shut everyone down. These people were suffering very badly with no jobs, no benefits, and now they're being foreclosed en masse on the Iron Range. So we got the dialogue going, we got the statement, we made some very fast friends. Lou-Anne and I had the distinct pleasure of delivering a statement to the governor's desk which said, "We in the iron mines understand what the basic problem is. We would like some short-term job programs up here to tide us through, especially through the winter months when things are very bad. Please don't funnel millions and millions of dollars up here to retrain and relocate us. We will try to tough it out with our farm friends to get the price for their commodities to restore their purchasing powers, so we will have our big customers again."

Lou-Anne Kling and Bobbi Polzine left the Iron Range to visit north-west Minnesota at the invitation of a local farm survival committee.

There was a five-county area up there that had separate three-, four-, and five-year disasters by weather. They had suffered some drought, usually too much rain or not enough rain, and these people just had exhausted everything. They had burned up their equity. They had pursued every avenue politically, trying to get their legislators to get them designated a disaster area. They weren't getting disaster loans. As a matter of fact, they not only were denied that, they were just being foreclosed on, and no mention was made. Living down here in the bottom quarter of the same side of the state, you'd think that we were in foreign countries. I have to admit that as involved as I have been, as many places as I've gone, as many people as I have met and worked with, I wasn't even aware that this disaster area in that corner of our state even existed. At least not to that degree.

So we went over there and ended up staying three days, and we took a swing through some of the Indian reservations. Having gone through what I've gone through now, I've often remarked since that time that I think I feel very much like the Indian leaders of old, when the chiefs tried every avenue they could, everything failed, they tried fighting every way they could, and slowly but surely, and then, toward the end, an accelerated process, the chief stood there and watched the people being driven from their own land. They'd seen the land taken away from their own people, and they were relegated to lands where you could raise nothing but poplar trees, your voice, and a little hell. But no crops.

207

Lou-Anne Kling, by this time, was on the verge of launching her Farm Advocates program with assistance and sponsorship from the Minnesota Department of Agriculture. The two being close, Kling successfully prevailed on Polzine to be part of the program, but the marriage of Bobbi Polzine with bureaucracy was an impossible one. Her main sticking point was her feeling of being muzzled as a representative of the state government, which, like most governments, is seldom comfortable sponsoring protest. While some have criticized her as a loose cannon or uncontrollable showboat, she says she felt a basic conflict between representing farmers and representing the government, although she thought they should be the same thing. The break came after only a few months.

I got a call that there was going to be a sit-in at a PCA office in Austin. Norm Larson went with me, and we drove to a meeting at a church in Austin. Someone had "cased the joint." This was in the dead of winter, piles of snow everywhere, and it was cold and kind of fun. First instructions were: anybody that's driving, put your car into a snowbank head first, set your parking brake, roll all your windows, and lock your doors, so you can't be towed. They'd have to pull you backwards. The next thing was, when we approach, walk very quickly and quietly around the side door and get as many people in there as you can before they slam and lock the door.

We went into the office to negotiate. There must have been between thirty-five and forty people, and it was not a large office. It was quite cramped, in fact. One woman carried her baby in there—diaper bag and all. The rest of us entered the office with sleeping bags, thermos bottles, lunch boxes, dinner pails, so they soon got the message that we weren't about to leave until we got our way. It was all very peaceful. They tried all the little tricks, like going in the next room to make phone calls. But there was someone on the outside who already knew where all the phones were, and they'd look through the outside window to a darkened room. They had memorized which buttons would light up if they called a national, a long-distance call, if they called the district man, so they knew where they were calling by looking from the outside into the office.

When they tried the threats of, "You leave or we're calling the police; we're warning you that you're trespassing," they did call, and the police did come. In preparation, the priest that was with us sat down on the floor and started singing protest songs and leading

208

everyone in joyful song, very peaceful and very entertaining, in fact. All the police found was a group of very peaceful people, sitting on the floor, just humming and singing this nice lullaby. They left, much to the consternation of the office personnel. When closing time approached, the media was really in there heavy. They had lots of TV coverage, good newspaper representation.

The hour kept getting later, and we started eating our lunches, sharing things, dragging out bunches of grapes and cheese curls. You start bringing out the really good storables like chunks of sausage, dried bread, and beef jerky, and they see that you've brought nonperishable food, your thermos, and your pillow, and you're not going to go anywhere until they negotiate. They agreed to negotiate, and we started working with them. They'd break down, and we'd start eating a little more and start talking about what we were going to do through the night, hoping the baby had enough diapers. Negotiations would pick up again. The joke on the media was that we hadn't gotten all the concessions that we really and truly needed to call this a successful negotiation session. We left right after, with all the intentions of being back well before opening in the morning to give the appearance we had indeed stayed overnight. Some of them did stay over. I came back home that night. In the end, the case was settled rather amicably.

There was a great deal of publicity over the next few weeks that brought a lot of support. This is the point where things started heating up with the lenders. They had always been in the driver's seat and just called the shots. Farmers had never known that they had borrower's rights. A lot of this was used later in other offices.

American Ag in Kansas had found out about a specific case where a black couple from Nicodemus, Kansas, was being unjustly foreclosed on. They were going to lose their land, they had already sold some of their equipment and pared back their operation. They wanted farmers from other states, and being with AAM—and them under NAFA's umbrella—I was obliged to drive to Nicodemus, Kansas.

Nicodemus is a very unique place. Only weeks before this action, the town had been lauded and honored and entered into the *Congressional Record* for having been an all-black town, built by black people 105 years before. Black people who had found their new freedom as slaves came from the Deep South to the center of Kansas and literally started with their hands and a handful of crude implements to clear the land and till the soil, and this town grew up. It was a

209

lovely town. They had their own school, they had lovely little churches, they had a downtown business area, they had a city park with a monument erected to the black people who had built this marvelous oasis in Kansas. Then they watched it start to degenerate and regress as a town that was going backwards in time. I did learn that black farmers were being foreclosed at a rate of three to one compared with the white farmers.

It gave some odd appearance when I came back from Kansas. They had no news of a protest action down there, and they see all these stickers on my car, saying "Save the Black Farmers." They look around, saying, "But there are no black farmers in Nobles County."

We had great hopes for pulling off a successful protest stopping the foreclosure on these people's farm, and we planned it out quite well. The night before, we had a meeting. We were very cautious there wouldn't be any "plants" there. When I first arrived in town, we met at the Baptist church, beautiful little church, and we had some coffee and donuts and very, very good speeches. Wayne Cryts showed up down there, Merle Hansen, Carol Hodne, Roger Allison, a group of wonderful people, and we all got together and had our meeting and later met over at the town hall. We ate outdoors, some of us slept outdoors, some slept in the park to watch for people coming into town. I slept with a bunch of mixed bodies on the floor in the Nicodemus town hall, and I got up very early in the morning. I didn't sleep very long that night. We'd stayed up quite late, practiced our strategy for the following day. We were anticipating some forces to oppose anything that we would plan. There was no problem agreeing that it had to be as we've always wanted it, totally nonviolent, that if anyone had any violent ideas or tactics, just forget it. We didn't want anyone even there that could be capable of it. We planned our strategy the night before, and the women began to practice their move. The women were going to manage carrying their very long banner. I don't even remember what was on the banner, but I do remember what we intended to do with it. The women would be leading the front line. We were going to march as we always do, with the American flag, singing traditional songs, things that probably characterize us best, like "God Bless America." We were going to march from the park to the courthouse the next morning, the flag preceding us, and Bernard and Ava Bates and their family would be walking in front to go to their foreclosure sale at the courthouse. The banner is a long sheet rolled up with the message on it, but if you

210

held the banner up and actually released the folds on it, it would be, I suppose, five and a half feet to the ground. The women had practiced the night before on a couple of dummies, but if we could get the sheet between buyer and seller, if we could manage to "depants" the gentleman, we didn't feel he would be in any "position" to buy or sell this black family's farm.

We had figured in our element of surprise, but we hadn't figured in the element of surprise they had planned for us. I got up early the next morning at 4:00. I got up and wandered into the city park and took a pseudo bath under a hydrant, brushed my teeth and brushed my hair, and noticed a red pickup truck sitting in an intersection. I walked over far enough to see. It was still quite dark, but I could see three men sitting in there with farm caps on, and two other caps for sure were American Ag hats, but I didn't recognize the faces under them. So I went back into the hall and woke the people and told them I thought we had company out there. I wasn't sure what they were up to, but I thought they were going to be out there to greet people coming into town for the protest action, and I knew they weren't our people.

I was right, but they had bases covered, too. They'd driven over to another town with PCA offices, a larger town, and they'd sent some people over there to keep an eye on things. They slept on benches in the park. I had all the comforts of home on the floor of the township hall, and they knew that this red pickup had left this other town with some people in it, and from somewhere they had bought American Ag hats, and they were sitting there as greeters. But it was mostly to keep an eye on us and see who was coming in. I suppose they figured it would be the leading activists from around the country.

We started our march through the streets. We went to Hill City by car caravan, with our signs, to their city park and assembled there and then marched up the street with our banner and flag and singing, a very beautiful and peaceful bunch of people. I remember the peaceful feeling when we did sing our songs and march with our flag down the street to save these people and their farm.

The courthouse is an ell-shaped building. They had put up the stand, a little elevated podium or stage where the business of buying and selling the farm was going to be conducted. I didn't notice too much as we approached, except that behind this line of trees leading up to the area in this courtyard, there were lines and lines and lines of police and patrol cars. Just in going by, you could see from the

211

numbers on the license plates that they were from different areas, all coming into town to watch this fistful of farmers out to do battle. Then, as we got closer, we could see the SWAT team, fully uniformed SWAT team. I don't know how many there were at the time. There had to be a thousand, but I would say of the police that were there and the SWAT team, at least 150, and on three sides from this dais they had put up in the corner, there were uniformed SWAT team members at arm's length, just perfect formation. They were helmeted, they had revolvers, nightsticks, tear gas canisters, tear gas bombs, tear gas guns, and I wonder why they didn't bring out dogs to turn loose on us. Past that was an unsettling feeling, as you looked up on the roof of this one-story courthouse. They had an equal number of people up there, I believe. I didn't know about the rifles on the roof until Senator Ernie Chambers[1] had arrived late for the proceedings, and he saw them, when it was over, taking the rifles off the roof of the building, coming out the back of the courthouse, so we knew they had been up there. We could see all the other guns and ammunition they had up there, plus they were videotaping our faces. Needless to say, it would have been futile when we're standing up there, no matter how long our sheet was, if they were looking down on us, to depants anyone or even crook your elbow. My God, there were times when they would hear a shutter on a camera, and all heads and eyes would turn. Everybody was just on a total alert, thinking a cocked rifle.

It's impossible for me to believe that they could think of the farmers in this way. The farmers don't go to town for a protest action armed with anything more than a protest sign, and you're not going to hit anyone with a little flimsy stick, not matched up against nightsticks and tear gas guns. Mace canisters they had. And while we were standing in that corner, we had hardly gotten through with our little statement we were allowed to make when Darrell Ringer[2] got up and presented them with our flag. They treated it like a hot potato, passing it back, trying to get rid of this damn thing. We presented them with an American flag and reminded them that we were there to see that justice was served, but that this is what they were hired to do, too: justice, simple justice. They're there to prevent and

---

[1] A black Nebraska state senator from Omaha.

[2] An American Agriculture Movement leader in Kansas who has twice run for Congress in the First District as a Democrat.

protect. They better be preventing and protecting for the farmer, too.

After we got into the corner there, we knew we were surrounded on three sides, and looked up and saw all this heavy artillery, for Pete's sake, on top of the building and, if you turned around, you could see the fireman pumping up the high-pressure hoses behind us. We were trapped, and there was very little we could do. I still contend, and I think everyone does, that the sale itself was illegal. They didn't take anyone else's bids. They didn't have any answers for us. We went away, not really too sad. It still was a victory in that so many people cared and came from so many miles, driving 1,500 miles or 15 hours to get down there in support of this man and his family. Many local people stayed quite a ways in the back, which really looked nice. It's like the farmers came in waves to support these people in their hour of need.

The following year brought with it a political campaign. In Minnesota, there was only one Democratic aspirant of consequence from the beginning: Walter Mondale, the native son. But even Minnesota farmers had another avenue for attempting to influence the party's stance on agricultural questions during the campaign. Texas Agriculture Commissioner Jim Hightower had organized hearings around the country to gather grass-roots testimony for use in formulating farm planks for the party platform at the convention in San Francisco. One of those was in Springfield, Illinois.

The ag leadership of the whole United States was invited to come to Springfield and put together concrete proposals for the 1985 farm bill. This was for the Democratic ag plank in the national platform. Geraldine Ferraro was chairing that day. Did you ever hear how she gaveled us down?

No.

Well, there were a number of workshops down there on the agenda. Some of them were price and supply management, income, farm credit, food quality and cost, ag research and development, world market, hunger and nutrition, soil and water conservation. In all of these workshops, the same basic message was coming back. Even in soil and water conservation, the greatest detriment to soil conservation is low farm prices because the farmer's forced to mine the soil, trying to make up in volume what he lacks in price. This same message was coming back over and over.

213

In getting into the workings of their panel, they had a number of leaders from different farm organizations coming up to testify. It was really good. They were all saying very basically the same song until we came to the Farm Bureau. This man got up, and he started saying the Farm Bureau's idea was not to raise commodity prices, my goodness, why, this would be the worst thing. They had their own program whereby we should subsidize the poor countries to buy more of our exports cheaper, in other words, break everybody on both legs. This is ridiculous. So when he started talking on all this, and this garbage is spewing out of this man's mouth and into the microphone, about 250 people get up.

We got up and walked out and went into the hall and, just as if it was planned, which it wasn't, a mighty cheer went up. I assume Geraldine told them on the inside of the room to lock the doors, bar the doors. So we were stricken from going back into the room until this Farm Bureau person had finished his testimony. I don't know if they thought we were going to come in and perhaps depants him, but when he finished we were allowed to come back into the room.

She felt the need to reprimand us like children or remind us that we had bad table manners. She was saying, "This man came here to speak, and we have the courtesy to sit here and listen to all of you, and this gentleman gets up to give his opinion, his philosophy, and you get up and you walk outside and you cheer." And there was cheering going on around the room. You know, we just kinda went "Yeaaa" and applauded ourselves, and she gaveled everything to a halt and called on the next gentleman to speak. It happened to be a gentleman from the labor union, I think it was the AFL–CIO, and he spoke right back to her, and he said, "Listen, if I wasn't serving on this panel, I'd have gotten up and walked out with the farmers in support of the farmers. I don't blame them."

Then she gaveled him all to pieces, so she didn't make a terrible big hit that day. Later, when we find out it comes to the committee platform meetings, and they just take all of our work and our feelings and our needs and our input, crumple it up and just discard it in the wastebasket, they have discarded in my mind and in my eyes the American family farm system. They chucked it in the garbage.

I wanted to get to Mondale or have somebody get to him to come out with a workable alternative. During his campaign, we had pressured for a very long time before we could even get our hands on anything related to ag issues. Finally, it came out and I read it, and my first remark, when asked my opinion, was that it had all the substance of diluted puke.

I had tried every conceivable way to get to him. We already knew at the state convention that Mondale was not going to be coming into the state. He was not going to be bringing materials in. I even warned my own people down here, "You know you aren't even going to have Mondale materials for your county fair," which they didn't—nothing arrived.

Anyway, the day before he and Geraldine Ferraro were to go to his old home town of Elmore, Minnesota, about a 2½-hour drive from me, I got a call from the NAFA office. "What can we do? He's going to Elmore; is there any way we can get to this man, any way we can talk to him and talk ag policy?"

I said, "I can't think of anything. Give me an hour and I'll see what I can cook up. This is awfully short notice." So I called them back a little later and said, "I've got this idea. Could you get me a bunch of Mondale posters? We'll put them on sticks and make signs, and then we'll put pieces of masking tape in a big X across Mondale's mouth, and one way it will say, 'FARM CRISIS,' and the other way it will say, 'FARM PRICES.' "

Well, it never came to fruition because nobody could find any Mondale signs. There wasn't a lot we could do except go to the little picnic and hand out materials, information packets, mostly *North American Farmer,* the new newspaper of NAFA. We handed that and some other printed sheets out, and it cost me half a pack of cigarettes. Just lucky for me that Mondale's staff smokes, and they're standing out in the street watching out for the staff cars, and they all ran out of cigarettes. So I swear, for every cigarette I handed out, I at least got to put an information packet on the seats of the cars. I know they left them there because I checked later, so Mondale and Ferraro, and even Joan Mondale, would have to get in the car and either sit on the packet or read it or put it in their lap.

We got that far, and apparently the staff did tell them that they were going to have to mention the word "agriculture." He'd gone all through his major speech for the media, hadn't said a darn word about the farmers or the problems, and then we got over to the press conference and it was almost panic time. We weren't sure we could get anything done yet. They went over to the church, and it was pretty hard to get near him anywhere in there, but, in the meantime, Julie and I both had very good interviews with the *St. Paul Pioneer-Press.* I never did see if anything came out in the *St. Paul Pioneer-*

Press, but the *Minneapolis Tribune* did quote in part a statement that I had made, which said basically that Mondale should be blushing with embarrassment to come back to his home state where there are 24,000 financially strapped farmers, and he's not even mentioning the word "agriculture." He did at the press conference say things like, "Yea, I support the rural sector because farming is important," big ideas like this.

Many in the farm movement maintain that Bobbi Polzine is not easy to work with. Throughout the summer of 1985, many complained about her unwillingness to support the Farm Policy Reform Act sponsored by U.S. Senator Tom Harkin, and backed by the North American Farm Alliance and many of the state coalitions and progressive farm organizations, such as Farmers Union. She maintained then that the bill's guarantee of 70 percent of parity in exchange for mandatory production controls was not enough—only 90 percent would be sufficient. Farm prices were averaging little more than 50 percent of parity that year.

But for nearly two years, until the summer of 1986, Bobbi Polzine rode the groundswell she helped organize in Minnesota. A movement with that name evolved from a loosely organized series of protests into a semi-institutionalized protest group complete with bylaws, charter, and board of directors. It marched on the state capitol by the thousands to repeat the demands that COACT had made in 1982. It organized rallies and tried to stop auctions. The Rev. Jesse Jackson led one tractorcade, riding a vehicle that, ironically, had a Reagan-Bush bumper sticker left over from the 1984 political campaign. Polzine became Groundswell's co-chair.

Her leadership of Groundswell evolved into a source of constant and considerable controversy by early 1986. Some other Groundswell leaders, like Delores Swoboda and Paul Sobosinski of Redwood Falls, Minnesota, say that her accounts of her increasingly extensive travels took on aspects of fantasy, including claimed requests from forty-five states to organize Groundswell chapters and offers of $5,000 lecture fees. According to Swoboda, members of the steering committee of the largely Minnesota-based organization became increasingly uncomfortable with the national and international focus of Polzine's activities and asked for an accounting of how they were funded, because Groundswell had no such money. Swoboda said Polzine offered conflicting and condescending accounts, particularly con-

216

cerning a trip to Nicaragua, and became even less accountable to the Groundswell board.

By May 1986, said Swoboda, the steering committee gave the Groundswell board a choice: oust Polzine as executive director or accept the steering committee's resignation. The members then did act, ousting Polzine amid charges that she spent too much time on international issues such as the Nicaraguan revolution, lacked accountability, and was primarily a publicity seeker. The ouster was promptly reported in Minnesota news media, which had grown to regard Groundswell as a primary voice of grass-roots farm activism.

Polzine's account of what happened next does border on fantasy. She said the group rapidly took a turn to the right politically after her departure. She also maintained that a number of "illegal" changes in the previously "democratic" bylaws followed in quick succession and that the group became increasingly secretive. She issued such accusations to the news media, including charges that the group was conspiring with radical right-wing farm activist Tommy Kersey, who had organized an armed confrontation in November 1985 to prevent a Georgia sheriff from foreclosing on a black farmer in Bleckley County. Swoboda said that news media fear of such connections, if true, created a temporary reluctance by reporters to stay in touch with the organization—a problem overcome only with patience and time.

Polzine maintained that she expected Groundswell to last about two years when she started, although it is not clear how or why she expected it to die out. Some Groundswell members pointed sympathetically to Polzine's family farm financial problems and impending divorce in 1986 as possible reasons for her inability to work out problems with Groundswell. Some friends did leave Groundswell in protest over Polzine's ouster. And Swoboda made clear that she does not like to "dump on Bobbi" and that she never objected to Polzine's interest in Nicaragua, but felt that a group with a limited budget was owed an accounting as to where its director's travel funds originated.

In January 1987, a far more bizarre development occurred. Some farmers were organizing a protest of a farm foreclosure sale on behalf of a southwest Minnesota farmer. Groundswell was invited but learned that Tommy Kersey had also been invited. According to Swoboda, the organization declined on the grounds of Kersey's planned presence and its fear that responding to such an invitation would only serve to confirm, in the public mind, Polzine's earlier charges that Groundswell had become a right-wing organization. The protest went ahead, but

217

with far fewer farmers attending than might have been the case had Groundswell participated.

Delores Swoboda, Lou-Anne Kling, Paul Sobosinski, and many other Groundswell members swallowed hard that night as they watched the evening news on television. For there, behind the microphone, hugging Tommy Kersey, was—Bobbi Polzine.

"We've had our differences in the past. . . . " she began to explain.

"I just don't know Bobbi anymore," says her longtime close friend and confidante, Lou-Anne Kling. Echoing a complaint offered by other farm leaders, she adds, "The publicity just went to her head."

Parking Lot Protest

CHARLIE PENISTON
Chillicothe, Missouri

May 1986. The parking lot in front of Donne and Katie Donahoo's backhoe, electrical, and concrete business, next to the USDA office building on Chillicothe's Washington Street, hosts tractors with license plates from across the Midwest and beyond. Most have bumper stickers: "Save the Family Farm," "America Needs Farmers." By the street is a portable neon sign: "Farmers Protest Day-73"—the number changes daily—"Honk Here." The arrow on the sign points to the quonset hut shed where a protest "park-in" has entered its seventy-third day, housing local volunteers with support from the Missouri Rural Crisis Center.

The protest began over alleged abuses of farmers by the Livingston County Farmers Home Administration office. Now, says Charlie Peniston, "I suppose there's 70 percent support among farmers" for the action, and "25 percent are down here working" out of the county's estimated 850 farmers. It has already become a cause célèbre *and made the network news with a John Cougar Mellencamp concert.*

Peniston and his family have been here too long to let the farm economy or any unhelpful farm lender push him out of farming. He, 37, and his father raise grain and hogs on 880 acres, of which 317 are his. His forebears came here in the 1830s from Kentucky. He and his wife have three boys and a girl and want to keep the farming tradition going.

OUR young farmers' group has been very active in the past. One night, we couldn't even decide which shoe to tie first because

219

all of our problems are stemming out of this office. We couldn't get operating money. Several of them were going to have to sell out. We talked a lot that night, and the next day we decided to meet at the local coffee shop to talk about this. We met and talked about it and decided we didn't have anything else to lose, so we decided to come down.

David Stallings[1] was very abusive and arrogant and was making our farm plans not work, so nobody could get any money. Of course, we all realize that loans are not the answer. We need prices for our products, but to survive this season we've got to have some money to operate. Then we've got to work on prices later, you know. We met and decided to have a meeting, invite all the bankers, loan institutions, PCA, Federal Land Bank, and FmHA out to the fairgrounds to talk to us about what they had planned and why they was puttin' so much pressure on everybody. I mean, we're the same people, the same land, the same machinery, and we're doing our job. We realize our debt load's getting bigger every year, but it's not our fault that our land prices have fell out of bed, and it's not our fault that we're selling below cost of production, and it's affecting every farmer here in the county, and it's affecting up and down Washington Street, and we wanted to talk to them.

But not a one of them showed up. Not one of them from FmHA, Federal Land Bank, PCA, the banks. We hand-delivered the messages and sent certified mail to Columbia to the state director, and certified mail to district PCA. We done our homework. They had to sign for all these letters.

It was gonna be an informational meeting. We were lost; our hands were tied. We decided to stand up and foreclose on FmHA. They were the main culprits in this area. We pulled in here March 17 with about forty tractors and two hundred farmers, in the rain, and foreclosed on 'em and had over three hundred signatures to ask for Stallings's resignation. Of course, he didn't resign, and we went to the state office the same day and presented the petitions to Mr. Foster. He didn't back up the petitions at all; said Stallings was doing a good job. Stallings has been kicked out of Schuyler County before this, but Foster would never admit this.

Anyway, one thing led to another, and the farmers come into Donne and Katie's office and asked to use the phone one day. The

---

[1]The FmHA county supervisor.

next thing you know, we moved in, and they said, "Come on in." The next thing you know, they said, "Use my whole building." Don and Katie have just been super to us. We virtually run 'em out of their business.

But we've had support all over town. Our agribusinesses and up and down Washington Street—there's just about five names here that you can see that haven't been real supportive to us, and we've got a list here. They've decided they don't need the farmers; we don't need them. We try to trade elsewhere. It's just that simple. The farm economy is really affecting the businesses in this area. On one street alone in a two-block area, there's eleven empty buildings. I can remember not too many years ago that it was plum full of businesses. It was active.

We've been very active in this protest, going to Washington twice since March 17. We saw Danforth, Nancy Kassebaum, Eagleton, Coleman, all the Missouri congressmen and senators. We either saw them personally or saw their aides. We tried to get in to see Dole, and we got into the head FmHA office and saw the third man in charge in FmHA. We went to the National Rainbow Coalition farmers' breakfast.

Of course, before we went to Washington, Jesse Jackson came to Chillicothe and stood up with the farmers, and we had a whale of a rally here that day. There was four thousand people. After we came home from Washington, we had different speakers come into Chillicothe and speak to us. We've had farmers from Iowa and California bring us their state flags and show support to this area and to this movement. And we got hold of John Cougar Mellencamp. He came in here and we had ten thousand plus people here, and it was a really exciting day. It showed the support that there really is out here in rural America.

If we had a president more worried about middle-class America and making it strong, instead of worrying about all these other bombs and missiles, we'd have a better America and stronger America, and we'd have a more peaceful America. And this is our whole deal. I mean, Stallings was the straw that broke the camel's back. He was the man that made the farmers stand up and say, "Enough's enough. We ain't gonna take this no more." And we've got the right to stand up just like any farmers across America. Missouri Rural Crisis Center has been very beneficial to us by coming in with support and helping us with the phones and food banks and distributing food. We couldn't have done it without 'em, but that is really the only banner that you might say we've been under.

221

And this is a crisis center to help people. There's a lot of need in this area. We've gave speeches and had tractor parades in Brookfield and Trenton and Kirksville and Macon, we've gave speeches in Savannah, and I'm going to Marysville. The farmers are hungry to stand up, and they're wanting to know what to do because they've been losing their homes and their farms and their traditions and their livelihood, and they're lost!

They don't know the rules and regulations about filing bankruptcy. They always thought in the past that bankruptcy was a sin, you know, and you don't deal or trade with somebody that's had bankruptcy. You know, he's no good. It's a tool, just like a tractor or a planter is, and farmers got to realize that they're gonna have to use this tool to survive the next two years of Reaganomics because the trickle-down theory is not going to work. It's not working. It's people helping people in the United States. It's not only a farmer's issue, but it's a national issue right now. If we don't start realizing this and waking people up across the United States, two years may be too late for everybody.

Two years ago Reagan carried Missouri. He carried most of this area around here. How much has changed in two years?

I don't know of very many people that you can still interview up and down Washington Street that would say that they voted for Reagan the second time. They might have done it, but they wouldn't tell you they did it the second time.

The vote count says they did.

Right. I understand that. And I understand that the farmers voted for Reagan, too. Fine. But people do make mistakes. Reaganomics is not working. Reagan also said that he would balance the budget. Look what the budget has done. It's quadrupled from what any president in history has done. Reagan tells us one thing and does something else, and he doesn't have real contact with the people that are out here in rural America.

A voice in the background: He's still living in a fairy-tale world.

Charlie: That's right. Eight farmers started this protest right here out of a coffee shop. And see what we've done. We're waking up America. People in North Carolina and South Carolina and Nebraska and Kansas and Oklahoma and Texas and California call us and ask, "What can we do to help? How you guys doing this?" The Minnesota

222

farmers said, "We're afraid to do anything like this 'cause they'll throw us in jail." For so long, big corporations have played the farmers against the labor unions, and the labor unions against the farmers. And they tell the labor unions that because of high farm prices, that's why everything's so high, and they tell the farmers, because of high labor prices, your tractors are so high.

That's a bunch of hogwash! I've visited and been in Austin, Minnesota, and talked to them, the P-9 people,[2] you know, making 8-something an hour, and by the time they take it home, it's 5-something. Hormel had the nerve to ask them for a 23 percent pay cut. You got to realize Hormel made profits of $84.6 million in the last quarter of 1985. And they did that by stealing hogs from the farmers and labor from the laborers. And yet their corporation gets bigger, stronger. Now they want to do it some more. They're not satisfied. You understand, 14 percent of the people in the United States own 85 percent of the wealth. And Reagan and his policies are pushing for these people. But there is another 86 percent of these people that's got the voting power that's gonna wake Reagan up.

When we started this, it was just one man. But after we got to visiting with each other, we realized that our problems are just not that one man. He was a problem, but it was more of a national issue, and it was more of a state issue, and it was bigger than all of us really realized. We didn't really realize that when we moved in here.

We picketed not only local FmHA, but state FmHA and national FmHA. We connected all of them together. And we connected the congressmen and the senators in this area, and we put pressure on them. Every day we set here, we put pressure on them because congressmen and senators don't like any big actions going on with the state office. Jeff City [the Missouri state capital] doesn't like it.

And you've got to remember there's never been a rock thrown. It's been peaceful all the way, and that's the way it's gonna be because farmers are peaceful people. We've just been like a sleeping giant out there. Farmers have been worrying about their own small little worlds. Now, we're standing up. We've changed a lot of things. And we've got more things to change. This is just the start of something that is really expanding day to day, it's getting bigger and bigger and bigger.

---

[2]United Food and Commercial Workers Local P-9, at the Hormel Co. meatpacking plant in Austin.

PART SEVEN
The New Leaders

Grass-Roots Democracy

DIXON TERRY
Greenfield, Iowa

Dixon Terry is no ordinary farmer. After all, how many farmers make Esquire's *list of the influential young men and women who are shaping America's future? How many have played, literally, a constant role throughout the past decade in formulating, strategizing, and organizing a national farm movement that, in its current dimensions, did not even exist a decade ago?*

Ruddy, red-haired, bearded, and usually wearing work clothes, Terry, with his wife, Linda, operates a dairy farm. His operation is organic, and he believes farmers need to experiment with alternatives to current practices, but he does not believe for one moment that there is any long-term solution without an adequate price for farm products.

He has been active in a number of organizations, serving on the board of the Iowa Farm Unity Coalition and the U.S. Farmers Association. In 1984, he played a role in the Gary Hart presidential campaign during the Iowa caucuses and became a delegate to the convention in San Francisco, where he helped to organize the Rural Caucus to advance agricultural issues.

THE Iowa delegates at the Rural Caucus had put in a lot of work between the state convention and the national convention in San Francisco in terms of pulling together a national caucus at San Francisco. We did a mailing to about 1,200 of the delegates nationally, assembled a list of conveners from six different states, including representatives of the three presidential campaigns:

227

John Stencel,[1] who was Gary Hart's main agricultural adviser, was a convener; Merle Hansen, who was Jesse Jackson's main ag adviser, was a convener; and so was Jim Hightower,[2] who worked with the Mondale campaign. We had another seven or eight conveners who were recognized rural leaders, mostly from the Midwest.

Before the convention started, we were at the hotels, and we did quite a bit of work. In light of that, we were a little disappointed with the turnout we did get. The first rural caucus we had scheduled was Monday morning, the first day of the convention, and about sixty delegates and alternates showed up. And, of course, a lot of the media, a lot of some other people. There was a good group of people. They were enthusiastic, but it wasn't a big enough bloc of delegates to really have an impact on the convention. That was apparent right away. Instead of taking on any platform battle at the convention, we thought it would be more realistic and more fruitful to utilize our time there getting organized with an ongoing rural voice in the Democratic party.

So we met daily before and during the convention. After the first day, we met at 7 o'clock each morning and consistently turned out about sixty people. The second day, the meeting was even better. They were quite enthused about the idea of getting together as rural people in our own caucus. We increased each day and increased the number of states represented in the totals. By the end of the convention, we had about sixteen states represented. And sixteen states in which we had volunteers to be state coordinators for the National Democratic Rural Caucus, in order to make it an ongoing part of the Democratic party. Many of the achievements through the week were decisions to structure the Rural Caucus as an ongoing organization within the party and development and approval by the Rural Caucus of an initial agenda.

We then also elected two national co-chairs, John Stencel and Karen Merrick,[3] of Iowa. It was agreed wholeheartedly by everybody there that we should maintain the Rural Caucus as a national network and continue to coordinate efforts, specifically on the '85 farm bill. Since then, we haven't done a lot to advance the structure of the rural caucus. We've more or less been working on our own in

[1]From Colorado, Stencel is president of the Rocky Mountain Farmers Union.
[2]Texas Commissioner of Agriculture.
[3]Mayor of Guttenberg.

each state, focusing on the issues with the candidates. We hope to maintain it as a national network. We think we'll be an ongoing presence that will lead to the increased representation of politically active rural people, who are going to the convention to raise the rural issues.

In the state of Iowa, we've moved ahead with the Rural Caucus in terms of initiating an effort to make the caucus an ongoing association of rural county parties within the state.

In '84, we were successful as a farm movement in getting the leadership of the Democratic party to take the farm crisis as a serious issue. Mondale never took a strong stand or offered a strong alternative, nor did the party as a whole. Some individuals like Harkin did and benefited from it. It was a reflection of the fact that the farm movement was younger, less well organized, with fewer people involved, but willing to move into the party process, write policy, and hold people accountable. A lot of people were individuals who saw the need, and by the seat of our pants we tried to pull the Rural Caucus together. To be effective, obviously, you have to have your act together before you go into the convention. You're then prepared to exert some influence.

We raised the issue in the campaign. We elevated the farm issue in the media. We got a lot of coverage. We got a lot of rural Democrats to think about it and take that next step and get politically involved. We were able to reach out to a lot of Democrats for future success.

In '86, we saw a lot of that success. That work was essential in moving the Democratic party in '86 to pretty much accepting our position as Democratic farm policy. The Harkin policy was no longer a marginal proposal. A majority of candidates was running on it. Nationally, candidates in farm states were running on it. It decided the balance in the Senate. In Texas, the bill is the focus of the farm issue.

We're making it a central issue in a lot of campaigns. Within Iowa, the Rural Caucus has met again with conventions, and the decision has been made that we should make an ongoing presence within the party. A rural development team has been organized as a policy committee with Arthur Davis, the state party chair, trying to get a representative from each county to serve on this team. A ten-page comprehensive policy statement endorsed the essentials of the Save the Family Farm Act and laid out other long-range goals. Davis and the State Central Committee endorsed this statement. They paid for a flyer, did press conferences, and released this report. They tried very hard to elevate this issue. It's a big change in two years from the cold shoulder. The key again here is organizing. If rural people are going to be effective, you must organize within the parties between election years. We'll see a very much changed attitude toward the importance of the farm vote.

To a large extent, a lot of rural people still are sitting back being cynical about the political process. There's a crisis in democracy in the whole society. If this scenario unfolds with grass-roots activity passing the bill and affecting the policy, it will be a tremendous demonstration of how politics can work in connection with personal problems.

It's a national problem, and we really need something to get people hoping again. People forced out of farming have to be given the hope that we can turn this thing around. We could change this thing dramatically if we just changed this policy. We have had this focus on saving everybody and fighting foreclosure but people think if we lose out, it's all over with. Five years from now, people could be looking at a lot of prosperity.

The greatest problem is demoralization and lack of hope. Everybody has neighbors who cheer you on and do nothing themselves.

You must provide an analysis for how you got here. You have got to show people that this isn't inevitable and show how you take the steps and how it can really happen. Even when they see that, a lot of times it isn't enough to give them hope. If we can give them immediately some camaraderie and moral support and be open with each other and give them some hope, that will help. Right now, too many farmers are staying home and watching TV, and that's what breeds hopelessness. We need to breed a cultural perspective on the rural community as a way of life.

With the onset of the 1988 Iowa caucuses, Dixon Terry, as chairman, geared up the Iowa League of Rural Voters—part of a national group of the same name organized in 1983—to play a role in influencing presidential candidates' farm policies. The group issued a series of five "Presidential Race Reports" during the year before the caucuses, monitoring the development of the candidates' positions and coaxing them into stronger statements on the issue.

The League, in cooperation with Prairiefire Rural Action and the Iowa Farm Unity Coalition, co-sponsored a presidential debate on farm policy in Ames, Iowa, on January 23, as it had done in 1984. It invited all candidates of both parties, but all the Republicans declined, so there was only a debate among Democrats. Of the Democrats, all but Sen. Albert Gore (Tenn.) accepted. Although there were differences among the candidates on specific points, the league and its co-sponsors showed their clout when all but former Arizona Governor Bruce Babbitt advocated the general principle of supply management as a means of improving farm income and terminating the farm crisis. Babbitt attacked the Harkin-Gephardt bill as the "Corporate Agribusiness Act," alleging that it would do more good for corporate than family farms and saying that he preferred a system of targeting farm program benefits to small farmers.

Dixon Terry, who had been a vice-chairman of the National Save the Family Farm Coalition, in January 1988 also became a co-chair of that organization when president Helen Waller resigned, thus increasing again his role in the national farm debate.

Farmers as the Solution

WAYNE CRYTS
Puxico, Missouri

Since becoming nationally famous as the farmer who illegally removed his soybeans from a bankrupt grain elevator in 1981, and then went to jail for refusing to name the farmers who helped him, Wayne Cryts has remained a national spokesman for the American Agriculture Movement and has served as its national president. His protest actions in 1981 led to reforms of the bankruptcy laws that allowed farmers to recover their claims for stored commodities before a bankrupt elevator's other obligations were settled, a matter of sheer survival for many farmers caught in such a situation. But the fines levied against him by a federal judge added considerably to his debt, which stood by 1986 at nearly $1 million.

I'M a sixth-generation farmer. We've got land that's been in our operation since the Civil War. And up until 1977, I'd never been involved in anything. I mean, we worked out there on the farm, and to be perfectly frank, we didn't even associate with people very much. Sort of kept to our farming operation.

In 1977, in the fall, I guess I was like a lot of other farmers. I heard about a bunch of farmers out west going on strike. I thought that was about the silliest thing I'd ever heard, a bunch of farmers going on strike. They got their tractorcades and everything like that. They started fanning out and going to meetings and speaking about what was happening to agriculture. If something wasn't turned around, you know, we was going to lose our family farm system. Finally, some of the farmers got down into our area, speaking, and I went out of

232

curiosity more than anything else because I just wanted to find out what these people were up to. And they were standing up there saying how bad it was on the farm, the directions it was going if we didn't turn it around, what not only was going to happen to agriculture but to the rest of the country. And at that time, I couldn't really identify with them. We had a very strong farming operation.

But what got me involved—when I got home after listening to these people—on our farming operation, we keep an explicit set of records. I can go back to 1956 and tell you what day we planted a particular field, what production cost was and yields, and I just charted our farming operation, and I found out about 1974 we started going broke. But it didn't really dawn on us because our financial statement was looking so much better. I mean, land values was going up. You could buy a tractor one year, and three years later trade it off, and the trade-in was worth more than the tractor. But what I noticed was I was going deeper in debt. I could see then, if something wasn't done, it was just a matter of time until we actually went broke.

And I got involved, started going to Washington, D.C. I got to see some people up there that, in the name of representing the farmers, wasn't. I belonged to different organizations just through doing business or probably had insurance. I got to listening to these people testify. And they wasn't representing me. Then I seen people in Washington, D.C., that set agriculture policy and knew absolutely nothing about agriculture. It was not uncommon to talk to a congressman that had been from a rural area, especially your southern congressmen, and they'd pat you on the back and say, "Son, I don't understand your problem. Why, I made money with 10 cent cotton." See, they wasn't relating to agriculture as it was today, they was relating to agriculture like it was when they was involved in it. They wasn't relating to $100,000 cotton pickers and $1-a-gallon diesel fuel.

And I could see right then that, if the individual farmer wasn't willing to get involved and start representing himself, we wasn't gonna get represented. So we came to believe that agriculture had a political problem, and we wasn't losing our farmers because they were bad managers or because they were inefficient, it was simply because we had government policies that allowed embargoes, bilateral trade agreements with trade sanctions, and an agricultural export policy that was taking away our ability to make a profit.

So that's the direction that we felt that we could change and put agriculture back on its feet: through the political process. We felt that we had a political problem. It was going to take a political solution. We don't have a supply-and-demand market. We believe the free-market system will destroy agriculture because they're saying if you're not a good enough manager, a good enough producer to compete in the world market, get out of business. But in the state of Missouri, our shoe industry used to be our second largest industry, and when they compete under a free-market system, they got to compete with Taiwan or Red China, that gets the equivalent of maybe 60 cent-a-day labor. The only way that we can compete with those countries is if our people are willing to reduce their standard of living.

These are the types of problems that we were seeing, and then we were seeing that the average man in the street was given a false impression of agriculture. They were saying, all right, we raise our prices, we're going to price ourselves out of the world market. But we have seen that the higher the price goes, the more of the share of the market we have. But for the competition and things like that, Argentina, you know, has got a cash flow problem, they're in debt, and they got to get enough money to pay the interest on their debt. So the higher the prices go, the less they have to export into the market, and the more they can convert to domestic uses.

So, it was all of these types of things that we seen had to be changed, had to get the attention of the American people on what was happening, to change that direction.

How would American Agriculture Movement rather see the market structured?

We believe that products have a value. We believe in parity. We have looked back at history, and we have seen that, when agriculture was at parity levels at the marketplace, then not only agriculture prospered, but the whole country prospered.

It's just like the big campaign issue now is to balance the budget. The last time we had a balanced budget in this country was 1974. The reason why we had a balanced budget was because, in 1973, agriculture received 100 percent of parity at the marketplace. 1973, we paid $10 billion in direct taxes. 1983, there was no taxable income in agriculture. That's our experience. What we have got to show the American people and our politicians and our legislators is that agriculture is not a problem; it is a solution to the problem. That's where we direct all of our energy, is to try to put agriculture out there

234

as a solution, and not as a problem. The American farmer doesn't want a welfare check; he doesn't want a subsidy payment. We want and deserve a fair price at that marketplace. But we want a farm bill that puts a floor under our prices, and what we're after is 90 percent of parity because that is the level that, if we have good weather conditions, if we have real good crops, then we can receive a profit, then we can start replacing this wore-out equipment, we can put the equipment companies back on their feet, we can put the people back to work. . . .

What potential does this give you for forming alliances around common interests, say, with labor or environmentalists?

That is something that we're just beginning to work in earnest on. It's just like southeast Missouri. Missouri is the second worst state in the nation for soil erosion. I realize as a farmer that it's not going to matter ten or twenty years from now what the price is if we lose our topsoil.

I like Louisiana, but I don't want to move to Louisiana just because my farm's moving there. And it's really what's happening. We're double-cropping and things like this, and this is the thing that we're trying to get conservationists and farmers to look at seriously: that the reason why we have a continuing increase in soil erosion reverted back down to price to the farmers. Because the lower the price goes, the more we have to try to produce, we're more intensive farming, we're into areas now double-cropping where we never did before. Because cattle was depressed for so long, a lot of people got out of the cattle, they broke up their land, and it's because of the financial situation confronting agriculture.

So if we can get a floor under our price above our cost of production, then, if we do have overproduction, if we feel that supply management has to be tied with this floor, if we have more production than can be used, then we're willing, and I believe the majority of the farmers in this country are willing, to have supply management, cut back those acres that we don't need in production, and tie it to good soil conservation practices on those acres. And halt this soil erosion. And I think we can get the support of the conservationist people and the environmentalists whenever we show them the benefits. But to farmers, these soil conservation practices are very, very expensive. And it's hard to get a farmer, even though he realizes that he's damaging soil, whenever he doesn't have the money, to do what's right.

235

I've had the opportunity to travel all across this country to speak about agriculture, and I've spoken in New York and Detroit, before banker associations and teacher associations and all other kinds of groups, and I've found out whenever you put agriculture in terms that they can understand it, and how it relates to them, they do stop looking at agriculture as a problem and start looking at it as a solution. A lot of people say, well, we raise the food prices, consumers are going to object, but I spoke right in the heart of Detroit last winter. There were people in that audience who were unemployed. They were in soup lines; there was food nutrition people there; there were city councilors. I got a standing ovation out of that audience telling 'em we had to double agricultural prices to American farmers. But I could relate why. And I can show them people why they were unemployed, how we could put 'em back to work, and I said, "What does it matter to you people whether steak is 50 cents a pound or $10 a pound? If you don't have a job, and you don't have any income, you can't buy it regardless of the price. But, if the American farmer makes a profit out there, we can put you people back to work and still produce this food at a reasonable enough cost that you can feed your family and maintain a high standard of living. And to double agricultural prices to farmers, it would raise food prices probably three percent." Well, you go back to the fact that, in a $1.50 box of corn flakes, there's 4 cents worth of corn. So, if you double the price of corn to the farmer, you're not going to double the price.

In 1986, Wayne Cryts, saying that he never expected that he'd have to go to Washington to save his farm, entered the Democratic primary for Congress in Missouri's sprawling eighth district, which stretches from the Arkansas border to within thirty miles of St. Louis. It was clearly a populist, grass-roots campaign, in which he was outspent two to one by incumbent Republican Rep. Bill Emerson.

Emerson had been a sponsor of the bankruptcy reform legislation passed in response to Cryts's earlier protest. Asked why he was now willing to oppose the man, Cryts tied Emerson to Republican farm policies under Reagan and said, "If I had a flat tire, and a man stopped to help me, I'd thank him, but I wouldn't let him steal my car."

Cryts won the primary with 70 percent of the vote. He won 48 percent against Emerson in a race that, he says, saw "our opponents throw everything at us but the kitchen sink." Among those flying

236

objects Cryts found suspicious was the service of papers on him, stemming from his earlier court cases and debts, just fifteen minutes before he was to go on stage in a debate with Emerson in the last two weeks of the campaign. But the 48 percent was encouraging enough, in a race many thought Cryts could not win, that he later prepared for a 1988 rematch. He spent much of 1987 working as an organizer for Rep. Richard Gephardt's presidential campaign.

Jesse's Right Arm

MERLE HANSEN
Newman Grove, Nebraska

In April of 1983, more than a hundred progressive farm activists from across the United States and Canada worked throughout a weekend in Des Moines to fashion a programmatic alliance that could organize around issues common to nearly two dozen farm groups that they represented. In many ways, they were a vanguard, recognizing the severity of a crisis that many farmers were still either denying or wishing would go away. The alliance they fashioned is the North American Farm Alliance, and they chose as its president Merle Hansen. The group located its office in Ames, Iowa, moved for about a year to Minneapolis, and returned, finally, to Ames.

Before his first year in this new role was out, Hansen acquired a new one as the Rev. Jesse Jackson's farm adviser for his 1984 presidential campaign. Jackson's appeals to farmers have continued, and Hansen's close ties to Jackson have grown. He worked for Jackson again in 1988.

THE North American Farm Alliance was formed in April of 1983. Our contribution is unique to the whole struggle, as far as farmers are concerned, because we've defined the farm problem in a different way than any other group has. We've given it some dimensions that no other group has had.

One of the first things that we did was that we had an international conference. The United States is so dominant in agricultural production, exports, and even imports, that we set the world price, and we set the whole game, how the agricultural game is played in the nonsocialist world. And so we had a conference in Ottawa where we had not only the Canadians and the U.S., but we had representatives there from Denmark, West Germany, the Netherlands, France, Italy, the Philippines, and Japan.

We learned a lot at that conference. It confirmed what we felt, that it was an international issue. We found out, for instance, that in the European Common Market, between 1960 and 1980, ten million farmers had been eliminated. It corresponded to what was happening in the United States. We had six million farmers in 1945, and now we're down to two and a third million farmers. We had common problems, and one of the main problems that farmers faced was the total inability to price their products. Also, the increasing problem of increased productivity, both in the United States and the European Common Market, but in many other countries. In some of the third-world countries, the farm problem is a little bit different, but it's primarily the same. An interesting sidelight is that in Nicaragua, they've canceled a lot of debt for farmers, they're trying to get them started, they have long-term, low-rate interest—and the Reagan administration says that one of the things that's wrong with Nicaragua is that they keep their farm prices too high.

We built these international ties, and we also concluded that with farmers as 2.4 percent of the population, with the dwindling number of farmers, we couldn't solve it ourselves. We began looking for allies and looking for other people who were victims, and one of the things that I think that we've done that no other farmer group has ever done before is that, when you examine the farm problem, you have to grant that it is institutionalized inequality and disparity. It has all the classic definition that you want to give to a social justice issue. It is entrenched, institutionalized, inequality and disparity. The farm problem is not a passing problem that just happened to come by the last few years. Never in the history of agriculture have farmers ever received a per capita equality of income with other people in our society, and we've constantly been a victim of the corporate marketing system, which is a system to buy raw materials as cheap as possible. The farm marketing system in 1932 reached a point where corn was as low as 10 cents a bushel, and hogs were 2 cents a pound, and eggs were 7 cents a dozen. All other prices were correspondingly low.

We voted and decided to support the [August 24, 1983] march on Washington for peace, jobs, and freedom. A group of North American Alliance people participated in the march. We had heard that someone else from AAM, Alvin Jenkins from Colorado, had been invited to be on the program. I got ahold of Alvin, and he was going to be in court. We were on the road going there, and I was trying to make some frantic calls, and we'd established some relationship with the committee that was running the march. By the time we got fairly near Washington, I called Alvin Jenkins again, and he said that he wasn't going to make it, so he wanted me to be on the program.

By that time, I had gotten acquainted with Preston Love, with the Jackson group and Operation PUSH, and they were very much interested also in having farmers participate. . . . Jackson was contemplating running, and they wanted to make some contacts with farmers.

So that day, right after the march, I got a hold of Preston Love again, so he gave me the good news. Preston said they had everything lined up for me to be on the program. We arranged to meet him with Jesse Jackson and his staff, and Frank Watkins [Jackson's press secretary] and they were interested in talking with us in connection with the campaign and what our ideas were on the farm question. That was the first time that we met Rev. Jackson. I think we hit it off right away. The thing that really cemented our relationship was our definition of the farm problem as a social justice issue. From then on, we just kept in contact and kept developing a little bit closer relationship all the time.

[Gary, Indiana] Mayor Hatcher had written to me and asked me my opinion about Jackson running. I replied to that, and also developed a pretty good relationship with Mayor Hatcher. Then he [Jackson] made his announcement. I think it was on November 3, and I was in Washington for that and participated in that. Later, he came to Des Moines for the presidential forum there. We spent maybe a couple of days, and by that time, he had taken on some advisers. The other advisers were telling him that they couldn't possibly come out for higher prices for farmers.

We had a real knock-down, drag-out debate over the farm question in the Fort Des Moines Hotel, with the staff and with Jesse. And I wasn't real sure that I won that argument, but Jesse went to a news conference, and I went along with him, and one of the reporters asked him what his position was on the farm question. And he came out and said that he was for 90 percent of parity price supports. He was for a moratorium on farm foreclosures, and he just went right on down the line and never missed a shot. I stood up, I had my Western hat on, I stood up and threw it out in the crowd. And startled the Secret Service.

240

And then, I think it was December 9, we'd arranged a meeting in Great Bend, Kansas, for him. To speak at a college and, also, to visit a farm. Darrell Ringer[1] was in on that a lot. I'd been up in Canada at Saskatchewan, and spoke to the National Farmers Union of Canada. It was 40 below zero when I left. I went down to Great Bend, Kansas, and it was thawing when I got there. Jesse flew in there, and there was a big bunch out to meet him, so he introduced me, then, as his farm adviser. We visited a farm, and I'm really impressed at how quick and sharp he is to pick things up, how he understands these issues. We had a rally at a college there, with college kids and farmers, and he was just super great. People were just standing up and shouting. Farmers just thought he was great. I am still running into a lot of people in rural areas, which would really surprise you, that say Jackson was the best candidate. He not only touched the issues, but he touched a certain emotional chord with a lot of people that feel his sincerity, and there's something real there.

Doesn't the umbrella of the Rainbow Coalition provide a common tie between many farmers and the other "powerless" that Jackson is appealing to, in that all these groups have heard similar justifications for their powerlessness that they are learning to reject?

Jesse had never been to Minnesota in the campaign, and he was up there after the campaign, and they had a big rally up there, and it was a great rally. Every one of these meetings is an emotional experience. And one of the things that people really responded to was when I said that what struck me about the campaign was the commonality of the problems that people faced, and the arguments that they use to defeat people, the things that they use to divide people. Most all of the problems that the Hispanics face, and native Americans, and blacks, and women, and farmers—when you face the arguments of why you are supposed to be where you are, it's just about the same, you know. The arguments that you have to use to overcome your plight are very common, too.

It's interesting that in the Jackson campaign, we were struggling with the platform committee to try to inject into the platform some things as far as the farm issue was concerned. Mainly around those three issues of moratorium and low interest and some kinds of price

[1]An American Agricultural Movement leader in Kansas who twice ran for Congress on the Democratic ticket. He also ran unsuccessfully in the 1986 Democratic senatorial primary for the right to challenge Sen. Robert Dole.

supports, because we had done some research on farm prices, and what determines farm prices is the government price support level. In the last fifty years, with the exception of the drought or corn blight or some severe aberration, the price that farmers get is the price that the government supports prices at. So this is an absolute key issue. It's just like the minimum wage for working people. In all those fights in the platform, the only ones who really held tough were the Jackson people. There was thirteen of them on the platform committee, but every time you could count on thirteen votes. Sometimes, some of them didn't know everything about what they were voting on, but they stuck with the farm issue, and they were on the right side all the way through.

Jackson asked me to give a seconding speech, and way over half of that was devoted to the farm question on national television, and so it's very touching that the coalition really did work. It really did work. I appeared before the National Conference of Black Mayors, where there's 258 black mayors in the United States on record for 90 percent of parity and price supports for farmers, and moratorium on foreclosures, and some long-term, low-rate interest. With those people representing the poorest people in this country having no objection to decent prices for farmers, a good question comes up as to where does all this opposition come from?

Drawing Battle Lines

ALAN LIBBRA
Alhambra, Illinois

Libbra and his wife farm just a couple of miles from the farm he grew up on. His background, he says, is "Joe Average": he studied agricultural economics at the University of Illinois and returned home to Madison County. But, he admits, his college experience probably left him more liberal than he had been and more predisposed to political activism. By the time the Illinois Public Action Council began organizing downstate in 1974, he was an activist waiting for a vehicle. Libbra was already involved in a local property tax assessment issue that drew large numbers of farmers to mass meetings. The resulting publicity drew Libbra to IPAC's attention when its organizer, David Zwick, began scouring small town newspapers for information on local leaders he could recruit to IPAC's banner. Within a year, Libbra was on the IPAC board.

In the late 1970s, IPAC, like some other citizen action organizations, was reconsidering its mission and contemplating direct involvement in supporting candidates for public office. But to be a force in Illinois politics beyond the Chicago area, IPAC needed to build downstate support. That inevitably meant rural support.

WE talked about the farm movement for a long time. One of the major constituencies we lacked, after organized labor came on with Illinois Public Action Council, was farm organizations. They were just almost nonexistent.

We found we were getting ready to jump off into electoral politics, and we're looking at this huge, mainly disorganized, not very active

243

rural part of the state. We just didn't have the contacts yet. And, for the most part, the progressive farm organizations in the state were not all that well organized, didn't have a lot of members. The Farm Bureau Federation, we'd run up against them, just on utility matters and things outside of farmers.

Larry Gallagher was on staff and had been working on property tax-related issues. I sat down with him and Bob Creamer and Janet Kelsey, who was our lobbyist at that time. It so happened that the assessment law on farmland that had been passed a year or two before was about to cause a huge increase statewide in farm real estate taxes. We looked at it, and we said if there's ever gonna be an opportunity, it'll be probably a year from now over an issue that at least gets this thing started in rural areas. So we decided we had better figure out if we could form a model for rural organizing because there really wasn't a book on it. There's a lot of documented and proven methods for organizing in urban areas and metropolitan areas, but rural organizing was just something that was kind of an unknown quantity. So Larry Gallagher essentially moved into my house, and we went about the business of creating a small town rural community organization, a multi-issue organization in Madison County.

We beat around for about a year to get it off the ground and test it out. We took on a tax issue in the county first. Then we took on some railroad crossing issues, and whatever came up. We tried the traditional model of organizing. We'd get a committee together and say, "We need to raise a $30,000 budget, and then we're going to create this organization." And then they [farmers] threw us out. So we had to kind of reinvent the wheel. After about a year and a half of work, we had what became known as the Organizing Committee for Eastern Madison County. It was a name that we adopted when the organizing committee from this organization finally started, and it just stuck.

The original project we took on was an assessment matter, and I had worked with people before on tax questions locally, and it was urban, it was small town, as well as rural, so it looked like a good issue. Larry and I looked at it and said, "Look, the assessment, you know, the tax business has a very definite cycle. And it starts here, there's a time for protest, but it ends on a certain date. So there's no way we can get on to this son-of-a-bitch and drag it out forever, because there's a very definite schedule, and sooner or later it's gonna end, and the issue will end."

So the organization will need something else?

That's right. But what we wanted to do was just get it rolling. It was a good issue. But we didn't want to get stuck on one issue. Unfortunately, in terms of an organizing strategy, when we got in this assessment, it seemed to be a very simple question of equity in your system of procedures, but we got into this big fraud thing. The supervisor of assessments was giving big tax breaks to Shell Oil and Denison Steel, and all kinds of bribe taking, and what we had planned in 1978 as a six-month, real easy, sweet-and-simple organizing drive to get people to protest their own taxes lasted until 1983, ending up with federal and state investigations of the supervisor of assessment, a subsequent indictment, now conviction, on bribery and all this kind of thing. . . . Having gotten the experience doing that, we looked at the upcoming question. What we needed was something to cut across rural areas and farmers in a like way. The issue was the same statewide, and at that point, back in the late seventies, there wasn't foreclosures and bankruptcies. Prices were relatively stable and a lot higher than they are today. Those kinds of issues weren't there, so what arose was another tax question. Very significant one.

Most farmers were looking at 200 and 300 percent increases in their property taxes. It was going to affect everybody exactly alike, so we grabbed it and formed the Illinois Farm Alliance. We went to all the major farm organizations. We were totally unaware of what was going to happen. Explained the situation, pulled together a coalition minus the Farm Bureau. Anyway, went into a two-year project [1980–81] which resulted in landmark assessment legislation in Illinois, which has been copied a lot since in other states. When that two-year project ended, at the culmination of successfully passing a decent piece of legislation, we collectively decided, since this was all planned anyway, to form a structured federation called the Illinois Farm Alliance and to go out and continue to organize. At that point, you know, Reaganomics began to rear its ugly head, and the farm crisis just kind of came. We moved directly into that arena, although we've done some other state legislative stuff like elevator bankruptcy bills.

But in the last couple of years, we've concentrated almost totally on the national issues and farm crisis issues because they're obviously up front. All the other issues are really irrelevant if we don't solve the central question. We have increasingly become more political in

245

nature, and, in fact, the board's stated goal, after the Reagan victory in '84, was by any means to systematically organize a network of leadership and contacts in this state that we could mobilize on either legislation or protest, whatever we need to do, but with an eye for mobilizing it around those issues and around candidates in electoral politics.

That's essentially what we're doing now. We've been involved doing this Farm Congress thing.[1] The most valuable thing coming out of this Farm Congress is the lists, the delegate selection. In the more productive parts of Illinois, we're hurting. They tend to be more conservative Farm Bureau Republicans. The one thing I do like with this Farm Congress scenario is that whoever comes to these meetings, in areas where we don't know a lot of folks or don't have good contacts, we don't have to go in and identify leadership or people who they look to because they're going to identify them themselves. I think that's the one real key to this thing. And then during the congress process, in contact with these people, we can even better refine it. What we should get out of that is a real big addition to the kind of network we're setting up.

You know, it is in the self-interest of the labor unions in the state of Illinois to see this kind of a progressive movement in the rural areas. We can be self-funded to some extent, but there are other contributors, I think, who would be part of that. That's why we need to go into Evans's[2] district, I think, to prove we can do it.

Our approach is overtly political, as opposed to more advocacy— and issue-oriented. In the final analysis, what our board and the leadership within the Farm Alliance have decided is that we'll be advocating for the rest of our lives, but until we at least have some leverage in the legislature—and we do have a lot of leverage in the legislature—the most important thing we can do is to work on the rural areas, the rural electorate, and prove that in a very Republican rural area, we can make major voter swings in that district *if* we have a congressman like Evans advocating the kind of policies we advocate. That was the case in the last election. He did very well relative to what he had done in '82. In '84, he did a lot better in the rural areas. I think he'll do better. We're out trying to reach a predominantly

---

[1]A national assembly of farmer delegates sponsored by Farm Aid in 1986 to draft proposals to Congress on farm policy.
[2]Rep. Lane Evans is a Democrat from western Illinois.

Republican constituency. There is no way that that can be done effectively without candidates like Evans. I mean, we did a hell of a good job in the 20th congressional district in '82. We got rid of Paul Finley, who had been a ranking member of the ag committee, and put in Dick Durbin. Our people did a lot of work for that, they raised a lot of money, contributed a lot. Some people I worked with personally the last five years put $400 to $500 in Durbin's campaign. And they don't do that traditionally. They're not political givers. They felt that strongly about changing Finley.

We can't do that again. We cannot replicate that in the 20th District because Durbin turned around and screwed us on the farm bill debate, when push came down to shove on the Bedell Amendment.[3] He voted wrong. Not only did he vote wrong, he went and did a speech on the floor of the House, and I've got the transcript of what he said, and we'd think Ed Madigan or Bob Michel [Republicans] were in there talking. Now he's destroyed what we had erected in the 20th District because, when we go back, people say, "Well, what the hell are you talking about? You said, if we elect a progressive Democrat, we're going to see a change. And Durbin is doing just like Finley always did!" And they revert back to old habits again.

He not only destroys us, but we sold Durbin on the credibility of our own people in that area. That's the plan. That's our plan. That's the only way it can be done. And now those people's credibility are washed out. Their neighbors call and say, "See what your buddy Durbin's doing?" And I'm irate about it, and he knows it. So are a lot of other people in that district. The problem we have in the coalition is that we have people coming to the coalition meeting and saying, "Not only are we pissed off at Durbin, but we want to beat him."

Then those people are very susceptible to some slick-talking Republican who's wrong on everything but comes in and talks a little bit about parity. Huge mistake by the Democratic party. No discipline. I don't know what else you would call it. The Democrats did not have a clear policy formulated on farm policy. And even when leadership put the word out that the Bedell Amendment was in, they broke ranks. There's absolutely no repercussions from the party for doing that. That is something we have to deal with.

---

[3]An amendment to the House version of the 1985 bill that would have established most of the supply management and producer referendum provisions of the Harkin proposal.

And when we talk about coalition building, there is nothing better than a political campaign to cement a coalition. We get in these meetings in these multi-issued Citizen Action organizations, and there's an agenda for labor, an agenda for disabled people, and we all get together quarterly and we have our board meetings, and we all love one another, and we pass resolutions to show our support, but, in the final analysis, when you're out on the line, when you're in the legislature, when you're in Congress, in committee, you fight your own battles. Farm people may come in and register in support of a trade restriction bill or something like that, but who's out there on the lines? Labor's out there. They're the ones who are going to do the bleeding and dying and raising the money. Farm issues are no different. The culmination of that joint action is in a political campaign. When you can find somebody like Harkin or Evans that adopts the entire agenda, and everybody can then work jointly, one thing becomes important: electing that person to office. Nobody's left out. Nobody voted no on the endorsement, nobody feels like they're having to give up their agenda for the betterment of others, and that pulls it together. There's nothing better in my view than a political campaign where the entire agenda's embodied in one person and ultimately in that campaign. The party elders had better look and see what Harkin and Evans and people like that are doing about pulling back that traditional Democratic coalition. There's no other way to do it.

How do you get those kinds of candidates?

It's one thing, quite frankly, to have Gary Hart come in and espouse the progressive agenda. But those people have to come to us; those positions have to be in their guts. They essentially have to come out of this universe of people, as opposed to going out and trying to find somebody and trying to mold them into your little mold. When we get an Evans who came out of this movement essentially, or we get a Jim Hightower, they understand, first of all, the dynamics of coalition work.

Evans didn't know about farm stuff, you know, he didn't know anything about it. But his commitment is to the people in saying, "These are the right folks, these are the people who have developed my program," and it really doesn't make any difference, I don't think, if it's a farmer or anybody else, as long as they have that kind of commitment and stick to the line. The worst thing is if they start going along to get along. It washes out everything you've done.

248

Some organizations view their goal in life as advocacy and pointing out problems, which include lobbying efforts and taking to the streets, and demonstrations. Our approach is that we have an agenda, and any and all of these tools are available. We use them to mix and match, as it becomes necessary and desirable to do so. In '84, we did the first foreclosure auction, and we did a couple of sale stoppages, but as opposed to Groundswell, and I really do like the folks up there, they see a very functional need to physically stop sales, essentially intimidate the system into stopping what they're doing. And to some extent they've done that. That's only a short-term objective, though. The system will, if not changed, ultimately crush you. The truck of economic change will run over you sooner or later. You can flatten its tires a few times.

So we use those things as we think they advance the goals of changing the people who are making the rules of the game. The two criteria to do legislative work: 1) Are they worth doing on their own? Would they be of value if we got the laws passed? 2) Do they raise the public debate? We choose issues on how they're going to divvy folks up. I hate issues where we let the Farm Bureau get on our side. I hate it. That's one thing farm organizations and people in this movement had to break themselves from doing was, well, who cares who gets the credit? Who cares who you're working with? I don't subscribe to that philosophy at all. The Farm Bureau is the enemy. It will always be the enemy, and therefore you should choose issues that divide them, clearly put them on the other side of the fence, and once they're on the other side of the fence, you ought to throw rocks at them the whole time you're working so they stay on their side of the fence. Because they're good for jumping over at the last minute and mucking up the waters. That's a fatal mistake that farm organizations, the more progressive farm organizations, have made for years.

That's something they did with the National Crisis Action Rally in Ames, February of '85. At the last minute, Farm Bureau, which had withheld its support, jumped on, and then they allowed Dean Kleckner[4] onto the platform.

And when they did, they should've just booed him off. And DeVon[5] should never have got up there, and said, "No, we don't want to do

4National president, but at the time, Iowa president, of the Farm Bureau.
5DeVon Woodland, president of the National Farmers Organization.

that, we want to be respectful." They should've booed him all the way back to his farm! That's a fatal mistake. Fatal mistake. Been doing it for years.

They allowed him to get the good press out of showing up?

Absolutely. You know, we had the same situation when we did that farmland assessment thing. It was a two-year project. They fought us for one year and eleven and a half months, and in the last two weeks, when it was obvious that, hell and high water, it was going to pass and be signed, they come on, they do a big press conference, and people said, "Well, it's all right, you know. We got the job done." They play on our good intentions, so that's one of the criteria we use for picking legislative work. The other thing is: Is there a good issue to organize around? You know, something we can always bring more people onto?

We've had some people leave, saying that we skew things and that we try to stage things so that it's for the best advantage of our friends, which are always Democrats. And it's all true! And the people who somehow have this false sense of fair play in my view are losers. And they will always lose. Because the other side never plays fair. They're never reasonable. And when you go into the thing laying your cards on the table, and always being a reasonable person, always being the one to compromise, you're going to get shafted!

That's never been my personal approach. If you don't win, it doesn't matter! It doesn't matter if you fought the good fight. I'm not up for that, you know, into the valley of death. Martyrs are dead people. And I'm not up for that. You have to win. You have to make a difference. In the last analysis, you have to be able to say we changed this, that, or the other, we put this person in office. And see a substantive, qualitative difference in the process. Just fighting the good fight, if that's all it's about, then I quit. I can fight the good fight by casting my one vote in each election and say I voted my conscience.

The other fatal flaw I see in a lot of the farm movements, that's this: The unwillingness—not the inability, because there are capable people out there, with good leadership qualities, good ability, good communication skills—but the unwillingness to get up in front of their neighbors and friends and say, "This is what I say we ought to do. And this is why I think we ought to do it, and this is why we are going to do it."

There's a terrible void, I think. It has to do, I guess, with cultural

250

differences between farmers and other people and some areas of religious beliefs, but that void is a serious one. They stop short. They organize, they get the people together, and once they're there, they stop.

American Ag and Illinois South[6] organized a big meeting in Greenville about a year ago. Had Wayne Cryts in to talk. There were a thousand people there. A thousand people. Wayne gave a very nice, very lovely speech, but everybody left that meeting with the same thought: He's enunciated our problems, he understands what they are, but what the hell are we supposed to do about them? Who's got the idea? They didn't come there to suggest solutions. They came there with a very definite problem, they heard their problem reiterated, but they heard nobody suggest to them what they could concretely do tomorrow and the next day to change that. And I don't quite understand that. I don't understand why people are loath to step into that void, other than you get responsibility.

[6]A rural advocacy group based in Herrin, Illinois, run by a staff cooperative that initially worked on coal stripmining issues and later added farm crisis questions.

No Time to Lose

ROGER ALLISON
Sturgeon, Missouri

Roger Allison and his attorney, Dale Riesman, left their marks on agricultural law in Allison v. Block, *a December 1982 decision by U.S. District Judge Scott O. Wright in the Western District of Missouri. Wright ruled that the "plain language" of the Consolidated Farm and Rural Development Act requires that the Farmers Home Administration give borrowers notice of their right to seek deferral and that it give them proper consideration for deferral on their loans. Judge Wright also characterized FmHA's "refusal to exercise" its loan deferral discretion under the law as an "abuse of discretion."*

But Roger Allison is not the kind of farmer to retire to his farm after a personal victory. He has grown rapidly as an activist since then. He is also impatient for change and unafraid of controversy. It was Allison who heckled President Reagan at the Missouri State Fair during the 1984 presidential campaign, and to whom Reagan then pointed, declaring to the Republican audience, "I'll raise his taxes!"

In December 1985, he joined in opening the Missouri Rural Crisis Center, headquartered in Columbia, with funds from the National Council of Churches, private individuals, labor unions, the North American Farm Alliance, FarmAid, and other sources. It has done food distributions to Missouri's rural needy and has distributed seeds to credit-starved farmers under the Sow Some Hope program. But for all its services, it is very much an advocacy organization.

I guess you'd say it all started in October of 1980. It was a hundred-and-some odd degrees. I was working on a combine on my farm when I heard cattle bawling over on my dad's place. My dad was going through an appeal with the Farmers Home Administration about a foreclosure on his 365-acre farm that he had just completed a new farrowing and nursery operation confinement building on. My dad was at the doctor's office in Columbia, Missouri, about twenty miles away, and here were all these trucks and all these semi trucks that were pulled up to his place, and his farm and my farm are joined. Our houses are probably about a mile and a half apart.

One of the neighbors called up. There were about six neighbors that were fighting farm foreclosure by the Farmers Home Administration. That area had been hit with droughts and floods, and people were behind on their payments, and then the commodity prices were low, even back in 1980.

So the neighbor called up, and I called Dale Riesman, who was just getting involved with the Farmers Home Administration. In fact, my dad was the first farmer to go to Dale Riesman and tell him about his problems, and Dale was trying to help out.

Dale called back on the phone and said, "Go over there in a peaceful manner, and tell them to stop loading up the livestock and hogs and all the machinery, that you don't want the machinery to go. Or anything else to go." And it turns out that the Farmers Home Administration view of voluntary liquidation is a liquidation where there's no resistance. If they can come in and bluff a borrower into letting his livestock and all his chattels go, well, then, they consider that a voluntary liquidation.

Even if you don't know any better. Hell, none of us knew any better. There wasn't any due process. We didn't even know that we had appeal rights until we started getting into it with Dale Riesman. And so I went over, and there was a deputy sheriff there, and that made it seem official to me. Of course, I'd known Tom Asbury for a long time, and he had known my dad for twenty years and knew my dad had never cheated anybody out of anything and was an honest person and a hard worker. He had raised a good family of kids. There were six of us. He had done everything that the Farmers Home Administration had ever told him to do. I asked Tom what was going up, and he said, well, he was a keeper of the peace. Well, I didn't know what that meant. I just figured that the Farmers Home Administration had him out there to try and make sure that we didn't try and stop them from foreclosing.

Well, what it did mean was, he wasn't there in an official capacity whatsoever. He was just there to make sure that nobody got hurt while they were doing their voluntary liquidation.

And so they opened up this confinement operation of my dad's, which had never had a foreign foot in it, it was completely disease-free, and everybody was real particular about how they went in it. And they had truck drivers and everybody else tramping through the damn place and moving hogs around. So I stood in the middle of the chute and told them that I was resisting the removal of my dad's livestock and that if they wanted to move those hogs, they were gonna have to run 'em over the top of me. And so then, the county supervisor, David Cox, says, whatever you do against me or my assistant, you're doing against the United States of America.

I'm a Vietnam veteran, I've got a Purple Heart, I've got two meritorious citations for things that happened during the heat of a battle, and I was thinking about what this guy said. That's the first thing that came to my mind, and I told him, "I'm not here to do anything against you or your assistant. But I'm here to do what I've got to do. You do what you think you've got to do." At that time the county supervisor had the deputy sheriff arrest me. The deputy didn't want to arrest me. But I told him to do his job, so he arrested me. He took me back to the house. I called Dale Riesman, and Dale lives about thirty miles away. He was coming on because they should have stopped. He had been in contact with the national office, but, you know, David Cox had the smell of victory and blood in his nose, and he was going to go ahead. As a matter of fact, he went up to my farm.

My dad and I shared some equipment. And I had a guy working for me that had worked for me for some time, and he said he didn't know who FmHA was. I wanted to keep him out of all of what was going on. Cox and an assistant drive up to my drive. I've got a half-mile drive, and so this friend of mine, Ed Bair, meets him. And Ed says, "Can I help you out?" And they said, "Yeah, we're friends of Roger's. Is he here?" And they started laughing, you know, it was so goddamned ridiculous that the county supervisor and his assistant started laughing so hard tears were coming out of their faces.

That was the type of mood that they were in. And so my friend told them to get the hell off my property. Anyhow, it came down to the point where they were going to try and move out more, they had already separated the calves, baby calves, and sent 'em down the road, in hundred-and-some-odd degree temperature.

Then it came down to the point where they were gonna move the

254

cattle out. And one guy had had problems with his heart, one of the livestock movers, so he had to leave because he was having heart problems. We told the other truck drivers, my brother's just as big as I am, that it takes sort of a low-rent son-of-a-gun to come out on a man's property and steal his stuff while he's gone. And they said, well, we were just doing a job.

Then it came time to move the rest of the cattle, and I left from the house, and I figured if they were gonna let me go, they were going to have to arrest me again. So when it came down to moving the cattle, it was a standoff between the truck drivers and my brother and myself. And needless to say, you know, the truck drivers didn't decide to press us on putting any more cattle up there. So my dad got there at about that time, the lawyer got there, and things started coming back to order a little bit, and I never forget what my dad told David Cox, the county supervisor. He said, "Your mom should've had you in a snow bank instead of under the porch." We'd been in a battle with this particular county supervisor since 1980.

Well, fifteen days after that, I got a notice from the Farmers Home Administration, David Cox, to come in and review my files, and he said, "We're gonna sell you out." I wasn't gonna go without a fight, and in April of 1981, I received my foreclosure notice. And through the process I found a little deal in *Pork Producers* magazine that said the Farmers Home Administration borrowers may have a legal leg to stand on with this 7 U.S.C. 1981(a) argument. So I clipped it out. I wrote a note to Dale and said, look into this, it could make a difference, and Dale did look into it, and November 1, 1982, I was the first farmer in the state of Missouri to stop a foreclosure of a farm. They were gonna sell it on the courthouse steps. We went to federal court, Judge Scott O. Wright decided that our argument that I hadn't been offered due process was right, and he permanently enjoined the Farmers Home Administration from foreclosing on my farm until I was given the opportunity to apply for a deferral under the 1978 Agriculture Act, 7 U.S.C. 1981(a).

At that time, the courthouse was filled up with farmers, and most of them had already lost their places and had gone by the wayside, and most of them have got pretty humble lives right now. But those farmers were there, I didn't know 'em, in support of me and in support of fighting for justice, and I made a determination that day that I was going to start helping other farmers. I'd been helping out a little bit before 1982, but I got really involved in 1982, and I've been all across the country, and, you know, I've probably done fifteen to sixteen direct actions. Most of them have been major. Whenever a farmer wanted someone to stand up at the courthouse steps with them, I was always there, and always put people together, and I've done demonstrations from as small as twenty-five people crying farmers' cases out on the courthouse steps to as many as fifteen thousand at the John Cougar Mellencamp protest. I stood up for a black farmer in Hill City, Kansas, which I think you're familiar with, back in April of 1983. I orchestrated a penny auction in 1984, where I sold $100,000 worth of equipment for $43 and some-odd cents. And all of it was to educate people that there's a crisis in rural America and that farmers have gotta stand together, and stand tall and ask for justice and demand it, and that what was going on was wrong. It was dead wrong, there was another way to go, a better way to go, and we just couldn't let our rural communities and our whole way of life go down the tube without a peaceful, nonviolent fight. We'd been orchestrating a fightback, really, since 1980.

Now it's a sudden death playoff. We're gonna lose more farmers in the next two years [1987–88] than we've ever lost before, and we've gotta make sure that those farmers fight back and stay on their farms, and they have to drag 'em off their farms. I'm not talking about draggin' 'em off dead, but I'm talking about draggin' 'em out of their houses, and when they drag 'em out of their houses, all their farm neighbors better be right in that house with 'em. It's of importance not only to rural America, but to a democracy as we know it in this country, but when we have consolidation of land ownership that we see going on, all you have to do is look at the Philippines and look at Nicaragua and look at El Salvador and then look at powerless people.

I think one of my biggest attributes is that I feel I've been a leader as far as coalition building throughout the country, where I've built a strong alliance between civil rights groups, labor groups, and farmers. And it isn't a sham. It's a real thing. We supported Rev. Jesse Jackson when he first started running for president. Even before he started running, we went out to Great Bend, you know, with Darrell Ringer. We had a big thing out there before he even announced his candidacy. He's probably been one of the single most important people as far as breaking down racism in this country, particularly in the rural areas. He's been putting the have-lesses and the have-nots and the misfortunates together, to fight for a common cause, and that is to have a certain amount of human dignity, to be able to feed ourselves and our families, have a roof over our heads, and be able to have gainful employment where we feel good about ourselves and each other. Farmers aren't gonna win justice in a vacuum. When farmers win justice, other people in this country who have been denied justice are gonna win, too.

You talk a lot about direct action. How does that fit into your philosophy on dealing with the farm issue?

People have put me off to the side and said I was radical and militant and that I was going to hurt my friends, you know. They aren't farmers themselves, they're organizers, saying that the right wing can come in and, my God, what if somebody hits a highway patrolman? Well, we don't have any choice in this matter but to stand up and be counted. Because, by God, time is running out. I want to go back to my farm and farm. I want my dad to be able to farm. And I want anybody else that wants to farm to be able to have that opportunity to do it. I see these corporations and these monopolies that are taking over. I'm not looking into a fifty-year-long struggle here. It may well turn out to be that. I hate to think about that. But farmers and rural people don't have any choice but to stand up with other people, with blacks, and with labor, and with other people that are gettin' shoved around, and together we make a majority. Direct action—it's just like Chillicothe here. There's a hell of a lot of ignorance going on out here because you've got this administration, and Democrats also, that run out this propaganda that they've dumped so much money on family farmers, but there's no way in hell we can save them.

Well, it's all gone the wrong way. If the farmers had received a fair price in the first place, we would have more family farmers instead of less. And they wouldn't have dumped all that money. But it isn't an issue of money. When Farmers Home Administration forecloses on these farmers, hell, the debt's gonna be written off. Write it off for the farmers; don't write it off for big stockholders and corporations and wealthy individuals that don't give a damn about the soil out here and don't care about whether there's a 4-H club in this community, or Boy Scouts, or a school or a church. They don't care about stuff like that. They look at the bottom-line profit, and if it means that Roger Allison's gotta go hungry so they can eke out a bottom-line profit, they're gonna do it. We have to save these people from themselves.

We've got to save the banks from themselves because they're going down the line of complete destruction.

There is going to come a point in the history of this country where we're not going to take it anymore. And it doesn't mean that we're not going to take it anymore in a nonviolent, peaceful manner. The people are gonna rise up and get justice. I see this as real important that we stand together; not just direct action.

I feel like I'm a well-rounded person. I can go and debate whoever wants to debate the issues. But the hardest thing is organizing farmers. They talk about the Iowa Farm Unity Coalition with this huge, vast number of people. Hell, what do they do? They go to the state legislature and talk about passing a bill that never gets passed. They go to Washington, D.C., and lobby. The only way that's going to be effective is if there's a real grass-roots movement out here that is together and understands what the issues are. In Chillicothe, Missouri, they can understand that this family farm liquidation act of 1985 is going to be the most expensive farm bill that we've ever seen. It's going to be the most destructive of family farmers. We had a farm bill that would've only cost $4.8 billion the first year, that would have done away with government subsidies, that would have ensured a little bit of economic justice for farmers. Why didn't we go that way? Because we're hell-bent to go towards consolidation, to go towards those ten thousand superfarms that government planners and corporate planners are talking about by the year 2000. That isn't healthy for this country, and it isn't healthy for us, as far as achieving goals of social and economic justice.

Hell, the slaves are gonna rise up. One of these days. It may not be in my lifetime, but if it keeps going in this path, they will.

Is there a race against time to line up farmers' support behind a progressive alternative versus having farmers turn to right-wing groups out of frustration?

Yeah, I really do see that. Farmers have had something, and they've put all the money back into it thinking they were going to retire, and their kids and these communities had a future. Now all they can see is depression, depression, depression, where hunger in rural America is pretty rampant. When you've got that vacuum, all kinds of people want to fill that.

Most agrarian movements in this country have always had the right wing flourishing on the fringes, but all the movements have always turned out to be progressive movements. You had Mary Elizabeth Lease, who was somewhat of an anti-Semite. Yet, she also had some progressive ideas, people working together and cooperatives, and so it's a mixed bag. You can't let the right wing scare you into just organizing against the right wing. Hell, you've got the right wing on the outside always passing out literature because they don't want to get their hands dirty. This is too hard. This type of organizing is just too hard to do. They think they're elitist and supremacist. It separates them. Right here in this area, where we're drawing all kinds of farmers, hell, they know who Lyndon LaRouche is. They don't want to have a damn thing to do with him. But in Iowa. . . .

I feel like I'm a populist. Taking control of the government through a grass roots type of an approach. Where you move masses of people toward social and economic justice. There's all sorts of things that fly up through putting those people together, but you can't get worried about it. You gotta keep moving forward.

The right-wingers don't bother me in the state of Missouri. They don't flourish here like they flourish in the state of Iowa, where they've had professional organizers for years that ought to be years ahead of us. And you notice I keep bringing up Iowa. I'm really down on friends of mine that are keeping farmers down and not showing them how they can come together and stand up in a peaceful, nonviolent manner, instead of putting them down for going to a machinery sale and saying, by God, it isn't right that my neighbor's being sold out, and don't bid on his equipment, let *him* buy that equipment. Or standing on the courthouse steps and crying the case about what's going on is just wrong, it's dead wrong. They have got themselves wrapped up in the political end of it where they have become elitist themselves. It's a lot more fashionable to fly to Washington, D.C., and talk to a senator and a congressman or go to a state legislator and do some backslapping and talk about, "We got 8,000 people here and if you don't do this, we're gonna vote you out." They were very successful organizing to get Harkin in, but Tom Harkin isn't gonna change the world. Iowa, the breadbasket of the world, ought to be a symbol for farmers standing together, which it has been in the past. I take my hat off to the Minnesota Groundswell, even though it's floundering now, for what they have done. They're on the right track. You can't forget the organizational part when you do the direct action. And you've gotta keep it so that people feel like they're part of something, and they're tied up with it.

259

I don't mind people perpetuating their jobs, and I don't mind talking about long-term approaches and solutions, but a lot of it is excuses for not moving in 1986. If you take a look back at history, you had the movement in the thirties, the Holiday, and then you had the Farmers Alliance in the 1890s. The Holiday, hell, that was six, nine months, a year and a half at the most. What happened? You saw real progressive politics in Minnesota, and you saw progressive politics in North Dakota. That didn't happen because it was long-term types of things. It happened because people were pushing an agenda forward and it all fell into place.

That's the way that the spark happened with the NFO. Then they lost it. Now, what our challenge is, and what's so important about these direct actions: maybe it will be Chillicothe, Missouri, that sparks the rest of the country to go. Maybe it will be. Or maybe it will be an action that we do in Kansas. Or an action that we do in central Missouri. It's going to be one of these actions where finally we've done the education job, where people have finally decided it's time to pull their head out of the sand and to stand up and be counted if they're ever gonna be counted. We dismiss this myth of us being out here with guns and all this other crap, where in Plattsburgh, Missouri, they beat the hell out of farmers and were vicious. I mean, the highway patrol was vicious about the way that they handled us because we dared to push back, because we were on the courthouse steps and they didn't like us being there.

That wasn't right the way that they treated us—period. And nobody was hurt there. They talked to one highway patrolman. They said somebody hit him on the foot with a hammer. I was right up there up front, and hell, you couldn't begin to bend over. I was sore for three days because of the pressure from that crowd. But it was a nonviolent demonstration. It was a firm demonstration. And it really forged the civil rights groups, the labor groups, and farmers. Boy, that was the first time that they stood together like that, where you had rank-and-file labor people that were arrested right along with the farmers and civil rights group people. And then, to go to stand up at a machinery sale where an old man was losing everything a week later, and the highway patrolmen had gotten their helicopters, and they're in helmets with battle gear, and a hundred deputies parked off down the road, and another hundred highway patrolmen getting ready to come in, and they tell us as we walk by, "We'll see you in Plattsburgh," you know, the second sale in Plattsburgh. "We'll get even with you in Plattsburgh."

That isn't the way that law enforcement ought to act, but it's just like the different movements, the civil rights movement that happened in this country, and the peace movement that happened in this country during Vietnam, where the Chicago police brutalized the hell out of people at the Democrat convention, where Martin Luther King and other people were beat the hell out of in Alabama. It's all part of the same thing. The cops in the city understand a little bit better, and they don't get as vicious, I guess, when these things happen. But it's all part of it.

We did this Hands Across America in Cape Girardeau. They pulled a whole division of highway patrolmen out, a whole division. Because they knew there was going to be trouble. And it was peaceful. Everything we've ever done has been peaceful and nonviolent. But they always want to confront.

We put 2,500 farmers down there. This is the type of stuff that went on because Roger Allison and the Missouri Rural Crisis Center were involved in organizing farmers and rural people to stand together for fifteen minutes and demonstrate that hunger and homelessness is also out here in rural America. They will spare no expense to cloud the issues.

I saw war and I know about violence, and I know about guns and rifles, and I know that there's no way in hell that farmers and rural people are ever going to get justice through the end of a rifle barrel. It's just not going to happen that way. Everybody else I know knows that, too, that we've got to do it through hard organizing and pushing the issues and crying the case. We've got thirty million people in this country that are going hungry, and they want to call the commodity cheese that they only distribute three times a year a surplus. We do have the capacity to overproduce, we certainly don't have a surplus because everybody is not well fed in this country. That's a political decision, too.

I've had a hell of an education since 1980. And a lot of other farmers have, too. I feel real good about what I'm doing. It's hell on personal lives, I can tell you that. It's one thing after another. No matter how organized you want to be, if you're really in this movement, this has got to be sporadic and spontaneous, and it is, and if you're a true leader out here, you're there. You're not in an office from 8 to 5, and "Can't talk to you on the phone until I get back into the office." You can't organize farmers that way.

I feel real good about the Missouri Rural Crisis Center. I got together with other farmers that I'd stood up with on the courthouse steps. All the staff of the Missouri Rural Crisis Center is farmers that are actively farming right now or have lost their farms or are in the process of losing their farms, but the bottom line of the crisis is we're gonna help farmers and rural people resist farm foreclosures. And you can't resist foreclosure unless you can feed your kids and unless you can put clothes on their backs and shoes on their feet and keep the lights going and keep the heat on. There's services out here we've got to make sure farmers get hooked up with, and so we do that. We run a hotline, and we know good attorneys out here, that when it gets down to the point to use an attorney, we're gonna hook farmers up. That's part of our services, but we organize. We organize farmers, and we coordinate. And we encourage—we don't discourage—farmers to stand together to take control of their lives because there isn't a lot of time left.

262

The Meaning of Progress

GARY LAMB
Chelsea, Iowa

In 1984, then-U.S. Representative Tom Harkin hired Lamb as a campaign spokesman for agriculture in his challenge of incumbent U.S. Senator Roger Jepsen. After winning the seat, Senator Harkin then made him an agricultural staffer in his Cedar Rapids office, a position Gary held until early 1986.

TOM asked me to go to work in March. I don't think Tom Harkin asked me to go to work for him because he thought I was some radical militant troublemaker out here that was raising all kinds of hell. He identified with what I was saying, and he recognized that there was a group of people that was concerned about the same things that I was concerned about, and that I could perhaps be an influence that could help him get elected as a United States senator.

He wanted me on his paid staff because he thought I could help him. I wanted to do that because Tom Harkin was one of the few people I had any faith left in at this point. When I met with him in March, and I asked him what he expected me to do, he told me, "Just go out and say the same things you've been saying for the last five years, only I'm gonna pay you a little bit to say it, instead of you having to take it out of your own pocket." I said, "Well, I think I can do that, Tom. But I learned something in the political arena, that every time you do something in the political arena, you try to do it in a manner that you strengthen yourself, you strengthen your own position down the road. If I go out here and I work for you the next five or six months, and we get you elected, there's something I want back."

263

Tom Harkin said, "I understand that, that's right. That's the way politics works. What do you want back?"

I said, "Well, Tom, I don't believe one man can really change the influences that are affecting us. But I do think one man can be a hell of an influence on change, and he can influence a lot of other people, you know. What I want in return is, if we get you elected, I expect you to stand out front, to lead the battle, to bring some positive changes out here, put some profit back in family farm agriculture." That's what I wanted back in return from me helping him get elected. And I told him at that time that if, any time in the next six years once we get him elected, I feel that he hasn't stood out front, that he hasn't tried, that at the end of those six years, if the good Lord was willing and I was still around, then I'd work twice as hard to get him defeated as I did to get him elected.

I wasn't looking at party politics, I was looking at individuals. A pretty high leader in the Democratic party, down at Tom's victory in Des Moines, came up and said, "You know, you did an excellent job for Tom. We really appreciate the fact that you were out working for the Democratic party."

And I've always been one that shot from the hip. I said, "No, I'm afraid you don't understand. I wasn't working for the Democratic party in Iowa. I was out working for a man by the name of Tom Harkin, who I have a lot of faith and respect in, and I was really out working for the *philosophies* of the Democratic party, which many of you people haven't had the damned political courage to back yourselves. What you fail to understand is, sometimes some of the leadership has used me and agriculture like a damned two-bit whore. When you wanted our vote, you expected it, and then you cast us aside until it was time to ask for our vote again."

I said, "Agriculture is not a two-bit whore that can just be used when you need us. You know, we're an industry very vital to the strength of Iowa and to this country, and until you have the political courage to back those philosophies and convictions, I won't work for the party, I'll work for the philosophies of the Democratic party.

"You know, you've got to give the Republican party some credit. They have some integrity. They tell us they're gonna lower our prices, and by God, they do it. You try to project the image, you elect us and we're gonna solve your problems. And then, because the problems are very complex and complicated, once we elect you, there's a great percent of you that don't want to face up to the complexities of that problem, just project an image that you're making an attempt when you're not."

I'm sure I didn't make any points with the Democratic leadership in the state of Iowa, but at least I got it off my chest. There was a look of amazement on his face, and he didn't argue too much. He probably wouldn't admit it openly, but I think he knew what I was saying, and I think to some degree you're going to alienate people when you say those kinds of things. But I think there's also a percent of people who're going to respect you because you're not involved for personal gain, and you do tell it the way you see it.

I'd like to think that we're going to get some people to recognize that the Democratic party is simply groups of individuals who make mistakes. Maybe not conscious mistakes at the time, but we make mistakes. And I think the Democratic party needs to recognize that they've made mistakes as well. Let's admit it, and let's correct those mistakes because then and only then are we gonna project a positive new direction out here that not only agriculture, but I think the nation, needs at this time.

What is that positive direction for agriculture?

I'm not against progress. I don't think any of us are against progress, but I guess the basic question that I begin to ask myself is: Progress within any industry should, first of all, benefit the industry itself, the people involved in it, and the people who consume our products, right?

So, let's analyze that. Has this so-called technological progress in agriculture with increased yield, the genetic improvement in both red meat production and feed grain production, benefited agriculture? In the thirty-two years that I've farmed, I've watched farm debt increase from $12 to $225 billion. If the industry's getting a decent, fair, equitable return, a system out there where you're getting a just economic system and a just treatment, you don't keep doubling your debt every five, eight, ten years. Yet, that's what we were doing in agriculture. So that tells me this hasn't been progress. Yes, it has been in terms of productivity and production of food.

But we've concentrated in the last thirty years on productivity alone. I think there's two other elements in agriculture that we've totally overlooked. And that's our ability to bring some young people into the industry; the second factor I think we've overlooked is what we have done to our nation's most valuable resources, our land and our water, in the process. We've speeded up erosion; we've polluted our water resources. That can't be progress, can it? So I say we haven't made progress in the industry. Have we made progress for the people involved in it? We know we're talking now about losing 40 percent of our farmers in the next five years—God, that's not progress! Have we benefited the consuming public out here? Well, we've got food pretty cheap. Cheapest any place in the world as a percent of disposable income. But we've got 40 percent of the people at John Deere laid off. We kept food cheap for those people, but we kept it so cheap that 40 percent of those people don't have any job today. That's not progress.

Of course, the last thing you think about when you talk about the progress in agriculture and the productivity is, well, at least we've fed the world's hungry. Have we fed the world's hungry? Have we gained on poverty and hunger not only around the world but in this country? Hunger's increasing in our own country and in our own cities, you know.

Well, what we fail to understand is that in the process, we've actually taken incentive away from third-world countries to develop their own agriculture. They realize there's so little return in agriculture; why would an underdeveloped country want to pump billions of dollars into agriculture development when there's no return on it? So what happens, I think, in the process, is the leadership of this country, the elite, the powerful, get all the cheap food they want to fill their stomachs, and do they really care about the masses of people within their country that are starving to death?

I've always found it a very strange and somewhat tragic paradox when we as a nation demand social, political, and economic reform in El Salvador because about fourteen families control 95 percent of the land involved. And we say we've got to break that down into smaller units, we say we've got to get more people to share in the wealth of El Salvador, and yet when we say that, we as a nation fail to understand, I guess, that time and progress itself have brought added changes and added influences into our own economic and social structure. And I think we've either adapted or adjusted to these economic and social changes that have taken place, and I really believe that one of the biggest challenges that faces our nation today, both in an economic and social sense, is understanding that and returning the land to the people. As we condemn El Salvador's type of social structure, we're leading ourselves down the same path, concentration of wealth in the hands of a few. We're not doing

266

anything to address it within our own nation. Can we demand economic and social justice in another country when we refuse to practice that policy in our own nation? There's something terribly wrong here; there's something wrong within the leadership of both parties.

Gary Lamb made another try for public office in the spring of 1986, entering the Iowa Democratic primary as a candidate for secretary of agriculture. In a four-candidate field, he faced State Representative Dale Cochran, longtime chairman of the House Agriculture Committee, liberal farm activist Theresa Sullivan, and a political unknown. Lamb, a board member of the Iowa Citizen Action Network, received an unanticipated jolt to his hopes when labor leaders on the ICAN board blocked his endorsement by backing Cochran, saying they owed it to him for his backing of organized labor. It was a classic example of the way wedges have often been driven between organized labor and farmers. But much to the chagrin of the Iowa Farm Unity Coalition, which Lamb represented on the ICAN board, Cochran was also endorsed by the Iowa Farm Bureau. This labor movement decision deeply embittered Farm Unity leaders, many of whom vowed it would be a long time before the wounds from the "betrayal" would heal. Only a year before, ironically, ICAN had cemented a new board membership arrangement that was designed to attract farm members.

In the primary, Cochran won with 36 percent of the vote to Lamb's 28 percent. Sullivan received 24 percent after being encouraged to run by a women's caucus that was recruiting female candidates for public office. Lamb says that Cochran's forces encouraged the caucus to foster her candidacy as a move to divide liberal farm movement votes. Some farm leaders also blamed Sullivan, who also had coalition ties, for splitting the farm reform vote and leading to Lamb's defeat. Others also suggested the Lamb campaign could have been better organized.

In the fall of 1986, the Iowa Farmers Union elected Gary Lamb its new president, and he left the Harkin senatorial staff permanently.

Political Sentinel

HELEN WALLER
Circle, Montana

In physical stature, in her frankness and spunk, and with her grandmotherly gray hair and good nature, Helen Waller in many ways could pass for the Dr. Ruth of the farm movement. Certainly, farmers are listening to her in greater numbers than ever before. But there is a difference. Whereas Dr. Ruth's mission is to reduce the naiveté of her audience about sex, Waller's mission is to reduce farmers' naiveté about politics.

That may yet yield another similarity. For both stress the value of meaningful relationships—in Helen's case, political ones. She is the president of the National Save the Family Farm Coalition.

M Y political experience and my experience in organizing began with the energy development issue. I was satisfied being a homemaker and a farmer and a mother of five, and I was pretty well caught up in this whole business of wiping noses and tying shoes, and the coal companies moved into our area and announced that they were going to stripmine a piece of land that was right across the fence from us. So, right away, we started asking questions and asking them specifically about how is that going to affect our water; what about air pollution; do you reclaim the land? These were pretty elementary questions for us. And, the more we learned, we found out it was going to have tremendous effects on us economically, environmentally, and socially. And we didn't learn it from the coal companies because they have rather devious ways sometimes of passing out information. We did our own research, our own digging of the facts.

So we started making them accountable. We basically told them that when they came in, they better be prepared to pay their own way and do the kinds of things that good neighbors do. I think that the lesson that I got out of that was that, if people in a community value the culture there enough, value the things that are important for a quality of life, it's up to you to save it because nobody else is going to look out for you. In the whole process of them talking about eastern Montana as the national sacrifice area, and the fact that they were going to build a synthetic fuels plant there, which would bring in fifteen thousand people during construction, we simply asked enough questions that they couldn't give us satisfactory answers for, that it aroused enough people.

Another factor was the lessening of the market for their commodity. It got to the point where they were going to produce synthetic fuels for $90 a barrel. Well, you know, what's crude now? Twenty dollars or less, probably. So they really didn't have a marketable product. But they really didn't care at that time because government was pumping so much money into the synthetic fuel industry that they didn't have to make money on their product. They were making it off the taxpayers. And we exposed it for what it was, and to make a long story short, they packed up and left town.

That doesn't mean that they're gone forever. We know that we have to watch what goes on from here. But they would go to the legislature every session and try to defeat our major facility siting act, or weaken it to the point where it didn't have any teeth in it anymore. So I think that experience kind of prepared me for the real fight. As tough as it was, and as real discouraging as it can be at times, I think there was a reason for us having to have fought that fight, because I think I'm much better prepared to take this one on.

Where'd the transition come?

We organized a local group around this issue. The energy development issue was big all over Montana. Various local groups sprung up, and then we created a statewide organization [Northern Plains Resource Council] that worked strictly on energy development issues.

And I got up at our annual meeting the fall of '83 and . . . I mean, I swallowed hard before I said this because this was a real diverse group organized around one issue. We could argue and debate heavily on a number of other issues because we had the most conservative, the most liberal, the most radical in every direction of philosophy on

269

other issues, but on energy development we thought alike, we worked together. That doesn't mean that we always agreed. We had some real tough debates in our meetings. But there was one thing about us. When we left the board meetings, whatever way the vote went, that's what we all did. And we hung together and we did a good job. But we were basically organized around the energy development issue, which in a way was a family farm issue. We were giving family farmers a voice to contrast the coal development voice. So, I didn't see it as a big shift in what I was doing. I was fighting to preserve family farmers at that time, too. The opposition was just coming from a different angle. But at that meeting, after one of our panels, I got up and I said, "You know, we have done some really significant things when it comes to preserving the history of our state and saving our state from the drag line. But I want you to think about it. What good has it done us to have done all the things that we have done and then lose the farm to the banker?"

And from that point on, we increased what we called the family farm task force. We had some real tough debates within that group to try to figure out why we should get into this issue, when the traditional farm groups that have been out there for a good number of years really haven't made much progress. We started looking at different ways we could attack it and why other organizations had failed. We discussed this very heavily for at least a year before we ever came out with a position. In the meantime, we were still trying to get our feet on the ground and figure out what we needed to do different from what other organizations had done.

I got an invitation to a meeting in Madrid, Iowa. This was the fall of '84. And I went there as an individual. I got up and said, "I've heard enough about everybody's problems. We've got two days. We've wasted half of our time talking about the problem. How about we talk about some solutions?" So we shifted gears about then, and the next day we talked about solutions.

We agreed that the price was the problem; that this was an economic crisis; we agreed that we had to influence the 1985 farm bill because prices are set in Washington; that we needed to begin to draft our own legislation; and that this legislation, number one, had to deal with price, and that, number two, it could not be at taxpayer expense.

Shortly after that, there was another meeting in Albert Lea, Minnesota. It was physically impossible for me to get to that meeting, but I was informed after that meeting that I had been put on a committee that was called the Coordinating Committee for the Farm Policy Reform Act. The responsibility of that committee was to be the sounding board while the legislation was being drafted. We tried to get as diverse a group as possible, especially geographically, because one thing I've learned in working on this farm bill is that what's good for one area is devastating to another. So we had people as far east as Kentucky, Hal Hamilton was on the committee; I was the farthest west. The leaders in their respective states were on the committee, and we had conference calls and other meetings as this Farm Policy Reform Act was being drafted.

Now, we had some pretty bitter discussions, too, because at one point in time Mark Ritchie[1] came out to Montana to give us an update on what was going on with the drafting, and there were a couple of sections of the bill I didn't like. One especially, and I told him unless that section was jerked, I'd actively lobby against the bill. So we had our problems in trying to formulate a bill that was acceptable to various areas.

But I think, for a first run, we did a pretty good job! I didn't like the targeting mechanism in the bill. I didn't like it when it was going through debate the fall of '85. And I was talking to Fred Lundgren,[2] still moaning and groaning about the targeting language, and he said, "If you don't like it, why don't you write something better?" So I went back to the hotel that night and put something together that I thought was quite a bit better, and Lane Evans introduced it in an amendment the next day. And the amendment passed, but then, of course, the whole bill failed. But it gave us an idea of what Congress would accept for targeting language, so that we could go back in the revision process and incorporate some of those same ideas.

Even though the bill didn't pass [in 1985], I think we should not underestimate the real progress that was made. You have to realize that we were asking for a total change in agricultural policy. The mindset in Washington was to set a target price and a loan rate, and pay farmers a deficiency payment. All they could think of was adjusting and tinkering with those figures. We were asking them to junk the whole idea and start over with a fresh idea. And this is not easy for those people to do.

In the first place, I think we're kidding ourselves if we believe that

[1]A researcher in the Minnesota Department of Agriculture.
[2]An assistant to Jim Hightower in the Texas Department of Agriculture.

those people in Washington, D.C., have a good grasp of the real farm industry, how a farm bill affects you when you're out in the field. I think the experts are the ones who handle the production end; I think that we can write a better bill. One of the best things we can do is find the loopholes. We've been finding them all the time in bills they write. Now let us find them and eliminate the loopholes. We're not going to eliminate them all because, I don't care what kind of a bill you write, there's gonna be somebody that's gonna try to connive around it. But I think we are more capable of writing a bill than the people who have been doing it previously.

After the Food Security Act[3] was passed, I was pretty disappointed. I went home from Washington swearing I'd never go back again. I was really discouraged not by the fact that we lost, but the reason why we lost and the misunderstanding and, in some cases, total ignorance of the real issue. And I swore I wasn't going back. Well, it wasn't a week and I was on the way back.

But we lost it. But the things that we really accomplished were that we found out who our friends were, we found out who our enemies were. It flushed out a whole array of pretty unsuspected opposition. Our own commodity groups came out in opposition, the processors, the bankers, the fertilizer companies. . . . We identified people in Congress that simply need cleaning out.

So it was a useful exercise, but the one thing I think we learned the most was that, even though we were a coordinating committee who had organizations that we represented, and we knew there were a lot of other organizations that were working on this issue and that were sympathetic to what we were doing, we did not have the coordination we needed to pull off anything as big as changing farm policy. So what that told us was that we had to set up a national structure that would bring in all of these organizations from the various states to head in the same direction. So we went back to Des Moines last February [1986] and organized the national structure. And I had no idea when I went there that I would end up in a leadership position because I had my hands full on enough other stuff, because I was chairing the rewrite of the farm bill.

Okay. So in January we started rewriting this bill. We knew that we had to be the only show on the road when we convinced Congress that they needed to move again. With the condition worsening,

[3]The current farm program, passed in 1985.

272

we knew the time had come, and we wanted to be in place.

I was really overloaded when I came back with the responsibility of chairing the national coalition. I worked out of my own home up until [October 1986]. We've opened an office in Circle, which gives me full-time secretarial help. But the people in the coalition are a tremendous group to work with. They're good organizers, and I think the one thing that makes our organization unique is that we have a very special feeling for the power of the people that are in the countryside. We don't want an organization that builds big buildings and sits in plush offices and loses track of what's going on in the countryside. We want there not to be a lot of levels between the people on the land and what our leadership is doing. And I think that we will remain flexible in that way. I think that we will be able to make decisions quicker. I think they'll be better decisions. I think our opposition will not know how to second-guess us as well. And within our coalition, the different elements to our rural crisis action campaign allow for a lot of flexibility in what we're going to do.

I mean, we have spent time and effort on this federal legislation, but that's only a part of the total program. We're working in the field of state legislation. There's a lot that can be done at the state level in dealing with the farm crisis issue. We're considering coordinating the efforts to pass grain marketing compact legislation[4] at the state level. And some states are working on emergency loan programs for farmers. North Dakota, you know, has the state bank there, and they're working in that direction. We need more than anything now to get going on a public education mass media program, which needs to be targeted not only at urban people and nonfarm people, we need to educate our own people.

There's a lot of people that don't realize the things that have happened, and the movements that have put us in the position we are in. I mean, this didn't just happen. It happened because we let it happen. People through the '40s got politically lazy about paying attention to what was going on. You know, farm people have—and I don't know if any of this is to our credit or detriment—a feeling that we elect our congressmen and senators, and they go down there and they look out for us. And it just doesn't happen. But I think we have been too trusting. We need to be a little smarter politically and take

[4]Legislation at the state level that would authorize a commission to study alternative methods of marketing grain for the greater benefit of the state's farmers.

care of our own. I think the National Save the Family Farm Coalition is allowing that to happen because we are organizing in the countryside. We don't lead our people to believe that this is a short-term effort, and that it's all going to be over, you know, and we can go home and do the things that we want to do after this bill is passed. We're going to have to hold on to it.

Not too long ago, I had a very serious discussion with our own son. He's out of high school one year. He has wanted to farm since he was a little kid. And I just plain said to him, you know, I don't intend to do what I'm doing now for him to get politically lazy and lose it for the next generation. We had parity pricing through the '40s. And we lost it in the '50s. And if we get it back again, we better treat the farm credit crisis of the '80s as though it was an occurrence never to happen again.

A farmers' holocaust?

Yeah. In Oklahoma alone, since November of '85 [to October '86], there have been thirty-one suicides directly related to the farm crisis. It doesn't even make news anymore. People are callous to it, I guess. At least the news media is. And that's a tragedy, that we don't look beyond what happened to why it happened, and should it have happened, and what could we have done to have prevented it from happening?

In January 1988, Helen Waller resigned as president of the coalition to run, with Democratic gubernatorial candidate Frank Morrison, Jr., for lieutenant governor of Montana in the June primary.

Afterword

A man with a formidable appearance walked into a banker's office. The startled secretary first gasped, then asked, "Can I help you?"

"Yes, I have an appointment," he replied.

"I'll let my boss know right away," she said, never able to take her eyes off the man while she dialed her boss to announce the man's presence. The man sat down. Still the secretary stared. Finally, she had to ask.

"Where did you get that peg leg?"

"A war injury," he replied.

"Oh, I'm so sorry to hear that," she said, her eyes still affixed. "I hope you don't mind my asking, but where did you get that hook for your hand?"

"Another war injury," he said sadly, his eye downcast.

"Oh, my goodness, I am really sorry about all that. I . . . I hope you don't mind one more question, but your glass eye. . . . "

"Oh, that," he said with a slight chuckle. "After I returned, I was wandering on the beach, contemplating what to do with my life, how to cope with my injuries, and I was staring into the sky, admiring the soaring flight of the sea gulls, when one dropped his doings right into my eye."

Noticing the slight chuckle, the secretary was incredulous. "I may look gullible, sir, but even I know that bird doo-doo won't do permanent damage to your eye."

"But ma'am," the ex-soldier protested, "it will if it happens just two days after you had this hook installed to replace your right hand."

In the midst of the war that editor Chris Nannenga describes, with all its rural casualties, two distinct but related agricultural crises vied for the American public's attention as Congress was debating the 1985 farm bill. One stemmed from an issue as old as the republic itself that engaged the minds of the U.S. Constitution's framers: Who should own the land, and how would their tenure affect the nation's emerging democratic system? The nation was nearing a seemingly irreversible decision by default to allow the land to fall under increasingly narrow corporate and plutocratic control. It is easier to preserve diversity of ownership than to regain it, some farmers were anxious to note; they pointed to the example of our Latin American neighbors.

Another crisis presented an even more daunting challenge: How could we feed ourselves and others while preserving our land's productivity for future generations and the health of our current generation? Groundwater contamination from pesticides, herbicides, and fertilizers had become a serious issue. Agricultural runoff and soil erosion were fouling our rivers while stripping the land of its long-term vitality. On the Great Plains, we had learned little from the Dust Bowl, mining the region's thin resource base to grow crops that were already in surplus. Nothing less than the nation's future was at stake.

The problem lay in reconciling proposed solutions to both issues. Family farm advocates like Helen Waller would see the institution of the family farm, like the apocryphal war veteran, suffering from wounds imposed during the farm crisis and vulnerable to aggravated injuries from seemingly minor new indignities. Farmers who supported the Harkin-Gephardt proposal, later known as the Family Farm Act, thus argued that the best way to preserve family farm agriculture was to eliminate direct subsidies and use supply management in concert with high support prices for staple commodities in order to allow farmers to earn a living from the marketplace, rather than from Uncle Sam. Giving farmers the ability to earn a decent living without abusing the land, they argued, would solve many environmental problems as well. Environmental advocates often saw the problem differently. Not all family farmers were environmental angels; some, in fact, could be stubborn, incorrigible culprits, often encouraged in their practices by old-line Extension agents and production-oriented land-grant college experts.

Environmentalists proposed ideas that were generally included in the Food Security Act Congress passed in 1985. Cross-compliance had been proposed in earlier years and had always taken a beating at the hands of conservative farm lobbyists. It involves limiting farm subsidies, such as deficiency payments to farmers to supplement farm income when commodity prices fall below target prices, to farmers who comply with environmental requirements like adequate soil conservation. The 1985 act requires farmers to have approved conservation plans for highly erodible acreage by 1990 in order to retain their federal farm program benefits. It also established a Conservation Reserve Program, whereby the federal government pays farmers lease rates to retire such acreage from production for up to ten years. It ended federal subsidies to farmers who engaged in swampbusting or sodbusting, that is, draining wetlands or plowing new dryland areas.

The two approaches were in obvious conflict. If farmers were to get their income through the market via the Harkin proposal's high price supports, environmentalists would lose the lever of subsidy denial to force compliance with the new farm bill's environmental provisions. For them, voluntary compliance was a failed idea whose time had passed. But Helen Waller, president of the National Save the Family Farm Coalition, which backs the Harkin proposal, had another point to make: Farmers must be able to afford to implement the requirements being imposed upon them. She does not oppose the environmental issues. She argues that they will be self-defeating if they are imposed at the expense of the family farm system. The litany is common to both conservative and liberal farm groups: Corporations don't care about the land as much as the family farmer does. On balance, family farmers will do a better job of preserving our resources for the future.

The Minnesota-based Land Stewardship Project, which champions the preservation of our topsoil, generally agrees. It reports a pattern of abuses where insurance companies have foreclosed on family farms and leased them as tenant farms. Unless the two issues are reconciled, advocates of *both* the family farm and the environment would seem to be damned if they do *and* if they don't.

Is there a way out? If so, it will take a more united front than the two reform blocs showed during the 1985 debate. The act's environ-

277

mental achievements have benefited farmers financially, through payments for retired land and consequent reduced input costs, but the difference it has made in preserving the family farm has been rather marginal. Grain prices have tended to stabilize—but at prices far below the target prices most family farms rely on to stay in business. Cattle and hogs have become profitable again. Land prices are not falling precipitously as they were in the mid-1980s, but then, how much steeper could their descent have been? The valley is still far below the peak. Exports are gaining slightly, but huge surpluses still hang over world grain markets. Net farm income is up, but as University of Missouri economist Harold Breimyer notes, the increase is mostly built on the thin reed of increased government expenditure.[1] Net cash income was high in 1987, he notes, because farmers were not replacing aging equipment. Net farm income, the figure achieved after properly accounting for depreciation, edged up only slightly above $30 billion. The U.S. Department of Agriculture was spending $25 billion that year. Payments to farmers for placing land in the conservation reserve have helped some farmers, but the long-term environmental gain remains to be seen. The program is scheduled to last only until 1995, at which time the public and Congress must reassess its value and its cost. Will the environmental lobby again prevail? Or will new assessments of the program's cost-effectiveness make it a victim of the federal deficit?[2]

Some conservation advocates have argued that the conservation reserve will help to restrain production and therefore raise prices by limiting surpluses. Farmers often know better, for they know all too well that in any voluntary program only the most marginal land will be bid into the reserve, while the most productive land will continue to generate record crops, often because it will be worked harder than ever. In the absence of supply management, and with the present price and subsidy structure, that is the inevitable thrust of the market. The swift current of financial pressure can sweep along in its path even environmentally conscious farmers.

The truth is that both the environment and the family farm are bucking powerful economic forces in their struggle for survival. Advocates on both fronts have a healthy distrust of the unfettered market and an even healthier distrust of some of the academic, business, and governmental institutions that have augmented the power of those market forces both through propaganda and government programs. But their distrust of each other has, at times, limited

Afterword

the potential of their cooperation. No Harkin bill will succeed without environmental support, so its supporters must seek an accommodation with environmental leaders to achieve their goals. But environmental leaders must also beware of the single greatest danger to their own goals: resentful, dispirited farmers struggling for survival and perceiving conservationists as just one more force bearing down on the already battered institution of the family farm. At that point, they would become the bird splat that hampered the vision of the old soldier. They would lose the friends they need for the most important campaign of all: the reeducation of Americans about the relationship between our society and its soil, and the changes that must take place in our attitudes, our institutions, and our farming practices to keep the American breadbasket both democratic in structure and sustainable in its fragile bounty. The time for achieving that alliance is short. The next farm bill debate will arrive in 1990, the tone for that debate established in the elections of 1988.

NOTES

1. Harold Breimyer, "Seems That Everyone Prefers to Be Optimistic," *Delta Farm Press,* July 10, 1987, pp. 8, 23.
2. Perhaps the most recent good analysis available on this question is by Thomas L. Daniels, "America's Conservation Reserve Program: Rural Planning or Just Another Subsidy?," paper presented at the American Planning Association annual conference, San Antonio, Texas, April 30–May 4, 1988.

APPENDIX A[*]

Historical Background on the Major Farm Lenders

FARM debt since 1950 has fast outstripped any growth in farm income. Net farm income in 1950 exceeded the outstanding U.S. farm debt by a slight margin (Table 1). By 1980, farm debt was well over eight times net farm income. In a rather unsteady fashion that reflected the erratic farm programs of the 1980s, that ratio grew slightly, but irregularly, until 1985. Only the drastic reduction of credit availability has reduced the ratio since then. Whatever else may be said of progress, it is unclear that the changes in U.S. agriculture over the last thirty-five years have made family farmers more solvent.

Table 1. Total U.S. Farm Debt and Net Farm Income, 1950–80

Year	Total Farm Debt	Net Farm Income	Ratio
	(in millions of dollars)		
1950	12,454	13,648	.91
1960	24,775	11,518	2.15
1970	53,027	14,151	3.75
1980	165,803	19,860	8.35

Sources: United States Department of Agriculture, *Agricultural Finance Statistics, 1960–1983*. Washington, D.C.: USDA, 1984, and *Economic Indicators of the Farm Sector*, various issues.

[*]This appendix is largely an updated revision of parts of a chapter from a report for Iowa's Legislative Extended Assistance Group at the University of Iowa: *The Farm Credit Crisis in Iowa* by James Schwab, February 1984, used courtesy of LEAG.

The major reason for this is that production expenses have kept the margin between gross and net farm income slim. While gross income rose from $33.1 billion in 1950 to $150.5 billion in 1980, production expenses rose from $19.5 billion to $130.7 billion. Thus, in terms of net income from farming, farmers have lost the battle against inflation. Increasingly, they have relied on second incomes to make up the difference. Off-farm income for farm families climbed from $8.5 billion in 1960 to $36 billion in 1980.

As prices initially climbed in the 1970s before leveling off, and the debt-carrying capacity of U.S. agriculture thus seemed to grow, the competition among lenders for market shares intensified. Where farm debt had doubled each decade from 1950 to 1970, it more than tripled during the 1970s. It continued to escalate into 1983, before declining slightly for the first time in four decades in 1984. The noose was tightening: Lenders grew wary of agricultural loans as farm prices declined.

Tables 2 and 3 demonstrate the distribution of the debt among classes of lenders in the United States. One of the most noticeable shifts in Table 2 is the aggressive inroads made into the farm real estate market by the Federal Land Banks, doubling their percentage between 1970 and 1983. Their sister institutions in the Farm Credit System, the Federal Intermediate Credit Banks, and local Production Credit Associations, while they did not increase their market share nearly as dramatically, still made gains in non-real estate farm loan volume. Banks, however, did lose part of their share, as troubled debt shifted steadily in the direction of the lender of last resort: the Farmers Home Administration. That shift was a clear sign of difficulties on the land.

The reason for offering two sets of percentages in Table 3 is the unique role of the Commodity Credit Corporation as a source of short-term credit for farmers. The CCC serves as a price-supporting mechanism whereby farmers can use their crops as collateral for loans from the government-owned corporation. These "nonrecourse" loans involve no repayment obligation. If the farmer does not pay them off with interest within nine months, the government simply takes possession of the grain, but has no other collection options. Loan rates for the grain are established in the federal farm legislation, but generally were lowered in the 1985 Food Security Act. The volatility of farm prices has caused the percentage of non-real estate farm debt owed to CCC to fluctuate dramatically. Although the

Table 2.   Farm Real Estate Debt: Percentages Held by Lenders on January 1 of Years Specified

Year	FLB	FmHA	Insurance Cos.	Banks	All Others*
1960	19.3	5.6	23.3	12.6	39.1
1970	22.9	7.8	19.6	12.1	37.5
1975	30.0	7.2	14.1	13.4	35.3
1980	34.7	8.3	14.2	10.1	32.6
1981	37.6	8.1	13.5	9.2	31.6
1982	41.3	8.3	12.4	7.9	30.1
1983	43.1	8.3	11.7	7.7	29.2

Source: United States Department of Agriculture, *Agricultural Finance Statistics, 1960-1983.* Washington, D.C.: USDA, 1984.
*Includes individuals such as relatives, farmers selling on installment contracts, partnerships, etc.

Table 3.   Farm Non-Real Estate Debt: Percentages Held by Lenders on January 1 of Years Specified

Year	Banks	PCA/FICB	FmHA	All Others	CCC
1960	38.0	11.4	3.1	38.3	9.2
	(41.9)	(12.6)	(3.4)	(42.2)	
1970	43.3	19.8	3.3	22.4	11.2
	(48.8)	(22.3)	(3.7)	(25.2)	
1975	49.3	26.6	2.8	20.4	0.9
	(49.7)	(26.8)	(2.8)	(20.6)	
1980	38.6	23.2	11.2	20.7	6.3
	(41.2)	(24.8)	(12.0)	(22.1)	
1981	36.5	23.6	13.6	20.5	5.8
	(38.7)	(25.1)	(14.4)	(21.8)	
1982	34.3	22.8	15.0	19.5	8.3
	(37.4)	(24.9)	(16.4)	(21.3)	
1983	33.8	19.6	13.8	18.3	14.4
	(39.5)	(22.9)	(16.1)	(21.4)	

Source: United States Department of Agriculture, *Agricultural Finance Statistics, 1960-1983.* Washington, D.C.: USDA, 1984.
(Percentages in parentheses eliminate Commodity Credit Corporation from total.)

percentage of debt held by CCC in the 1970s was relatively low historically, percentages in this decade have not been exceptionally higher than in 1970, before the large expansion in export trade. Even with declining price support levels, however, the debt exposure of

CCC has been growing under the 1985 legislation because of precipitous drops in farm prices. The percentages in parentheses, in any case, provide a comparison of market shares of conventional credit sources without the wide fluctuations of CCC loan volume.

Farmers Home Administration

The financial straits of farmers during the Great Depression, with growing numbers of bankruptcies and a rapid rise in already serious rural poverty, led to the creation of the Farm Security Administration, renamed in 1946 the Farmers Home Administration. Although there were earlier federal government ventures into the field of farm credit, FmHA is the agency that specifically inherited the mission of aiding low-income and inexperienced farmers, and of trying to insure the viability of small farms by expanding opportunities for farm ownership. The key to the whole program lay in making supervised farm ownership and operating loans to farmers unable to qualify for traditional sources of credit. That supervision necessarily involved a good deal of counseling and advice in an effort to bring these farmers to the level of competence and credit that would allow them eventually to qualify for normal credit. Created by passage of the 1937 Bankhead-Jones Farm Tenant Act, it was not merely farm legislation, but a major piece of New Deal social welfare legislation that expanded federal responsibilities for preserving a system of family agriculture in the United States.

FmHA gained new authority to authorize loans for "acquisition, improvement, and operation of farms" under Title III of the Agricultural Credit Act of 1961. It also gained authority for various kinds of rural home improvement loans and rural community development loans, making it, in effect, a source of credit for rural economic improvement both on and off the farm. But its major mission remains agricultural.

Within that realm, it has a number of farmer loan programs for which the following glossary may be helpful:

Farm Ownership Loans (FO). These are made to farmers who cannot obtain credit elsewhere, for the purchase or improvement of farms or additions to farms, for refinancing debt, or for financing nonfarm enterprises, and are secured by real estate. The limit is $200,000, and the general period of amortization is 40 years. Although this program still legally exists, it is not currently funded.

284

Operating Loans (OL). These are made to farmers who cannot obtain credit elsewhere; they offer chattel credit and short-to-intermediate-term production credit. Examples would be purchases of livestock or machinery. Repayment is limited to seven years, and the loans are usually secured by crops, livestock, or machinery. The limit is $100,000. The current trend in FmHA is to push these borrowers toward guaranteed loans (see below).

Emergency Loans (EM). These do not require the same "last resort" test, but are made to farmers in designated disaster areas to cover physical and production losses from drought, flood, tornadoes, and the like. They can be secured by real and/or nonreal property, and there is now a $500,000 limit on individual loans.

Economic Emergency Loans (EE). These were created in 1978 to deal with economic conditions resulting from a cost-price squeeze on a temporary basis. This has been the most controversial program, largely because of the high volume of loans to larger farms claiming economic difficulties. Its original date of expiration was March 1980, but it was extended by Congress. It is now defunct. It had a $400,000 individual loan limit.

Insured vs. Guaranteed Loans. "Insured" loans in FmHA terminology are those FO and OL loans made directly from the Agricultural Credit Insurance Fund, a revolving fund supported by small insurance fees paid by borrowers, and from which all FO and OL loan moneys are drawn. Guaranteed loans are those FO and OL loans that simply involve 90 percent FmHA backing, while coming from participating banks or Farm Credit System institutions to the borrower, who would not qualify for them without the FmHA guarantee. The relative emphasis on these two tools is a focus of policy debate over the future of FmHA itself, with the Reagan administration preferring guarantees.

Limited Resource Loans (LR). A long-standing FmHA real estate loan rate of 5 percent jumped to a higher floating rate in 1978. In passing the Agricultural Credit Act of 1978, Congress raised the FO loan rate from that fixed rate to a cost-of-money rate. To compensate for the adverse effect on many low-income farmers, Congress simultaneously created a new LR program, first at 5 percent, then later at higher LR rates for both FO and OL loans. The present provision has been to offer LR/FO loans at one-half regular FO rates and to discount LR/OL loans by 3 percent below regular OL rates. In 1980, Congress also established a 20 percent minimum quota for use of both FO and OL loan funds for LR borrowers. There are wide variations around the nation, however, in the actual percentage of loan moneys used for LR borrowers. Iowa, for instance, used over 60 percent of its FO and OL funds for LR loans in fiscal year 1984, while California used only 12.4 percent of its FO, and only 10.4 percent of its OL funds, for this purpose. Arkansas used 19.3 percent of its FO, and only 2.9 percent of its OL funds, for LR borrowers.

LR borrowers must not only meet the regular criteria for FO loans, but also must meet some additional criteria. These are: 1) inability to obtain sufficient credit under the regular program; 2) ownership or operation of a small or family farm (including new farmers); and 3) a low income and a need to maximize income from farming operations.

Nationally, FmHA is headed by a presidentially appointed national administrator and is a part of the U.S. Department of Agriculture. Each state has a state director, district directors, and county supervisors. There are also program directors at the state level, including one for the Farmer Program, which oversees the loan programs discussed above. The county offices are the field operations where lending activity actually takes place, with local personnel operating under the guidance of the county supervisor.

A key aspect of the county FmHA office operations is the county committee, made up of local farmers who pass judgment on the eligibility of program applicants, but leave administrative decisions and operations to the county supervisor. As can easily be imagined, the exercise of discretionary authority by both the county supervisor and the county committee has, in the recent years of farm stress, had considerable impact upon local perceptions of the agency and its attitudes toward its clientele.

One recent change in FmHA structure may affect that profoundly, although only time will tell. Where the county supervisor previously appointed the county committee, two of its three members will now be local farmers elected by farmers in the county. The members must *not* be FmHA borrowers in order to be eligible for nomination, which occurs through petitions circulated among local farmers eligible to vote.

Another aspect of the crisis of recent years is that the strain that increased credit stress combined with decreased federal loan resources has placed on FmHA personnel has resulted in escalating rates of personnel turnover in many areas, though FmHA officials, at least in the author's experience, have not always been notably willing to divulge or discuss the numbers involved. Common sense, however, dictates that a high turnover rate inevitably leads to a deterioration of the experience and expertise of the agency's loan personnel, and increased resulting strain between those personnel and indebted farmers.

Farm Credit System

There is an old saying that when the only tool you have is a hammer, every problem looks like a nail. Before the advent of the Farm Credit System in 1916, agriculture indeed looked a nail to many banks. Farm real estate loans were for terms of only one to five years, and renewal often depended more on the banks' needs than on the farmers' ability to make the farm work. If another source of credit did not materialize, the farmer was often headed for another line of work.

It was with these problems in mind that Congress in 1916 created the Federal Land Banks under the Farm Loan Act. The idea was to use a pool of farm mortgage money to collateralize long-term mortgages that would give farmers greater security. The money was secured through bond sales initially handled by the Federal Farm Loan Board. In 1923, in response to the need for farm operating loans as well as real estate loans, Congress created the Federal Intermediate Credit Banks. Later, in 1933, the creation of local Production Credit Associations followed. Just as Federal Land Bank borrowers became cooperative owner-members of those banks through their local Federal Land Bank Associations, the PCA borrowers became cooperative owner-members of those associations, which in turn were eventually to become the owners of the regionally organized FICBs. Congress also, in 1933, created the final leg of the three-part Farm Credit System, the Banks for Cooperatives, whose mission was to provide financing for farmer-owned marketing and production cooperatives. These banks were to be owned by the cooperatives themselves.

The method of "purchasing" the ownership of the system, for farmers, was to be the sale of stock to farmers as a percentage of their loans when they borrowed money from a member institution. The profits of the system eventually paid back the initial federal investment in the banks. The Federal Land Banks first paid back all government capital in 1932; however, the intervening Great Depression forced new government assistance for the FLBs, and the FLBs repaid that investment for the final time in 1947. The FICBs, PCAs, and Banks for Cooperatives repaid their government capital in full as of 1968.

After this successful transition to full private ownership of the entire system by farmers and their cooperatives, the Farm Credit Administration, an independent agency that, since 1933, has acted in a supervisory and regulatory capacity over the system, developed a legislative plan to provide greater independence for the Farm Credit System. Congress approved this plan as the Farm Credit Act of 1971 (Public Law 92-181). The Farm Credit System and its components now operate as autonomous entities, privately owned and self-governing. The Federal Farm Credit Board is the national policy authority for the Farm Credit Administration and appoints its governor, who until 1969 had been a presidentially approved appointee nominated by the board. The members of this body are chosen from district farm credit boards, which govern all three components of the system in each district. Finally, each local association has its own board and elects members to the district board. Although local PCAs generally are freer to exercise discretion over the making of individual loans than are FLBAs, most of the actual administrative and financial work throughout the system is handled by the district Farm Credit Banks. In all, there are twelve districts in the national system.

Once turned loose in the pastures of private enterprise, the Farm Credit System institutions wasted little time in adopting an aggressive lending posture, as can be discerned from Tables 2 and 3. Although the Federal Land Banks held just 22.9 percent of the farm real estate debt nationally in 1970, they produced a little over half of the new loan volume between 1970 and 1982. The comparison of PCA/FICB debt volume to overall totals is not quite so striking, but the growth in debt volume was still substantial, particularly in the Midwest. The PCAs were also the first to show a clear retrenchment in loan volume, once difficulties began to become apparent in agriculture after 1980. Many critics now maintain that the Farm Credit System was too willing to extend credit during the 1970s, and overly restrictive once the same farmers encountered economic difficulties following the Federal Reserve Board's deflationary policies after 1979. National farm debt held by the Farm Credit System peaked in the early 1980s at more than $82 billion, but that loan portfolio had shrunk to about $70 billion by early 1987, and continues to dwindle steadily. Both the loss of creditworthy farmers fleeing the system's financial difficulties and the denial of new credit to less fortunate farmers contribute to the steady decline.

Sheer volume makes the Farm Credit System a major actor in the farm credit problem. Its actions and policies have consequences that extend far beyond the impact on the system itself. Aggressive lending may well have played a part in bidding up farm land prices in the 1970s. Restrictive policies and a growing number of liquidations, used in an effort to salvage a deteriorating balance sheet, serve as a depressant on the farm land and equipment market. It does not require Federal Land Bank, either, to put the land on the market. A borrower up to date on a real estate loan may still be forced into liquidation because of difficulties in meeting his or her operating expenses. Thus, the sizeable drop in PCA loan volume in the last few years is a key factor in the depressed land market.

And PCAs have been at the forefront of Farm Credit System problems and controversies. Throughout major farming areas of the United States, PCAs became insolvent in domino fashion throughout 1985 and 1986. A few were liquidated; others saw their "stock" frozen, which essentially meant that farmers who had not already fled to another institution had probably waited too long to do so. The ultimate solution, which required some arm twisting among a dispirited membership, was the consolidation of local PCAs into single districtwide PCAs. For instance, thirty-seven local PCAs in the states of Iowa, Nebraska, South Dakota, and Wyoming in late 1985 became a single Omaha PCA with branch offices. One result was to erase the authority, such as it was by then, of local PCA boards.

A source of great controversy by 1985 was the issue of federal intervention into the financial crisis of the Farm Credit System, and what demands, if any, Congress or the administration might make in return for any form of bailout. A temporary answer was offered in a bill Congress passed at the end of that year, signed by President Reagan in January 1986, that provided access to emergency credit through the Federal Reserve Board only after the system had exhausted all internal resources in solving its credit problems. Among the losers in such a deal were those more financially healthy districts, like Texas, which then had to honor loss-sharing agreements, the nature and provisions of which were the source of rancorous debate among some farmer members of Farm Credit System institutions, particularly the Texas Federal Land Bank. As the financial position of the entire Farm Credit System was still deteriorating in early 1987, the system's future and its internal sovereignty—or lack thereof—remained a volatile issue in the Farm Belt.

Projections for 1987 were that the Farm Credit System would suffer losses of up to $1.5 billion. With the sense of urgency about the system's solvency that such projections created, Congress in December 1987 passed a bailout bill to allow units of the Farm Credit System to float up to $4 billion in bonds whose proceeds would be used to aid the system. The measure also contained provisions dealing with farm borrowers' rights. The bill, signed into law by President Reagan, created a Federal Assistance Board consisting of the secretary of agriculture, the secretary of the treasury, and a presidentially appointed farmer member, which would be responsible for disbursing the aid. Farm Credit Administration chairman Frank Naylor expected at least four Federal Land Bank districts to apply: Jackson, Mississippi; Omaha; Louisville; and Spokane, Washington.[1]

Farm debt was falling quickly from its earlier peak. Economist Neil Harl of Iowa State University estimated that farmers paid off about $30 billion of their debt in 1987, lowering it to $141 billion. (The 1984 peak was $215 billion.) Of that paydown, Harl estimated, only 60 percent was voluntary. The rest resulted from foreclosures, liquidations, repossessions, and similar payoffs under pressure. As a result, most of the projected 1987 losses did not ultimately occur. But the Farm Credit System was still far from finding its way out of the woods.[2]

NOTES

1. "Never Mind, Thriving Farm Credit System Says," *Des Moines Register,* January 22, 1988, p. 5S
2. Ibid.

APPENDIX B
Farm Organizations

Even the casual rural reader may be excused for discovering organizations in this book that are unfamiliar. Rural groups, like those in virtually any other sector of American society, spring up like dandelions and grow like weeds. Throughout the history of rural America, there have always been a few that accidentally found themselves in the right place at the right time, with the right message, and evolved into national voices on farm policy, whereas many others remained small or burst upon the scene for a short period, only to wither away just as quickly. Many of their organizers consider the latter fate appropriate once a protest movement has served its purpose, although a few groups hang on for years as a mere shell of what they were in their heyday.

The following glossary is by no means comprehensive, but merely seeks to acquaint the reader briefly with those groups that found their way into the interviews and stories that, in turn, found their way into this book. There are many others that deserve to be mentioned, and many are—in other books, journals, and publications.

American Agriculture Movement. In late 1977, four farmers sat around a coffee table in Compo, Colorado, and decided agriculture should go on strike for parity farm prices. Often unstructured, the grass-roots movement spread across the United States and organized the now-famous tractorcade protests in Washington, D.C., in the late 1970s. It later split into two groups, AAM–Grassroots and AAM Inc. The former has largely disappeared, but the latter maintains a Washington office, lobbies on farm legislation, and raises money for a political action committee that contributes to various political candidates, mostly those running for Congress.

Center for Rural Affairs. Founded in 1973, the center operates out of Walthill, Nebraska, as a research and advocacy organization. It is member-supported and used to publish *Small Farm Advocate,* a source of information on family farm programs, laws, and problems. It was a prime mover behind Initiative 300, which effectively banned corporate farm ownership in Nebraska.

Citizen Action. This multi-issue network of state citizens' groups has added farm problems to its agenda in the last few years. It is a federation of groups whose primary fundraising technique is door-to-door canvassing and whose politics are basically left-wing populist. Common issues have been control of the energy industry, national health care, environment, and neighborhood development. Most of its groups have recognizable state name tags that include "Public Interest Coalition," "Citizen Action Network," or some similar label. Common elements of the coalitions are labor organizations, farm groups, senior citizens, politically progressive church groups, and neighborhood groups.

COACT (Citizens Organizations Acting Together). This group originated in rural Minnesota, but in recent years has organized affiliates elsewhere, the largest being in Indiana. It participates in Citizen Action, and its politics are much the same. The group, because of its rural origins, has put considerable emphasis on farm issues, including state legislative issues dealing with farm credit, such as foreclosure moratoria, debt restructuring, and the like. Since 1985, it has worked closely on these issues with the Center for Rural Affairs. It was also the organizing force behind the St. Paul-based Family Farm Organizing Resource Center.

Farm Bureau Federation. Begun around 1920, the Farm Bureau has built a veritable empire that now includes insurance and agribusiness elements. Its politics are fundamentally conservative and geared to advocacy of the benefits of the free market, although it had a somewhat more liberal tilt during the turbulent years of the New Deal. It was a prime supporter of the 1985 farm legislation passed by Congress and supported by the Reagan administration.

Farmers Union. Launched in Texas in 1902, Farmers Union has one of the longest track records of any agricultural organization in American history. It organized many of the farmer-owned marketing cooperatives that still exist. In recent years, it has lost some of the clout and membership it once had, but it is still considered a major force among the more liberal farm organizations. It lobbies, but was a reluctant endorser, at first, of the Harkin farm legislation, although it has since lent stronger support to a coalition effort to back the bill.

Groundswell. This group, using many direct action tactics to rally its followers, swept much of rural Minnesota in the mid-1980s and organized many of the largest farm-related demonstrations Minnesota's capital has ever seen. Like most protest groups, its structure has been somewhat loose from the beginning, but has allowed it to move quickly to do what it does best. It became somewhat smaller in the aftermath of the Polzine controversy.

Illinois Farm Alliance. This came into being basically as the farm wing of the Citizen Action-affiliated Illinois Public Action Council (see Citizen Action). Not originally a membership organization, it has become one and also is a potent organizing force around populist solutions to the farm crisis. Its office is in Edwardsville.

Iowa Citizens for Community Improvement. Primarily and originally a neighborhood advocacy group located in several Iowa cities and headquartered in Des Moines, it has sought in the last few years also to organize farmers. A key issue, which caused it to part company in 1984 with other state farm groups over priorities, was minimum price legislation that would mandate prices for farm products in much the same manner as minimum wage laws do for workers. The bill passed the legislature, but was vetoed by Governor Branstad. It is an affiliate of the Iowa Farm Unity Coalition.

Iowa Farm Unity Coalition. Conceived at a meeting of various liberal and populist farm leaders in the basement of a bank in Atlantic in 1982, this group now has about a dozen affiliates, including the United Auto Workers, whose membership has been devastated by tractor factory layoffs, plus state affiliates of some of the major national farm groups, except the Farm Bureau. The coalition has basically shaped the farm reform agenda at the state level since hitting its stride as a lobbying force after 1984. At the local level, it organizes county survival groups, many of whose members first contact the coalition through its farm crisis hotline, which offers farm debt counseling. It is headquartered in Des Moines.

Missouri Rural Crisis Center. Organized only in late 1985, the center has responded quickly to organizing opportunities through direct action tactics, while also locating referral and emergency aid for farmers and getting it distributed under crisis center auspices. It is headquartered in Columbia.

National Farmers Organization. Launched in 1953 by Oren Lee Staley, a fiery orator who advocated withholding actions as a farmer's means of getting a fair price, NFO became the center of considerable controversy as those holding actions drew national publicity during the early 1960s. It has evolved into primarily a marketing organization that negotiates prices for farmers' products in bulk and went through some difficult times in the 1970s, when some farmers' withdrawals from group marketing agreements nearly forced it into bankruptcy. In 1987, it began to work in combination with Farmers Union on some state-level joint marketing agreements. Its national office is in Corning, Iowa.

North American Farm Alliance. More than two dozen state and national farm organizations sent representatives to a special conference in Des Moines in the spring of 1983, which led to the formation of NAFA, now headquartered in Ames, Iowa. Its focus has been on promotion and public education for the Harkin farm bill, and on assisting grass-roots farm movement organizing where such help is needed. It provided much of the initial support needed to create the Missouri Rural Crisis Center, for instance. It has sporadically published *North American Farmer,* a movement newspaper covering farm events.

Northern Plains Resource Council. This Montana-based group organized in the late 1970s in response to the threat to the area's rural environment posed by energy development, primarily coal strip mining. While those issues remain an important focus, it branched out in the early 1980s into some family farm issues as well, with one of its leaders now heading the Save the Family Farm Coalition.

Pennsylvania Public Interest Coalition. A Citizen Action-affiliated state advocacy group.

Prairiefire Rural Action. Originally its staff was the branch office staff in Des Moines for Rural America, before that group had to shrink its commitments for financial reasons. The staff then set up its own independent organization to continue its operations in Des Moines, where its office also houses the headquarters for the Iowa Farm Unity Coalition and runs the farm crisis hotline.

Rural America. A national rural advocacy group, it opened two field offices around 1981, one in Jackson, Mississippi, and one in Des Moines, the latter later becoming Prairiefire Rural Action. It used to publish a magazine, *Rural America.* It now lobbies primarily on issues of rural concern, such as rural transportation.

Save the Family Farm Coalition. This single-issue national coalition of other farm organizations has its office in Circle, Montana, and its priorities in Washington, D.C. It supports the Save the Family Farm Act introduced by Iowa's Senator Tom Harkin.

Wisconsin Farm Unity Alliance. Another state-level farm coalition, the alliance has organized a farm advocate network like that in Minnesota, as well as concentrating many of its organizing efforts on direct action confrontations with farm lenders like the Farmers Home Administration and the Farm Credit System. One of its first such operations was a sit-in at a PCA office in Mondovi. The alliance is also an unequivocal supporter of the Harkin farm bill.

Index

Index

Index

About the Author

Born in New York in 1949, Jim Schwab grew up in Cleveland, where he earned a B.A. in political science at Cleveland State University. He moved to Ames, Iowa, in 1979 to become executive director of the Iowa Public Interest Research Group. Three years later, he began graduate work at the University of Iowa, in Iowa City, where he earned two master's degrees, in journalism and in urban and regional planning. In 1985, he joined the American Planning Association as assistant editor of its monthly magazine, *Planning.* He has also contributed freelance articles to more than a dozen magazines and newspapers. While at the University of Iowa in 1984, he produced a study of the farm credit crisis for the Iowa legislature, *The Farm Credit Crisis in Iowa.* This is his first book.